SOUTH AFRICA

TAX GUIDE

VOLUME 1
BUSINESS TAXATION

International Business Publications, USA
Washington, DC, USA - South Africa

SOUTH AFRICA

TAX GUIDE, Volume 1. BUSINESS TAXATION

Editorial content: International Business Publications, USA

Editor-in-Chief: **Dr. Igor S. Oleynik**
Editor: **Natasha Alexander**

Published by
International Business Publications, USA
P.O.Box 15343, Washington, DC 20003
Phone: (202) 546-2103, Fax: (202) 546-3275.
E-mail: rusric@erols.com

UPDATED ANNUALLY

We express our sincere appreciation to all government agencies and international organizations which provided information and other materials for this guide

Databases & Information: International Business Publications, USA
Cover Design: International Business Publications, USA

2006 Updated Reprint International Business Publications, USA
ISBN 0-7397-9459-0

For customer service and information, please contact:

in the USA: **International Business Publications, USA**
P.O.Box 15343, Washington, DC 20003
Phone: (202) 546-2103, Fax: (202) 546-3275.
E-mail: rusric@erols.com

Printed in the USA

SOUTH AFRICA
TAX GUIDE
VOLUME 1
BUSINESS TAXATION

TABLE OF CONTENTS

STRATEGIC AND BUSINESS PROFILES

SOUTH AFRICA: STRATEGIC PROFILE

Capital	Cape Town (Legislative) Pretoria (Administrative) Bloemfontein (Judicial) 33°55′S 18°25′E
Largest city	Johannesburg
Official language(s)	Afrikaans, English, Zulu, Xhosa, Swati, Ndebele, Southern Sotho, Northern Sotho, Tsonga, Tswana, Venda
Government	Parliamentary democracy
- President	Thabo Mbeki
Independence	From the UK
- Union	31 May 1910
- Statute of Westminster	11 December 1931
- Republic	31 May 1961
Area	
- Total	1,221,037 km² (25th)
	471,443 sq mi
- Water (%)	negligible
Population	
- July 2005 est.	47,432,000 (26th)
- 2001 census	44,819,278
- Density	39/km² (163rd) 101/sq mi
GDP (PPP)	2005 estimate
- Total	$527.4 billion (18th)
- Per capita	$11,900 (54th)
HDI (2003)	0.658 (120th) – medium
Currency	Rand (ZAR)
Time zone	(UTC+2)
- Summer (DST)	not observed (UTC+2)
Internet TLD	.za
Calling code	+27

STRATEGIC PROFILE

COUNTRY OVERVIEW

Independence: May 31, 1910 (from United Kingdom)
Population: 43.4 million
Location/Size: Southern Africa/1.2 million square kilometers (471,445 square miles, nearly twice the size of Texas)
Major Cities: Pretoria (capital), Johannesburg, Durban, Cape Town
Languages (official): Afrikaans, English, Ndebele, Northern Sotho, Southern Sotho, Swazi, Tsonga, Tswana, Venda, Xhosa, Zulu
Ethnic Groups: Black (76%), White (12%), mixed race (Colored) (9%), Asian (3%)
Religions: Christian (Dutch reformed, other Protestant and Catholic denominations) 60%, Jewish, Hindu, Muslim, and traditional African religions
Defense: Army, 79,440; Navy, 8,000; Air Force, 11,140; Medical Corps, 6,000

ECONOMIC OVERVIEW

Minister of Finance: Trevor Manuel
Minister of Trade and Industry: Alec Erwin
Currency: 1 rand (R) = 100 cents
Market Exchange Rate: US$1 = 6.29 R
Nominal Gross Domestic Product : $129.5 billion
Real GDP Growth Rate : 0.5%: 2.8%
Inflation Rate : 6.0%: 7.7%
Merchandise Exports : $28.2 billion
Merchandise Imports : $25.1 billion
Trade Balance : $3.1 billion
Major Exports : Gold, metals and metal products, minerals,
Major Imports : Machinery and equipment, chemicals, finished goods
Major Trading Partners: Japan, Germany, Italy, United Kingdom, United States
Current Account Balance : -$0.6 billion
Total Reserves, Non-Gold: $4.2 billion

GEOGRAPHY

Location: Southern Africa, at the southern tip of the continent of Africa
Geographic coordinates: 29 00 S, 24 00 E

Map references: Africa

Area:
total: 1,219,912 sq km
land: 1,219,912 sq km
water: 0 sq km
note: includes Prince Edward Islands (Marion Island and Prince Edward Island)

Area—comparative: slightly less than twice the size of Texas

Land boundaries:
total: 4,750 km

border countries: Botswana 1,840 km, Lesotho 909 km, Mozambique 491 km, Namibia 855 km, Swaziland 430 km, Zimbabwe 225 km

Coastline: 2,798 km
Maritime claims:
continental shelf: 200-m depth or to the depth of exploitation
exclusive economic zone: 200 nm
territorial sea: 12 nm
Climate: mostly semiarid; subtropical along east coast; sunny days, cool nights
Terrain: vast interior plateau rimmed by rugged hills and narrow coastal plain

Elevation extremes:
lowest point: Atlantic Ocean 0 m
highest point: Njesuthi 3,408 m

Natural resources: gold, chromium, antimony, coal, iron ore, manganese, nickel, phosphates, tin, uranium, gem diamonds, platinum, copper, vanadium, salt, natural gas

Land use:
arable land: 10%
permanent crops: 1%
permanent pastures: 67%
forests and woodland: 7%
other: 15%

Irrigated land: 12,700 sq km
Natural hazards: prolonged droughts

Environment—current issues: lack of important arterial rivers or lakes requires extensive water conservation and control measures; growth in water usage threatens to outpace supply; pollution of rivers from agricultural runoff and urban discharge; air pollution resulting in acid rain; soil erosion; desertification

Environment—international agreements:
party to: Antarctic-Environmental Protocol, Antarctic Treaty, Biodiversity, Climate Change, Desertification, Endangered Species, Hazardous Wastes, Law of the Sea, Marine Dumping, Marine Life Conservation, Nuclear Test Ban, Ozone Layer Protection, Ship Pollution, Wetlands, Whaling
signed, but not ratified: none of the selected agreements

Geography—note: South Africa completely surrounds Lesotho and almost completely surrounds Swaziland

PEOPLE

Population: 43,426,386
note: South Africa took a census 10 October 1996 which showed a population of 37,859,000 (after a 6.8% adjustment for underenumeration based on a post-enumeration survey); this figure is still about 10% below projections from earlier censuses; since the full results of that census have not been released for analysis, the numbers shown for South Africa do not take into consideration the results of this 1996 census

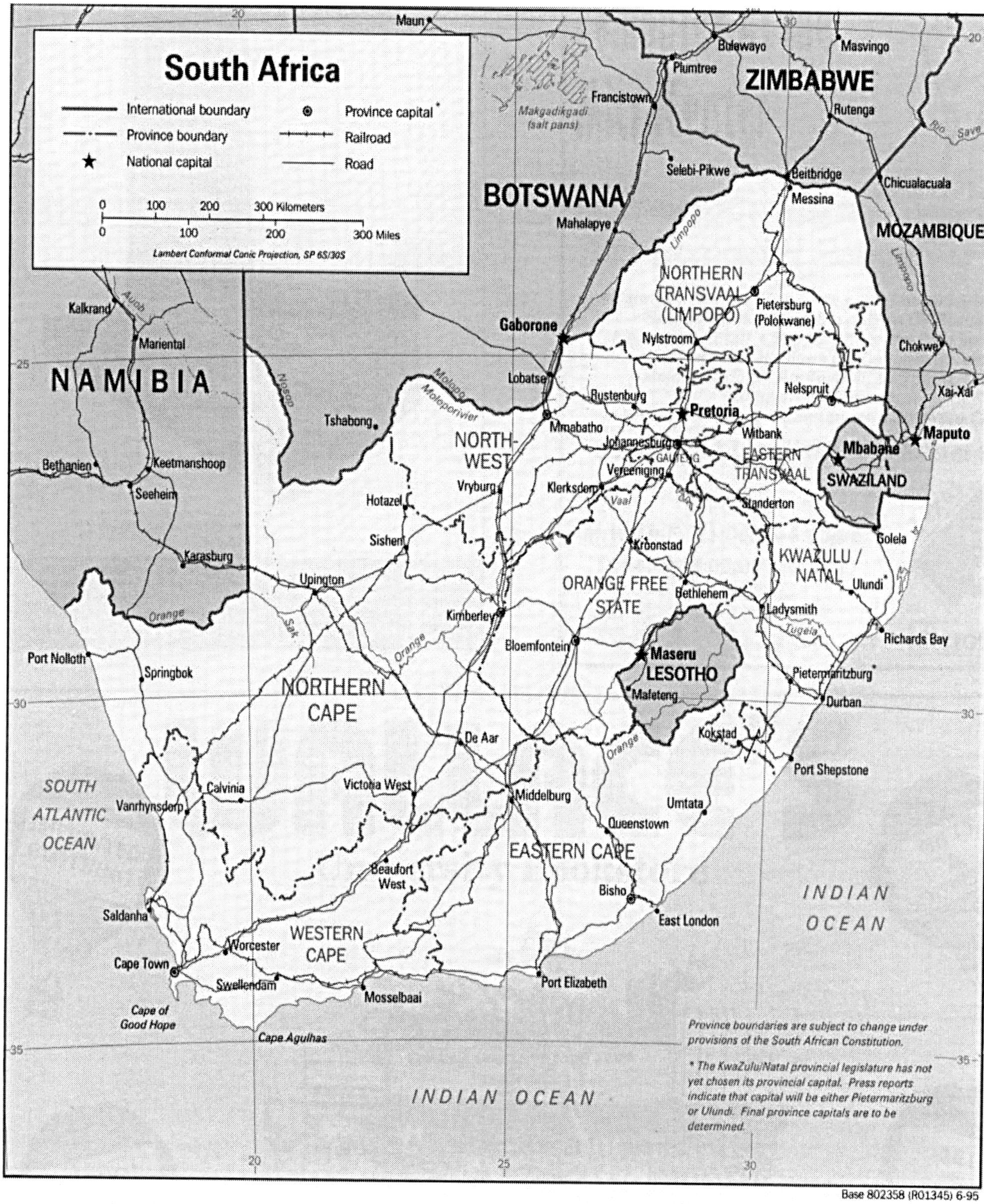
South Africa
International boundary
Province boundary
National capital
Province capital*
Railroad
Road
0 100 200 300 Kilometers
0 100 200 300 Miles
Lambert Conformal Conic Projection, SP 6S/30S
NAMIBIA
BOTSWANA
ZIMBABWE
MOZAMBIQUE
SWAZILAND
LESOTHO
NORTHERN TRANSVAAL (LIMPOPO)
NORTH-WEST
EASTERN TRANSVAAL
GAUTENG
ORANGE FREE STATE
KWAZULU / NATAL
NORTHERN CAPE
EASTERN CAPE
WESTERN CAPE
SOUTH ATLANTIC OCEAN
INDIAN OCEAN
Maun
Bulawayo
Masvingo
Plumtree
Francistown
Rutenga
Makgadikgadi (salt pans)
Selebi-Pikwe
Beitbridge
Messina
Chicualacuala
Mahalapye
Limpopo
Pietersburg (Polokwane)
Kalkrand
Auob
Mariental
Gaborone
Nylstroom
Chokwe
Lobatse
Nossop
Molopo
Moloporivier
Tshabong
Rustenburg
Pretoria
Nelspruit
Xai-Xai
Mmabatho
Johannesburg
Witbank
Maputo
Mbabane
Bethanien
Keetmanshoop
Seeheim
Vryburg
Klerksdorp
Vereeniging
Vaal
Standerton
Hotazel
Sishen
Kroonstad
Golela
Karasburg
Upington
Bethlehem
Ulundi*
Orange
Sak
Kimberley
Ladysmith
Tugela
Richards Bay
Bloemfontein
Maseru
Port Nolloth
Springbok
Pietermaritzburg*
Mafeteng
Durban
De Aar
Kokstad
Port Shepstone
Calvinia
Victoria West
Middelburg
Umtata
Vanrhynsdorp
Queenstown
Beaufort West
Bisho
East London
Saldanha
Worcester
Cape Town
Swellendam
Mosselbaai
Port Elizabeth
Cape of Good Hope
Cape Agulhas
Province boundaries are subject to change under provisions of the South African Constitution.
* The KwaZulu/Natal provincial legislature has not yet chosen its provincial capital. Press reports indicate that capital will be either Pietermaritzburg or Ulundi. Final province capitals are to be determined.
Base 802358 (R01345) 6-95

Age structure:
0-14 years: 34% (male 7,541,840; female 7,403,235)
15-64 years: 61% (male 13,180,925; female 13,312,917)
65 years and over: 5% (male 798,825; female 1,188,644)

Population growth rate: 1.32%
Birth rate: 25.94 births/1,000 population
Death rate: 12.81 deaths/1,000 population
Net migration rate: 0.08 migrant(s)/1,000 population

Sex ratio:
at birth: 1.03 male(s)/female
under 15 years: 1.02 male(s)/female
15-64 years: 0.99 male(s)/female
65 years and over: 0.67 male(s)/female
total population: 0.98 male(s)/female

Infant mortality rate: 51.99 deaths/1,000 live births

Life expectancy at birth:
total population: 54.76 years
male: 52.68 years
female: 56.9 years

Total fertility rate: 3.09 children born/woman

Nationality:
noun: South African(s)
adjective: South African

Ethnic groups: black 75.2%, white 13.6%, Colored 8.6%, Indian 2.6%
Religions: Christian 68% (includes most whites and Coloreds, about 60% of blacks and about 40% of Indians), Muslim 2%, Hindu 1.5% (60% of Indians), traditional and animistic 28.5%
Languages: 11 official languages, including Afrikaans, English, Ndebele, Pedi, Sotho, Swazi, Tsonga, Tswana, Venda, Xhosa, Zulu

Literacy:
definition: age 15 and over can read and write
total population: 81.8%
male: 81.9%
female: 81.7%

GOVERNMENT

Country name:
conventional long form: Republic of South Africa
conventional short form: South Africa
abbreviation: RSA

Data code: SF
Government type: republic

Capital: Pretoria (administrative); Cape Town (legislative); Bloemfontein (judicial)

Administrative divisions: 9 provinces; Eastern Cape, Free State, Gauteng, KwaZulu-Natal, Mpumalanga, North-West, Northern Cape, Northern Province, Western Cape

Independence: 31 May 1910 (from UK)
National holiday: Freedom Day, 27 April (1994)
Constitution: 10 December 1996; this new constitution was certified by the Constitutional Court on 4 December 1996, was signed by President MANDELA on 10 December 1996, and entered into effect on 3 February 1997; it is being implemented in phases
Legal system: based on Roman-Dutch law and English common law; accepts compulsory ICJ jurisdiction, with reservations
Suffrage: 18 years of age; universal
Executive branch:

State President	**Mbeki,** Thabo Mvuyelwa
Executive Deputy President	**Zuma,** Jacob
Min. of Agriculture & Land Affairs	**Didiza,** Angela Thoko
Min. of Arts & Culture	**Jordan,** Pallo
Min. of Communications	**Matsepe Cassaburri,** Ivy
Min. of Correctional Services	**Balfour Ngconde**
Min. of Defense	**Lekota,** Mosiuoa
Min. of Education	**Pandor,** Naledi
Min. of Environment & Tourism	**Van Schalkwyk,** Marthinus
Min. of Finance	**Manuel,** Trevor
Min. of Foreign Affairs	**Dlamini Zuma,** Nkosazana
Min. of Health	**Tshabalala-Msimang,** Manto
Min. of Home Affairs	**Mapisa-Nqakula,** Nosiviwe
Min. of Housing	**Sisulu,** Lindiwe
Min. of Intelligence	**Kasrils,** Ronnie
Min. of Justice & Constitutional Affairs	**Mabandla,** Bridgette
Min. of Labor	**Mdladlana,** Membathisi
Min. of Mineral & Energy Affairs	**Mlambo-Ngcuka,** Phumzile
Min. of Provincial & Local Government	**Mufamadi,** Sydney
Min. of Public Enterprises	**Erwin,** Alec
Min. of Public Service & Administration	**Fraser-Moleketi,** Geraldine
Min. of Public Works	**Sigcau,** Stella
Min. of Safety & Security	**Nqakula,** Charles
Min. of Science & Technology	**Mangena,** Mosibudi
Min. of Social Development	**Skweyiya,** Zola
Min. of Sport & Recreation	**Stofile,** Makenkesi
Min. of Trade & Industry	**Mpahlwa,** Mandisi

Min. of Transport	**Radebe,** Jeff
Min. of Water & Forestry	**Sonjica,** Buyi
Min. of the Presidency	**Pahad,** Essop
Governor, Reserve Bank	**Mboweni,** Tito
Ambassador to the US	**Sisulu,** Sheila
Permanent Representative to the UN, New York	**Kumalo,** Dumisani Shadrack

Legislative branch: bicameral parliament consisting of the National Assembly (400 seats; members are elected by popular vote under a system of proportional representation to serve five-year terms) and the National Council of Provinces (90 seats, 10 members elected by each of the nine provincial legislatures for five-year terms; has special powers to protect regional interests, including the safeguarding of cultural and linguistic traditions among ethnic minorities); note—following the implementation of the new constitution on 3 February 1997 the former Senate was disbanded and replaced by the National Council of Provinces with essentially no change in membership and party affiliations, although the new institution's responsibilities have been changed somewhat by the new constitution
elections: National Assembly and Senate—last held 26-29 April 1994 (next to be held 2 June 1999); note—the Senate was disbanded and replaced by the National Council of Provinces on 6 February 1997
election results: National Assembly—percent of vote by party—ANC 62.6%, NP 20.4%, IFP 10.5%, FF 2.2%, DP 1.7%, PAC 1.2%, ACDP 0.5%, other 0.9%; seats by party—ANC 252, NP 82, IFP 43, FF 9, DP 7, PAC 5, ACDP 2; Senate—percent of vote by party—NA; seats by party—ANC 61, NP 17, FF 4, IFP 5, DP 3

Judicial branch: Constitutional Court; Supreme Court of Appeals; High Courts; Magistrate Courts

Political parties and leaders: African Christian Democratic Party or ACDP [Kenneth MESHOE, president]; African National Congress or ANC [Thabo MBEKI, president]; Democratic Party or DP [Tony LEON, president]; Freedom Front or FF [Constand VILJOEN, president]; Inkatha Freedom Party or IFP [Mangosuthu BUTHELEZI, president]; National Party (now the New National Party) or NP [Marthinus VAN SCHALKWYK, executive director]; Pan-Africanist Congress or PAC [Stanley MOGOBA, president]; United Democratic Movement or UDM [Roelf MEYER, Bantu HOLOMISA]
note: 11 other parties won votes in the April 1994 elections but not enough to gain seats in the National Assembly

Political pressure groups and leaders: Congress of South African Trade Unions or COSATU [Sam SHILOWA, general secretary]; South African Communist Party or SACP [Charles NQAKULA, general secretary]; South African National Civics Organization or SANCO [Mlungisi HLONGWANE, national president]; note—COSATU and SACP are in a formal alliance with the ANC

International organization participation: AfDB, BIS, C, CCC, ECA, FAO, G-77, IAEA, IBRD, ICAO, ICC, ICFTU, ICRM, IDA, IFAD, IFC, IFRCS, IHO, ILO, IMF, IMO, Inmarsat, Intelsat, Interpol, IOC, IOM, ISO, ITU, MTCR, NAM, NSG, OAU, OPCW, SACU, SADC, UN, UNCTAD, UNESCO, UNHCR, UPU, WFTU, WHO, WIPO, WMO, WToO, WTrO, ZC

Diplomatic representation in the US:
chief of mission: Ambassador (vacant)
chancery: 3051 Massachusetts Avenue NW, Washington, DC 20008
telephone: [1] (202) 232-4400
FAX: [1] (202) 265-1607
consulate(s) general: Beverly Hills (California), Chicago, and New York

Diplomatic representation from the US:
chief of mission: Ambassador James A. JOSEPH
embassy: 877 Pretorius St., Arcadia 0083
mailing address: P.O. Box 9536, Pretoria 0001
telephone: [27] (12) 342-1048
FAX: [27] (12) 342-2244
consulate(s) general: Cape Town, Durban, Johannesburg

Flag description: two equal width horizontal bands of red (top) and blue separated by a central green band which splits into a horizontal Y, the arms of which end at the corners of the hoist side, embracing a black isosceles triangle from which the arms are separated by narrow yellow bands; the red and blue bands are separated from the green band and its arms by narrow white stripes
note: prior to 26 April 1994, the flag was actually four flags in one—three miniature flags reproduced in the center of the white band of the former flag of the Netherlands, which has three equal horizontal bands of orange (top), white, and blue; the miniature flags are a vertically hanging flag of the old Orange Free State with a horizontal flag of the UK adjoining on the hoist side and a horizontal flag of the old Transvaal Republic adjoining on the other side

ECONOMY

Economy—overview: South Africa is a middle-income, developing country with an abundant supply of resources, well-developed financial, legal, communications, energy, and transport sectors, a stock exchange that ranks among the 10 largest in the world, and a modern infrastructure supporting an efficient distribution of goods to major urban centers throughout the region. However, growth has not been strong enough to cut into the 30% unemployment, and daunting economic problems remain from the apartheid era, especially the problems of poverty and lack of economic empowerment among the disadvantaged groups.

Other problems are crime and corruption. The new government demonstrated its commitment to open markets, privatization, and a favorable investment climate with the release of its macroeconomic strategy in June 1996. Called "Growth, Employment and Redistribution," this policy framework includes the introduction of tax incentives to stimulate new investment in labor-intensive projects, expansion of basic infrastructure services, the restructuring and partial privatization of state assets, continued reduction of tariffs, subsidies to promote economic efficiency, improved services to the disadvantaged, and integration into the global economy. Serious structural rigidities remain, including a complicated and relatively protectionist trade regime, and concentration of wealth and economic control.

GDP: purchasing power parity—$290.6 billion
GDP—real growth rate: 0.3%

GDP—per capita: purchasing power parity—$6,800

GDP—composition by sector:
agriculture: 5%
industry: 39%
services: 56%

Population below poverty line: NA%
Household income or consumption by percentage share:
lowest 10%: 1.4%
highest 10%: 47.3%
Inflation rate (consumer prices): 9%
Labor force: 15 million economically active (1997)
Labor force—by occupation: services 35%, agriculture 30%, industry 20%, mining 9%, other 6%
Unemployment rate: 30%
Budget:
revenues: $30.5 billion
expenditures: $38 billion, including capital expenditures of $2.6 billion (FY94/95 est.)
Industries: mining (world's largest producer of platinum, gold, chromium), automobile assembly, metalworking, machinery, textile, iron and steel, chemical, fertilizer, foodstuffs
Industrial production growth rate: -1%
Electricity—production: 186.949 billion kWh
Electricity—production by source:
fossil fuel: 93%
hydro: 0.7%
nuclear: 6.3%
other: NA%
Electricity—consumption: 181.404 billion kWh
Electricity—exports: 5.575 billion kWh
Electricity—imports: 30 million kWh
Agriculture—products: corn, wheat, sugarcane, fruits, vegetables; beef, poultry, mutton, wool, dairy products
Exports: $28.7 billion (f.o.b., 1998)

Exports—commodities: gold 20%, other minerals and metals 20%-25%, food 5%, chemicals 3%

Exports—partners: UK, Italy, Japan, US, Germany
Imports: $27.2 billion (f.o.b.)
Imports—commodities: machinery, transport equipment, chemicals, petroleum products, textiles, scientific instruments (1997)
Imports—partners: Germany, US, UK, Japan
Debt—external: $23.5 billion
Economic aid—recipient: $676.3 million
Currency: 1 rand (R) = 100 cents
Exchange rates: rand per US dollar - 6.3593 (2005), 6.4597 (2004), 7.5648 (2003), 10.5407 (2002), 8.6092 (2001)
Fiscal year: 1 April—31 March

COMMUNICATIONS

Telephones: 4.729 million

Telephones - mobile cellular:19.5 million

Telephone system: the system is the best developed, most modern, and has the highest capacity in Africa
domestic: consists of carrier-equipped open-wire lines, coaxial cables, microwave radio relay links, fiber-optic cable, and radiotelephone communication stations; key centers are Bloemfontein, Cape Town, Durban, Johannesburg, Port Elizabeth, and Pretoria
international: 1 submarine cable; satellite earth stations—3 Intelsat (1 Indian Ocean and 2 Atlantic Ocean)

Radio broadcast stations: AM 15, FM 164, shortwave 1
Radios: 7.5 million
Television broadcast stations: 556 (includes 156 network stations and 400 privately-owned low-power stations; in addition, there are 144 network repeaters) (1997)
Televisions: 7.5 million

TRANSPORTATION

Railways: *total:* 21,431 km
narrow gauge: 20,995 km 1.067-m gauge (9,087 km electrified); 436 km 0.610-m gauge (1995)

Highways: *total:* 331,265 km
paved: 137,475 km (including 1,142 km of expressways)
unpaved: 193,790 km
Pipelines: crude oil 931 km; petroleum products 1,748 km; natural gas 322 km
Ports and harbors: Cape Town, Durban, East London, Mosselbaai, Port Elizabeth, Richards Bay, Saldanha
Merchant marine:
total: 9 ships (1,000 GRT or over) totaling 274,797 GRT/270,837 DWT
ships by type: container 6, oil tanker 2, roll-on/roll-off cargo 1
Airports: 749

Airports—with paved runways:
total: 144 *over 3,047 m:* 10 *2,438 to 3,047 m:* 4
1,524 to 2,437 m: 45 *914 to 1,523 m:* 75 *under 914 m:* 10

Airports—with unpaved runways:
total: 605 *1,524 to 2,437 m:* 35 *914 to 1,523 m:* 304 *under 914 m:* 266

MILITARY

Military branches: South African National Defense Force or SANDF (includes Army, Navy, Air Force, and Medical Services), South African Police Service or SAPS
Military manpower—military age: 18 years of age
Military manpower—availability:
males age 15-49: 11,330,692
Military manpower—fit for military service:
males age 15-49: 6,889,631
Military manpower—reaching military age annually:
males: 453,610
Military expenditures—dollar figure: $2 billion

STARTING BUSINESS IN SOUTH AFRICA

ESTABLISHIGN A BUSINESS

FORMATION PROCEDURES

All South African companies are governed by the Companies Act which was originally based on English company law. The Act prescribes the procedures to be followed to form a private or public company. The Companies Act is administered by the Companies and Intellectual Property Registration Office (CIPRO - formerly the Registrar of Companies), whose offices are in Pretoria.

All South African close corporations are governed by the Close Corporations Act, which is also administered by CIPRO. There are no formal procedures relating to the formation of partnerships and sole proprietorships. The trustees of a trading trust must be authorised to act as trustees by the Master of the High Court. Actions by trustees prior to the issue of such authorisation are void.

REGISTRATION

Incorporation of a company entails the following steps -

- reserving a company name;
- filing the memorandum and articles of association of the company; and
- filing the written consent of auditors to act for the company.

A company name must be reserved with and approved by CIPRO. It is advisable to suggest alternative names in case the first name is deemed unsuitable by CIPRO.

The memorandum and articles of association must also be filed with CIPRO. The memorandum of association must indicate, among other things

- the name of the company;
- the company's main object, although there may be any number of ancillary objects; and
- the amount of authorised share capital (not all of which is required to be issued).

There is no minimum capital requirement. However, for a company which is controlled by non-residents, if the tax authorities consider the ratio between equity capital and borrowings to be inadequate, they will disallow the deduction for tax purposes of interest and similar amounts paid by the company to the non-resident shareholders.

A standard format for the memorandum and articles is available and can be adapted to the company's requirements. Incorporation takes about four to six weeks to complete and costs approximately R3 300 (excluding VAT and disbursements).

It may in many cases be more convenient to purchase an existing "shelf company" (for a cost of approximately R3 500 (excluding VAT and disbursements) plus a fee for ancillary company secretarial work) and adapt it to suit the requirements of the new business. The "shelf company" has no assets or liabilities and no previous trading history, ie it is effectively a "clean" and dormant company. When compared to incorporating a new company, buying a "shelf company" saves time and this is an important practical advantage.

If a foreign company wishes to establish a branch or external company in South Africa, registration is required as an "external company". This is accomplished in much the same way as for a domestic company. A certified copy of the memorandum and articles (or their equivalent) of the foreign company, authenticated by a South African diplomatic representative or in certain circumstances notarised by a registered notary, must be filed with the Companies and Intellectual Property Registration Office. An external company is in most respects subject to the same regulations as a South African company. Registration also takes about four to six weeks and costs about R2 500 (excluding VAT and disbursements).

Registration of a close corporation (CC) is much simpler and quicker. It does not have a memorandum or articles of association. The only constitutional document required is a founding statement, which must be filed with CIPRO (which has also taken over the function of the former Registrar of Close Corporations). Registration takes about four to six weeks and costs approximately R1 000 (excluding VAT and disbursements). A private company that meets the requirements of a close corporation may convert to a close corporation, and a close corporation may convert to a private company.

In addition to meeting the requirements of the Companies Act (and/or the Close Corporations Act, where applicable) a business generally has to register with the authorities that regulate VAT, employees tax, provincial and regional services levies, workmen's compensation and the unemployment insurance fund. Companies and individuals must also register for income tax purposes. Business licences are required for certain activities and are generally easily obtainable from the licensing authorities, subject to compliance with the relevant requirements.

The establishment of a factory generally requires the consent of several different Government departments. The industrial development branch of the Department of Trade and Industry provides an advisory service covering all aspects of the establishment or expansion of industrial undertakings in South Africa.

SHAREHOLDERS AND DIRECTORS

For a private company, the minimum number of shareholders and directors is one (the sole shareholder may also be the sole director), while a public company must have at least seven shareholders (unless it is a wholly-owned subsidiary of another company) and two directors. No residence or nationality restrictions apply to either shareholders or directors.

The minimum number of members of a close corporation is one member and the maximum number of members is ten members. Certain disqualifications apply - a juristic person such as a company may for instance not be a member of a close corporation. A close corporation is managed by its members and does not have a separate board of directors.

LABOUR SUPPLY AND REGULATIONS

Labour Relations

The Labour Relations Act and a number of other Acts promulgated since 1996, have fundamentally altered the legal framework in which labour relations are conducted. Before embarking on any venture which has labour implications, it is advisable to consult with a specialist labour lawyer or consultant to establish the legal position. This is particularly so in the light of the aforementioned changes.

Principles Governing Employment in South Africa

The contract of employment and the employment relationship are regulated by the provisions of the Basic Conditions of Employment Act and the provisions of the Labour Relations Act.

In addition to these statutes, the Employment Equity Act provides for the eradication of discrimination in all employment policies, practices, procedures and the working environment in all work places as well as the implementation of affirmative action programs by certain designated employers in respect of previously disadvantaged persons.

Basic Conditions of Employment

The Basic Conditions of Employment Act (BCEA) provides for minimum terms on which employees must be employed in relation to, inter alia, annual leave, sick leave, overtime and daily and weekly maximum working hours. Certain provisions of the BCEA are regarded to be terms of an employment contract whether or not the employer and employee intended differently. The BCEA prescribes minimum terms and conditions of employment such as maximum ordinary hours of work and overtime, minimum payment for overtime worked including work performed on Sundays and public holidays as well as minimum meal intervals, rest periods and leave provisions, including minimum annual leave and maternity leave.

The BCEA encourages transparency in the workplace by obligating employers to furnish employees with particulars of employment as well as information in respect of their remuneration. In recognising that the unique nature of particular industries may necessitate variations to the prescribed terms and conditions of employment, the BCEA makes provision for employers to vary the prescribed conditions of employment either through collective agreements concluded with trade unions, individual agreements concluded with employees or formal variations granted by the Minister of Labour.

The Labour Relations Act

The BCEA also allows the Minister of Labour to make sectoral determinations establishing basic conditions of employment for employees in a particular sector. Labour inspectors appointed by the Minister of Labour are empowered to monitor and enforce the BCEA. Failure to comply with the provisions of the BCEA may result in fines being levied. These fines can be between R100 and R500 per employee in respect of whom a failure to comply occurs (where the contravention does not include an underpayment) and between 25% and 200% of the amount due, including interest owing (where the contravention involves an underpayment).

The Labour Relations Act (LRA), which came into operation on 11 November 1996, aims to give effect to the constitutional right to fair labour practice. The LRA confers on employees the right to join trade unions and on trade unions the right to represent their members in all employment related matters. The LRA provides a framework within which employees can exercise their right to strike and within which employers can exercise their right to lock out employees from the workplace. Significantly the LRA confers on employees the right not to be unfairly dismissed and the right not to be subjected to unfair labour practices by prescribing the grounds on which employees' services can be terminated as well as the procedures to be followed before dismissal can be contemplated.

The LRA establishes the Labour Court, the Labour Appeal Court as well as the CCMA tasked with adjudicating employment disputes. By imposing limits on the compensation that may be awarded to employees for unfair dismissal the LRA also endeavours to create certainty between employers and employees.

Prior to the enactment of the LRA a trend of appointing employees on fixed term/limited duration contracts developed in order to avoid the onerous obligations imposed on employers seeking to dismiss employees. This trend of avoidance was addressed in the LRA by extending the definition of what constitutes "dismissal". As a result, a dismissal can also occur where an employee reasonably expected the employer to renew a fixed term contract of employment on the same or similar conditions but the employer offered to renew it on less favourable conditions, or did not renew the contract at all.

Where a dismissal is based on the employer's operational requirements the LRA adopts a more prescriptive approach in terms of the procedure to be adopted by the employer in order to safeguard employment as far as possible. Although an employer is not obliged to adopt a purely checklist approach to the prescribed procedure, the employer is required to

- disclose to the employee, or their duly authorised representatives, in writing, all relevant information to enable the employees to participate constructively in the process including, for example, the reasons for the proposed dismissal, the number of employees likely to be affected, alternatives considered before proposing dismissal, the severance pay proposed, any assistance to be given to affected employees and the possibility of future employment; and

- engage with the employees likely to be affected by the process in a meaningful joint consensus seeking process. If consensus cannot be reached on the need to retrench and the employer remains of the view that retrenchments are required the employer will be entitled to nevertheless retrench its employees. In the case of large employers embarking on large scale retrenchments, the LRA allows the employees to strike in order to oppose the pending retrenchments.

The LRA aims to encourage voluntary collective bargaining and the settlement of disputes, and does so by enhancing the powers of new forums designed to facilitate those objectives.

Collective Bargaining and Dispute Resolution

Under the LRA, the concept of "Bargaining Councils" has been introduced which extends the concept of the previous Industrial Councils. A Commission for Conciliation Mediation and Arbitration (CCMA), a Labour Court and a Labour Appeal Court have been established in terms of the LRA. Disputes regarding dismissals (other than multiple retrenchments and dismissals based on a prohibited ground of discrimination) must be resolved in accordance with statutory conciliation, mediation and arbitration requirements through the CCMA and, in certain instances, the relevant Bargaining Council. Disputes regarding multiple retrenchments, dismissals based on a prohibited ground of discrimination and disputes requiring the intervention of a court (for instance, where applications for interdictory or mandatory relief are made) must be resolved in the Labour Court and the Labour Appeal Court. The Industrial Court and the Conciliation Boards have been abolished. The LRA also introduced requirements for the establishing of workplace forums in certain enterprises, which promote employee participation in decision-making and require employers to furnish a wide range of information to employee representatives in those workplace forums.

Transfer of Contract of Employment if a Business is sold as a Going Concern

Section 197 of the LRA provides that where a business is directly acquired as a going concern (but not through the acquisition of shares in a company) the contracts of employment of the employees of the business will be automatically transferred to the purchaser unless an agreement to the contrary is reached with all or any of the affected employees or their duly authorised representatives. In addition

- the purchaser will automatically assume the rights and obligations of the previous employer in respect of all employees, despite any agreement by the parties to the contrary;

- the seller remains jointly and severally liable with the purchaser for claims concerning any terms or condition of employment that arose prior to the date (transfer date) of transfer of the business to the purchaser;

- the seller and the purchaser are obliged to agree (and disclose to the employees transferring to the purchaser)
  - the leave pay accrued to the transferring employees as at the transfer date;
  - the severance pay that would have been paid (as at the transfer date) to the transferring employees in the event of their dismissal by reason of the employer's operational requirements;
  - any other payments that have accrued (as at the transfer date) to the transferring employees but which have not been paid;

- the seller will (for a period of twelve months after the transfer date) be jointly and severally liable with the purchaser to any employee who becomes entitled to receive any such leave pay, severance pay and/or other payment as a result of the employee's dismissal for a reason relating to the purchaser's operational requirements or the purchaser's liquidation or sequestration. The seller will however not incur such liability if it can show that it has complied with all the provisions of section 197 of the LRA.

Skills Development

The Skills Development Act is designed to develop the skills of the South African workforce and increase investment by employers in the education and training of their workforce. This is achieved by way of the Skills Development Levies Act imposing on employers a levy equal to 1% of their total wage bill, payable to the South African Revenue Services. Portions of this levy can be recovered by the employer as a grant on meeting certain requirements set out in the Skills Development Act and its regulations.

Employment Equity and Affirmative Action

The Employment Equity Act (EEA), which came into operation on 9 August 1999, provides generally for the promotion of the constitutional right to equality, the elimination of unfair discrimination and the implementation of employment equity in the workplace to address historical discrimination and to achieve diversity in the workplace. The EEA prohibits unfair discrimination and confers on employees and applicants for employment the right to refer unfair discrimination disputes to the CCMA and thereafter the Labour Court. The Labour Court may award unlimited compensation where it finds that an employer has discriminated against an individual unfairly.

The EEA also obliges employers employing more than fifty employees (so called designated employers) to implement affirmative action measures aimed at achieving employment equity, to prepare and implement employment equity plans and submit regular reports to the Director General of the Department of Labour. Designated employers must also appoint a senior manager to take responsibility for and oversee the implementation of the EEA. It is critical to note that failure to comply with the EEA can expose a designated employer to fines of between R500 000 and R900 000 per contravention.

The EEA furthermore establishes a commission for employment equity and provides for the monitoring of employment equity compliance by employees, trade unions and labour inspectors.

SOCIAL SECURITY

The Government-operated social welfare system is not as comprehensive as those to be found in Europe and North America. A number of constraints prevent the extension of South Africa's social welfare system. These include finance, manpower, difficulties experienced in maintaining accurate records of those eligible for pensions and the long distances people must sometimes travel to reach welfare centres. More than 6,5 million South Africans currently receive grants from Government.

Pensions

There is at present no national pension scheme, but a Government appointed committee is examining the issue. Apart from pension funds operated for civil servants, the Government provides social pensions, old age pensions, pensions for the blind, disability pensions and war veterans' pensions. Private pension funds are operated by employers and administered in various ways, often by insurance companies. Pension funds are subject to statutory regulation, and contributions to a pension fund are usually made by both employer and employee.

Unemployment Insurance

The Unemployment Insurance Fund provides benefits for unemployed people and for the dependants of deceased contributors (provided certain criteria are met). Illness and maternity benefits are also paid. Revenues are obtained from the contributions of employees, their employers and the Government.

Workmen's Compensation

The Compensation for Occupational Injuries and Diseases Act provides a system of "no fault" compensation for employees who are injured in accidents that arise out of and in the course of their employment or who contract occupational diseases. The Act compels employers to insure their employees against industrial accidents or illness that could result in death or disability. The Act provides for the compulsory insurance cover of employees.

Medical Aid

South Africa does not have a national medical insurance scheme. Private medical aid schemes are operated under the Medical Schemes Act and cover most types of medical expenses in accordance with scales of benefits (tariffs) established by each scheme, which are revised from time to time. These expenses include the costs of private medical and dental services, prescribed medicines, and hospital and nursing home fees. Contributions are usually made by both employer and employee in equal shares. However, the scales of benefits usually do not equal the charges actually levied. The excess must be borne directly by the patient. A number of insurance schemes are available to cover these excesses and other medical expenses which are not provided for by the medical aid schemes. Medical schemes are increasingly establishing and operating managed health care programs in an effort to control steeply escalating claims and abuses of the benefits provided by them.

The Medical Schemes Act provides for the establishment of a Council and Registrar of Medical Schemes and contains provisions relating to the registration and control of certain activities of medical schemes and the protection of the interest of medical scheme members. The Act also seeks to extend the ambit of medical aid cover to less advantaged South Africans.

Occupational Health and Safety

The Occupational Health and Safety Act (OHSA), which came into operation on 1 January 1994, places an obligation on employers to reduce risks to health and safety in the workplace and provides for the regulation and monitoring of workplaces in order to protect the health and safety of employees and other persons in the workplace and in the use of plant and machinery.

In terms of the OHSA the chief executive officer of every employer is liable for contraventions of the OHSA. Contraventions can result in criminal convictions, fines and/or imprisonment. The maximum period of imprisonment, depending on the portion of the OHSA contravened can be between one and two years.

The OHSA also obliges all employers to report accidents or incidents which occur in the workplace.

The Mine Health and Safety Act (MHSA) is established to protect the health and safety of persons at mines and to require both employers and employees to identify hazards and eliminate, control and minimise the risk relating to health and safety at mines.

In terms of the MHSA every chief executive officer must take reasonable steps to ensure that the functions of the employer as contemplated in the MHSA are property performed. Without derogating from any responsibility or liability of the chief executive officer, he may entrust any function contemplated in the MHSA to any person under his control.

Every employer must establish and prepare a health and safety policy that, inter alia, describes the organisation of work, establishes policies to protect employees and other persons who may not be employees but who may be directly effected by the activities of the mine, outline the procedures to carry out and review policies and outline the arrangements for carrying out and reviewing policies.

The MHSA is regulated and endorsed by the Department of Minerals and Energy which appoints inspectors with wide and extensive authority to ensure compliance with the MHSA. An inspector may enter any mine without a warrant or notice and inspect the mine's compliance with the MHSA. If an inspector has reason to believe that any activity at a mine may endanger the health and safety of any person at the mine the inspector may instruct that the operations at the mine or a part of the mine be halted. Less severe instructions may also be issued by the inspector.

In terms of the MHSA any person who, by a negligent act or by a negligent omission, causes serious injury or serious illness to a person at a mine commits an offence. In terms of the MHSA a conviction of an offence may result in fines and/or imprisonment. Depending on the provision of the MHSA contravened, the maximum term of imprisonment can be either one, two or three years.

BUSINESS TAXATION

Most taxes in South Africa are levied by the central Government. The new Constitution gives some taxing powers to the provinces. These mainly involve assessment rates and other taxes based on immovable property.

Before 1 January 2001, a "source" based system applied, ie tax was only payable on income from (or deemed to be from) a South African source. Income is generally regarded as being from a South African source if its originating cause is situated in South Africa. Non South African sourced income was accordingly not taxable in South Africa. However with effect from years of assessment after 1 January 2001, South African residents (as defined in the Income Tax Act) are taxed on their worldwide income, ie any income derived by South African residents from outside South Africa will be taxable in South Africa. This includes the income of a controlled foreign company, being a company where residents collectively or individually hold more than 50% of the participation rights (either directly or indirectly) or where 50% of the participation rights is imputed to residents pro rata to their shareholding (provided that such shareholding is not less than 10% of the participation rights of the company in question). However some categories of income and income from certain activities outside South Africa will be exempt and credit will be given for foreign taxes paid. Non South African residents will continue to be taxed on their South African sourced income only.

Companies will be tax resident if they are either incorporated or have their place of effective management (the day to day activities involving a level of senior management) in South Africa. Individuals will be tax resident in South Africa if they are either ordinarily resident here or are physically present in South Africa for a certain number of days. Treaty residence overrides the local residence laws - ie if, in terms of a treaty, a taxpayer is not treaty resident in South Africa, but meets the above (local) requirements for tax residency, the taxpayer will not be tax resident in South Africa.

For many years married couples were taxed as a unit. From the 1996 year of assessment, under the influence of the Constitution's emphasis on equal treatment for all, the individual has been adopted as the basic taxpaying unit, and no distinction is made between males and females or between married or single people.

The Government and tax authorities have not yet adopted any formal position or measures on the issue of electronic commerce and taxation. The Electronic Communications and Transactions Act does not specifically deal with taxation issues.

Due to the complexities involved, and constant changes to tax legislation, readers are advised to seek specific advice on the application of and changes to the tax system.

PRINCIPAL TAXES

Direct Taxes

Direct taxes, which are covered in more detail later in this chapter, may be summarised as follows

Income Taxes:

- individual income tax - an annual tax on the income of partnerships, trusts and individuals (see below for further details);
- company tax - an annual tax on the income of companies and close corporations (see below for further details);
- secondary tax on companies - a tax imposed on dividends declared by companies and distributions made by close corporations, payable and borne by the companies and close corporations (see below for further details);
- a tax on certain dividends from foreign registered or incorporated companies, including retirement funds and insurers (see below for further details).

Capital Taxes:

- donations tax - a gift tax payable by the donor on the value of property disposed of by donation by South African residents (see below for further details);
- estate duty - an inheritance tax payable by the estate on the value of property of a deceased who was resident in South Africa at the date of death (see below for further details);
- capital gains tax was introduced with effect from 1 October 2001 and applies to the disposal of any asset that takes effect after that date (see below for further details).

Indirect Taxes

South Africa imposes the following indirect taxes -

- value added tax - an invoice based value added tax which is levied on supplies of goods and services (see below for further details);
- excise and customs duties (see below for further details);
- stamp duties - charges levied on certain documentary instruments (see below for further details);
- securities tax on the transfer of securities (see below for further details);
- transfer duty on the transfer of fixed property (see below for further details);
- regional services council levies (see below for further details);
- skills development levies (see below for further details);
- unemployment insurance contributions (see below for further details).

Administration

Company tax is payable for the fiscal year that coincides with a company's financial year. The tax year of individuals ends on the last day of February in each year.

Tax is payable in installments by all companies and close corporations and by those individuals who are classified as provisional taxpayers (for example directors of companies and members of close corporations). Provisional tax consists of two payments, the first falling due six months after the commencement of the year of assessment and the second at the end of the year of assessment. A penalty and interest is payable for late payment. A third top-up payment must be made within seven months after the end of the year of assessment if the total amount paid by way of provisional taxes is less than the amount of tax actually payable. Interest (non-deductible) is payable on the shortfall at a prescribed rate currently 11,5%. Conversely, if the total amount paid exceeds the tax assessed, interest is payable to the taxpayer at a prescribed rate - currently 7,5% - on the amount overpaid. That interest is taxable in the hands of resident taxpayers.

Employers are required to deduct employees' tax from their employees' remuneration and to pay such amounts over to the authorities on a monthly basis. Employees' tax thus deducted is allowed as a credit against the total amount of an employee's liability for tax as finally assessed on the basis of his or her annual return. Under the SITE system (Standard Income Tax on Employees) however individuals earning less than R74 000 a year from employment are not required to file an annual income tax return, and the employees' tax deducted from their salaries represents their full and final liability for tax.

CORPORATE TAX

Before 1 January 2001, companies were subject to income tax only on their income from South African sources excluding capital gains. However, South African resident corporates are taxed on their worldwide income for years of assessment after 1 January 2001.

In addition, companies pay secondary tax on companies, which is generally imposed on all dividends declared by them. In most respects, a company is defined for tax purposes to include a close corporation.

Rates

Companies are taxed on income at the rate of 30%. Gold-mining companies are taxed according to a special formula. However, due to the secondary tax on companies (see below for further details), which is levied at 12,5% on the net amount of dividends declared by a company, the effective rate is higher than 30%. The combined rate is however not 42,5%, but is effectively 37,78% of all profits distributed. Thus, broadly speaking, it can be said that a South African company will be taxed at the rate of 30% on so much of its profits as are retained, and at an effective 37,78% on so much of its profits as are distributed by way of dividend. Because secondary tax on companies is not a withholding tax on dividends, but a corporate tax, the rate is normally not reduced in terms of double tax agreements.

Small business corporations (namely corporations having an annual turnover of less than R5 million and which meet certain specified requirements) are taxed at the rate of 15% for the first R150 000 of taxable income and at 30% for amounts in excess of R150 000 (exclusive of secondary tax on companies - the effective rate will increase in respect of profits distributed by way of dividend).

"Employment companies" (namely certain labour brokers or companies on whose behalf a "connected person" renders services to clients) are taxed at a rate of 35% (exclusive of secondary tax on companies - the effective rate will increase in respect of profits distributed by way of dividend).

Dividends Received

Local dividends are exempt from tax in the hands of the recipient and are deducted from dividends paid by a recipient that is a company or close corporation in determining the net amount on which secondary tax on companies is calculated. Certain foreign dividends received by South African residents may also be exempt in certain circumstances (see below for further details).

Determination of Taxable Income

The assessment is based on taxable income determined in accordance with the Income Tax Act. Taxable income is calculated as gross income less exempt income less deductible expenses plus capital gains (see below for the inclusion rate of capital gains). Taxable income generally coincides with profit calculated in accordance with generally accepted accounting practice. Capital receipts are excluded from gross income. To be eligible for deduction, expenditure must be incurred in the production of income, must be for the purposes of trade and must not be of a capital nature. In addition, a number of special allowances (set out below) are allowed as tax deductions in calculating taxable income.

Industrial Plant and Machinery

The cost to the taxpayer of plant or machinery used in a process of manufacture can be written off over periods varying between three to five years, depending on the circumstances (eg the date when the plant or machinery was acquired and brought into use by the taxpayer for the first time and whether the plant or machinery is new and unused when acquired by the taxpayer). An accelerated depreciation rate of 100% per annum applies for small businesses.

Industrial Buildings

Industrial buildings, the erection of which was started by 31 December 1988 and which were brought into use by 31 December 1989, qualify for an initial allowance of 17,5% of their cost. An annual allowance is available on the balance of the cost after deduction of the initial allowance. The annual allowance (which is also available for buildings erected and brought into use outside the above time window) depends on the date when erection of the building commenced and the use (the building must be used in a process of manufacture or, during certain periods, a similar process is also acceptable) to which the building is put and varies between 2% and 10% of the cost of the building. The latest allowance is calculated at 5% (that is for buildings acquired and brought into use on or after 1 April 2000).

Housing Projects

Housing projects consisting of five or more residential units qualify for a 10% initial allowance and a 2% annual allowance, provided that the units are for the use of employees or are to be let at a profit.

General Capital Allowances

Capital allowances are also available for expenditure on any buildings or machinery used for the purposes of scientific research, certain intellectual property, wear and tear depreciation, hotels, aircraft, ships, plant and buildings of agricultural co-operatives, agricultural capital expenditure (including dams, roads, fences and machinery), buildings in designated urban development zones, pipelines, transmission and railway lines and mining capital expenditure. There is an investment allowance for approved strategic industrial projects.

Special Deductions

The Income Tax Act provides for certain special deductions for expenses incurred relating to repairs, scientific research, legal expenses, medical and dental expenses, restraint of trade payments, bad and doubtful debts, leasehold improvements, lease premiums, donations to public benefit organisations, trading stock and contributions to pension and provident funds and retirement annuities.

Tax Losses and Group Relief

Companies in a group may not share their tax losses with profitable companies in the same group. Tax losses may not be carried back but may be carried forward indefinitely, provided that there is trading in every tax year. Individuals may carry forward assessed losses even if there is no trading in the following tax year.

Roll-over relief applies for most transactions between groups of companies (which generally requires a chain of at least 75% equity shareholding). Roll-over relief may, in certain circumstances, result in an increased tax cost for the parties which needs to be weighed against the benefit of a deferral of tax.

Secondary Tax on Companies (STC)

The secondary tax on companies is a tax on dividends declared by a company (or a distribution declared by a close corporation). The tax liability is based on the net amount calculated by subtracting dividends accruing to the company from those declared by it. That net amount is taxed at the rate of 12,5%, and the tax is borne and paid by the company. Dividends paid by distributing equity capitalization shares do not give rise to STC liability. STC is also payable on amounts distributed by companies to shareholders which are deemed to be dividends, like certain loans to shareholders or where the South African tax residence status of the company ceases. Pursuant to the introduction of a tax on certain foreign dividends (see below for further details), a South African resident company will not be able to claim a taxable foreign dividend as a credit in the determination of its liability for STC.

Branches of Foreign Companies

An "external company" (namely the South African branch of a foreign company which has its place of effective management outside South Africa) is subject to an income tax of 35% on taxable income derived from a source within South Africa. External companies are exempt from STC.

Interest received by or accrued to foreign companies

Interest received by or accruing to a non-resident company is exempt from tax, if the company does not carry on business in South Africa. Otherwise normal tax will apply.

Transfer pricing and thin capitalisation

Transactions between residents and related non-residents as well as between residents and their offshore establishments need to comply with transfer pricing guidelines. For example, where a non-resident holding company charges excessive interest to its South African subsidiary, the excessive portion of the interest will not be allowed as a deduction in the South African company's hands and will be treated as a dividend attracting secondary tax on companies.

In addition, the thin capitalisation rules prescribe that interest charged on financial assistance granted by a non-resident company to its related South African resident company will be disallowed as a deduction in the hands of the South African company to the extent that the financial assistance, in relation to the non-resident's equity shareholding in the resident, exceeds the debt:equity ratio of 3:1 and the excessive portion will be treated as a dividend subject to secondary tax on companies. There is room to negotiate a higher ratio with the SARS in appropriate circumstances.

OTHER ENTITIES

Partnerships

Partnerships are not separate legal entities and are accordingly not taxed separately. Partners are required to file returns for the portion of the partnership income that has accrued to them. Income received or accrued in common by the members of a partnership is deemed to have accrued to them individually (in the proportions of their partnership interests) on the date that it accrued to them in common.

The tax loss that a limited (sleeping) partner in an en commandite partnership may claim may not exceed the income received or accrued from the partnership, plus the amount for which such partner is at risk - that is, the amount he or she has invested.

Trusts

Where a trust is simply a "conduit" for income (generally taken to mean that income is vested in the beneficiaries in the same tax year as that in which it is earned), the trust is not taxed separately and the beneficiaries are taxed on their benefits, which retain the character of the income concerned. For example rental retains that character and is taxable, South African dividends retain that character and are not. Where the income is not so vested, the trust is taxed as a separate taxpayer at 40%. Trading trusts which do not distribute their entire profits are taxed separately.

Losses of a trust are not allowed to flow to beneficiaries for tax purposes. Such losses may instead be retained in the trust, where they may be carried forward to the following tax year to be set off against the income of the trust in that year.

An exception to the application of the 40% trust tax rate has been made in the case of a trust created solely for the benefit of persons who suffer from a mental illness or serious physical disability and testamentary trusts established for the benefit of minor children. These trusts are taxed at individual rates.

INDIVIDUALS

South African residents are taxed at progressive rates on their worldwide income with effect from 1 January 2001. An individual's tax year ends on the last day of February in each year.

In general, individuals earning less than R74 000 a year from employment are not required to file tax returns if they do not have other taxable income. See Appendix 3 for the tax rate schedules for the years ending February 2004 and February 2005.

The tax threshold for persons below the age of 65 years is R30 000 for the tax year ending February 2004 and R32 222 for the tax year ending February 2005. The corresponding thresholds for persons aged 65 years or older are R47 222 and R50 000 respectively.

PERSONAL INCOME TAX REBATES

The following rebates are deductible directly from the income taxes payable by individuals for tax years ending in February 2004 and February 2005. These rebates are not available to trusts.

	2004	2005
Primary Rebate	R5 400	R5 800
Secondary Rebate	R3 100	R3 200

TREATMENT OF DIVIDENDS

Local dividends from all companies and distributions from all close corporations are exempt from tax. Generally speaking, foreign dividends received by South African residents with a holding of less than 25% in the company declaring dividends, are taxable insofar as the profits they are distributed from have not been taxed in South Africa (see below for further details).

TREATMENT OF INTEREST AND FOREIGN DIVIDENDS

The first R11 000 of interest and non-exempt foreign dividends received by an individual resident taxpayer under the age of 65, is exempt from tax. The exemption is R16 000 for each individual resident taxpayer aged 65 or more. The first R1 000 of the exemption applies to foreign dividends.

Interest accruing to non-residents (other than non-residents who are residents of countries in the common monetary area) is generally exempt from tax. To qualify, a non-resident individual must be absent from South Africa for not less than 183 days during the year of assessment. A natural person who was at any time resident in South Africa and who has been carrying on business in South Africa during the year of assessment will not qualify for this exemption. A non-resident company will only qualify if the interest it receives is not connected with any business it carries on in South Africa.

TAXATION OF TEMPORARY RESIDENTS

In accordance with South Africa's source-based rules, remuneration from services rendered in South Africa is taxable in South Africa. Foreign nationals temporarily residing and working in South Africa are therefore taxable on their remuneration, regardless of where their employer resides or where payment is made. Such income may be exempted, however, under one of South Africa's double taxation agreements. That exemption will usually be available if the temporary resident is present in South Africa for less than 183 days in any one tax or fiscal year and is paid by a foreign employer.

WITHHOLDING TAXES

Royalties

A withholding tax of 12% on gross royalties paid to a non-resident, is levied and is payable by the South African entity which is liable for the royalty, on behalf of the non-resident. Relief may however be provided in terms of double tax treaties

OTHER TAXES

Value-Added Tax

An invoice-based value-added tax (VAT) has been in force since 30 September 1991. The value-added tax system is similar to those used in Western Europe and New Zealand. Most transactions involving goods (including immovable property) and services attract VAT. The rate of VAT is 14%. The tax is levied on the value added in each transaction.

Donations Tax

Donations (gift) tax is payable by the donor at 20% of the value of property disposed of by donation by South African residents (other than public companies). There are exemptions for donations -

- of up to R30 000 a year for an individual donor and up to R10 000 a year for a non-public company;
- by a public company;
- under a trust;
- to public benefit organisations;
- between spouses;
- which only come into effect on the donor's death; and
- of property that was acquired from non-residents or derived from trade outside South Africa.

Estate Duty

Estate duty is levied at the rate of 20%. Overseas property that the deceased acquired by inheritance or held before taking up residence in South Africa is exempt. The first R1.5 million of an estate is exempt. Bequests to a surviving spouse are exempt.

Capital Gains Tax (CGT)

Capital gains tax was introduced with effect from 1 October 2001 on the disposal of assets on or after 1 October 2001. Those liable for the tax are -

South African residents on worldwide assets;

non South African residents in respect of immovable property in South Africa (including immovable property held through a company) or assets of a branch or agency in South Africa.

The tax is triggered by the disposal or deemed disposal of a capital asset on or after 1 October 2001. A capital gain or loss is the difference between the "base cost" (as defined) of an affected capital asset and the consideration realised or deemed to be realised on the disposal or deemed disposal of such asset. A portion of the "net capital gain" will be included in the taxpayer's gross income for income tax purposes. Capital losses may be deducted against capital gains or carried forward to future years of assessment, but are not available for set-off against revenue income.

The portion of the gain (or inclusion rate) that is taxable (by way of inclusion in taxable income) is 25% for a natural person, special trusts and an insurer's individual policyholder fund and 50% for all other taxpayers like a company, close corporation or business or family trust. For example if a company makes a gain of R100, 50% thereof (ie R50) must be included in its taxable income for income tax purposes and taxed at the corporate rate of 30%. The effective rate of CGT is accordingly -

Inclusion rate (50%) x statutory rate (30%) = effective rate (15%).

Certain assets are however exempt. These include a primary owner occupied residence (up to R1 million of the capital gain), assets owned by institutions exempt from normal taxation (like Government departments), lump sum benefits of most superannuation and life assurance policies (excluding "second-hand" policies), private motor vehicles, gambling proceeds, small business assets and personal belongings and effects.

CGT liability will not arise with regard to -

transactions eligible for roll-over relief (eg company formations, share for share transactions, intra-group transactions, amalgamations, unbundlings, etc.). The CGT liability is essentially rolled over and thus not avoided;

transfers of property from a deceased estate;

transfers between spouses;

transactions subject to income tax.

Excise and Customs Duties

South Africa imposes excise duties on the local production of certain commodities, such as automobiles, jewellery, beer and wine, without regard to their sale. Clothing, basic foods, medicine, rent, certain utilities and professional services are exempt from excise duties.

Imported goods are subject to similar treatment in the form of customs duties. The rates of such customs duties, however, are not always the same as the rates of excise duties. A rebate of customs duty can be obtained if the imported goods are to be used in manufacturing for export.

Local Taxes on Immovable Property

Real estate taxes are levied by local governments. Agricultural land is taxed at a lower rate than dwellings or business properties. The value of real estate on which such local taxes are levied will, in certain circumstances, include land together with improvements and buildings on the property.

Regional Services Council Levies

Regional Services Councils, Metropolitan Councils and Joint Services Boards are responsible for the supply of basic services within their regions. A regional establishment levy is payable by businesses to these councils, calculated on the gross consideration received in respect of the sale or letting of goods, the sale or letting of fixed property and any trade, business or professional service rendered.

A regional services levy is also payable on the salary paid by an employer to employees.

The amounts of these levies vary from region to region, but the amounts are very small - for example, in the Johannesburg area, the regional establishment levy, payable on income, is 0.1408% while the regional services levy, payable on remuneration, is 0.3509%. VAT is added to these amounts.

Unemployment insurance fund contributions and Skills development levy

Employers are liable to pay unemployment insurance fund contributions to a maximum amount of 1% of salaries (limited to a maximum monthly salary of R8 836) as well as a skills development levy of 1% of remuneration. To the extent that there is appropriate training for the staff, some of this levy may be reclaimed.

Uncertificated Securities Tax

A tax is currently imposed on the transfer of ownership of listed securities excluding debentures. The tax is currently 0,25% of the consideration paid in the transaction. Warrant issuers and registered brokers are however exempt.

All listed shares have been dematerialised in terms of the Share Transactions Totally Electronic system (STRATE) of the JSE Securities Exchange South Africa in a Central Securities Depository (CSD). Ownership of the dematerialised shares is electronically transferred without the necessity of filing any paper. Amendments to the Stamp Duties Act and the Marketable Securities Tax Act have been effected to ensure that Uncertificated Securities Tax is paid on the transfer of ownership of shares which have been dematerialised on the CSD.

Stamp Duties

Stamp duties apply to a number of documents in South Africa. The duty is on the document itself, not the transaction. Some stamp duties are at a fixed amount and others are at ad valorem rates. Government's policy remains to eventually remove stamp duties. Currently stamp duties only apply to debit entries in bank, credit card and Postbank accounts, installment credit agreements for movables, lessees of immovable property and the issue and registration of transfer of non-listed securities.

Duty on Transfers of Immovable Property

Transfers of immovable property where the seller is a vendor for VAT purposes are subject to VAT at 14% unless the property is transferred to a VAT vendor as part of a business sold as a going concern in which case VAT is chargeable at 0%.

Where the seller is not a vendor for VAT purposes, acquisitions of immovable property by companies or close corporations or trusts are normally liable to duty at the rate of 10% of the property's value. Acquisitions by individuals are liable to duty at the rate of 0% on the first R140 000 of the value, 5% on any excess value up to R320 000, and 8% on any further excess value.

Pensions, Provident and Retirement Annuity Funds

Tax at a rate of 18% is imposed on monthly gross interest, non-exempt foreign dividends and net rental received by or accrued to pension, provident and retirement annuity funds.

Non-exempt foreign dividends

The exemption that applies to most local dividends is not equally available for dividends received by residents from foreign resident companies (including retirement funds and insurers) and these are generally part of the taxable income of South African residents unless one of the exemptions referred to below applies.

Foreign dividends declared during tax years commencing on or after 1 June 2004 will qualify for tax exemption in certain circumstances, including -

dividends received by shareholders holding certain minimum holdings (currently 25%);

dividends declared by listed companies where South African residents hold certain minimum holdings (currently 10%);

dividends declared out of profits that were already subject to South African tax.

Mining Taxes

In terms of recent legislation, mining companies will become obliged to pay a royalty to the Government in respect of mining rights held by them. The introduction of the mining royalty will be delayed until five years after the introduction of the Mineral and Petroleum Resources Development Act (which came into effect on 1 May 2004). It is proposed that the royalty be levied at a differentiated rate to take account of the industry's diverse production dynamics and market structures. Other areas under review include mining depreciation allowances, rate differentiation for mining sectors, allowable deductions and STC exemptions. The gold mining tax formula (which provides income tax exemption and STC relief for certain gold mines) is under review. This is to be replaced by a royalty regime that would make adjustments for profit levels, thereby automatically benefiting marginal mines.

TAX TREATIES

South Africa has a number of double taxation agreements with various countries. Most are comprehensive agreements. Some relate only to sea and air transport. The comprehensive agreements include relief in respect of withholding taxes on royalties and know-how.

In addition, double tax agreements have been signed with several countries and will come into force as soon as they are ratified. With other countries, double tax agreements have been initialed but have not yet been signed, or are under negotiation or renegotiation.

PERSONAL INCOME TAX RATES

The income tax rates for the year of assessment ending February 2004 and 2005 are as shown in the following table. These tax rates change from year to year. Changes are usually announced in the annual budget and become effective from 1 March in the year in question.

The adjustments to personal income tax rates have afforded meaningful relief to taxpayers.

Individuals - Year of Assessment ending on 29 February 2004	
Taxable Income (R)	**Rates of Tax**
R0 - R70 000	18% of each R1 of taxable income
R70 001 - R110 000	R12 600 plus 25% of the amount over R70 000
R110 001 - R140 000	R22 600 plus 30% of the amount over R110 000
R140 001 - R180 000	R31 600 plus 35% of the amount over R140 000
R180 001 - R255 000	R45 600 plus 38% of the amount over R180 000
R255 001 and above	R74 100 plus 40% of the amount over R255 000

Individuals - Year of Assessment ending on 28 February 2005	
Taxable Income (R)	**Rates of Tax**
R0 - R74 000	18% of each R1 of taxable income
R74 001- R115 000	R13 320 plus 25% of the amount over R74000
R115 001 - R155 000	R23 570 plus 30% of the amount over R115 000
R155 001 - R195 000	R35 570 plus 35% of the amount over R155 000
R195 001 - R270 000	R49 570 plus 38% of the amount over R195 000
R270 001 and above	R78 070 plus 40% of the amount over R270 000

DOUBLE TAX TREATIES

During the first half of 2004 further agreements were reached with other countries on the avoiding of double taxation of income accruing to South African taxpayers from foreign sources or to foreign taxpayers from South African sources. The position at June 2004 is as follows

- Comprehensive agreements are in place with Algeria, Australia, Austria, Belarus, Belgium, Botswana, Canada, Croatia, Cyprus, the Czech Republic, Denmark, Egypt, Finland, France, Germany, Greece, Hungary, India, Indonesia, Iran, Ireland, Israel, Italy, Japan, Korea, Lesotho, Luxembourg, Malawi, Malta, Mauritius, Namibia, the Netherlands, Norway, Oman, Pakistan, the People's Republic of China, Poland, Romania, the Russian Federation, the Seychelles, Singapore, Slovak Republic, Swaziland, Sweden, Switzerland, Thailand, Tunisia, Uganda, the United Kingdom, the United States of America, Zambia and Zimbabwe. The newly updated treaty with the United Kingdom also extends to Grenada and Sierra Leone.
- Comprehensive agreements have been ratified in South Africa with Brazil, Nigeria, New Zealand and Rwanda.
- New or updated comprehensive agreements have been signed, but not ratified, with Ethiopia, Kuwait, Swaziland and Ukraine.
- Comprehensive agreements have been negotiated or renegotiated, but not signed, with Bulgaria, Democratic Republic of Congo, Estonia, Gabon, Germany, Ghana, Kuwait, Latvia, Lithuania, Malawi, Malaysia, Morocco, Mozambique, Namibia, the Netherlands, Portugal,

Qatar, Saudi Arabia, Spain, Sri Lanka, Tanzania, Turkey, United Arab Emirates, Zambia and Zimbabwe.

- Comprehensive agreements are being negotiated or renegotiated but have not been finalised with Bangladesh and Cuba.
- Limited sea and air transport agreements exist with Brazil, Portugal and Spain.

Other

No other withholding taxes are imposed on amounts paid to non-residents.

ANTI-AVOIDANCE LEGISLATION

The Income Tax Act contains anti-avoidance provisions which enables the Commissioner to assess a taxpayer for any taxes which have been avoided, postponed or reduced. A wide business purpose test is applied, the question being whether the relevant transaction was entered into in a manner which would have been utilised for bona fide trade purposes. If not, the Commissioner is entitled to levy tax as if the transaction had not been entered into.

Common law anti-avoidance rules are also applied to prevent tax avoidance.

It is proposed to tax hybrid investments (such as convertible loans, perpetual debt and redeemable or interest yielding preference shares) according to their underlying economic substance rather than their form, in conjunction with suitable anti-avoidance legislation. The anti-avoidance measures will focus on convertible instruments, debt instruments of which the capital is effectively never repayable, shares with a required capital repayment and the introduction of special rules for domestic and hybrid instruments.

Finally recent amendments have been introduced which ring-fence the tax losses of certain trades (or so called "hobby activities") and thereby restrict the netting off of tax losses arising from these hobby activities against the taxable income derived by a person carrying on a trade. Only natural persons in the maximum marginal tax bracket are affected.

ACCOUNTING AND AUDIT

THE ACCOUNTING PROFESSION

The accounting profession is well established in South Africa and all of the major international firms are represented. The generally accepted standards of auditing and accounting in South Africa have been developed to meet the strict requirements established by the profession. These requirements have been influenced to a large extent by the standards promulgated by the International Accounting Standards Committee and the International Federation of Accountants.

STATUTORY REGULATIONS

Accounting Records

In terms of the Companies Act, all companies must keep accounting records in one of the eleven official languages. At a minimum, these records must include -

- the assets and liabilities of the company;

- a fixed-assets register;
- cash receipts and payments;
- details of goods purchased and sold; and
- annual stock-taking (inventory) statements.

The accounting records must be such as to fairly present the state of affairs and business of the company and explain the transactions and financial position of the trade or business of the company.

Annual Financial Statements

In terms of the Companies Act, the directors of every company must prepare annual financial statements and present them to the annual general meeting of the company. At a minimum, the annual financial statements must consist of -

- a balance sheet and notes;
- an income statement and notes;
- a directors' report;
- an auditors' report; and
- a cash flow statement.

The annual financial statements must fairly present the state of affairs of the company as at the financial year-end and its profit or loss for that year in conformity with generally accepted accounting practice (GAAP). If a company has subsidiaries at the end of its financial year and is not a wholly-owned subsidiary of another company incorporated in South Africa, it has an obligation to prepare group financial statements. These must, in the same way as the company's own financial statements, fairly present the position and results of the group and must also conform to GAAP. Both the company and group financial statements must set out certain additional information prescribed by the Companies Act, must be approved by the directors and must be signed by two directors or, if there is only one director, by that director.

Every company that is not a wholly-owned subsidiary of another company incorporated in South Africa must submit a directors' report, which must cover such matters as -

- the state of affairs of the company.
- a description of the company's business; and
- the profit or loss of the company and its subsidiaries.

Any material matters in any of these areas and certain other matters specifically identified in applicable legislation must be addressed in the directors' report.

Interim Reports

Public companies and branches of foreign companies (external companies) are required to send all members and debenture holders a half-yearly interim report, fairly presenting the business and operations of the company (or, if applicable, the group). It is not required that such interim reports be audited, but they must be approved by the directors and signed on their behalf by two of the directors. Private companies are not required to provide an interim report to members.

Provisional Financial Statements

If a public company has not issued annual financial statements within three months after its year-end, it must (within such three-month period) issue provisional financial statements to its members and debenture-holders. These must fairly present the business and operations of the company or, if applicable, the group. The requirements for private companies are less stringent. If a private company has not issued its financial statements within six months after its year-end, the Companies and Intellectual Property Registration Office (CIPRO - formerly the Registrar of Companies) may, on application by a member and for good cause shown, require that provisional financial statements be submitted to that member. It is not necessary that such provisional annual financial statements be audited but they must be approved and signed by the company's directors.

Close Corporations (CCs)

For a close corporation, the requirements relating to the maintenance of accounting records are similar to those for a company. A close corporation's annual financial statements must be drafted within nine months after its year-end. The annual financial statements must be approved and signed by or on behalf of members holding at least 51% of the members' interest in the close corporation and must consist of -

- a balance sheet and notes;
- an income statement or any similar financial statement (if such alternative is appropriate); and
- a members' net investment statement.

The financial statements must fairly present the state of affairs and the result of the operations of the close corporation, in conformity with GAAP as appropriate to the business of the close corporation.

Annual Audit Requirement

The financial statements of both public and private companies are subject under the Companies Act to an annual audit. Only chartered accountants registered with the Public Accountants and Auditors Board may be appointed as auditors for the purposes of the annual audit.

Close corporations are not subject to a compulsory audit. However, the corporation is required to appoint an independent accounting officer, who is responsible for the preparation of the financial statements and who must be a member of one of the recognised professional accounting bodies.

Filing and Disclosure Requirements

Copies of a company's annual financial statements and group annual financial statements (if any) must be sent to the shareholders and debenture holders of the company not less than twenty-one days before the date of the company's annual general meeting. Public companies and external companies are required to file a copy of their annual financial statements with the Companies and Intellectual Property Registration Office within six months from the end of their financial year. Private companies are not required to do so, although the Second King Report on Corporate Governance has recommended that the Companies Act be amended to require this. An external company must also file a copy of its annual financial statements as prepared in terms of the requirements of the jurisdiction in which it is incorporated. External companies can apply for exemption from this and other requirements and such exemption is fairly readily granted.

The annual financial statements of companies must comply with the disclosure requirements set out in the fourth schedule to the Companies Act and as prescribed by GAAP. It should be noted that listed companies must also comply with the requirements of the JSE Securities Exchange South Africa.

The disclosure requirements for a close corporation are not as stringent as those for a company and are subject to the overriding requirement of fair presentation. The complexity of the financial statements would depend on the needs of the members, who, as owners and managers of the corporation, are the primary recipients of the financial information.

ACCOUNTING PRINCIPLES

Statements of Generally Accepted Accounting Practice are drafted by the South African Institute of Chartered Accountants and, after a period of publication for comment, approved by the Accounting Practices Board (APB). The APB consists of representatives from the accounting profession, commerce and industry.

South Africa's GAAP statements can be broadly categorised as introductory statements, general statements, statements on fieldwork and statements on reporting. When international auditing guidelines are issued, they are compared to the existing standards and procedures in South Africa (regardless of whether codified in the form of statements) to determine whether there are significant differences between the two. If there are significant differences, steps are taken, if appropriate, to seek the harmonisation of South African practice with international auditing guidelines.

Statements of GAAP must be followed in the preparation of the financial statements of companies subject to the Companies Act. They are also relevant to the financial statements of other entities purporting to achieve fair presentation.

FORM AND CONTENT OF FINANCIAL STATEMENTS

The Companies Act does not require a company to specify how its net profit for the year is made up, but does require certain items of income and expenditure to be detailed, for example turnover, depreciation, directors' remuneration, interest paid and provision for taxation. If a company or group is involved in more than one type of business, the directors' report must indicate the proportion of profit attributable to each type of business. Notes to the financial statements usually provide details of all significant items shown on the balance sheet.

In addition to the Companies Act requirements, GAAP requires the disclosure of information concerning the company's accounting policies, details of taxation, extraordinary items, prior-year adjustments in the income statement and other matters. Additional disclosure requirements apply to companies listed on the JSE. These requirements call for the disclosure of directors' interests in the share capital of the company, employee share incentive schemes and borrowing powers and also require interim and preliminary reports to the members. The Second King Report on Corporate Governance has also recommended disclosure of directors' remuneration and benefits on an individual basis.

Under the Close Corporations Act, a close corporation's accounting officer is required to ensure that the annual financial statements accord with the books and records of the corporation.

The Companies Act and Close Corporations Act do not apply to unincorporated partnerships or sole traders. Other corporate bodies, such as co-operative societies and pension funds, are governed by their own statutes, which in most cases prescribe the form and content of their annual financial statements. If no such requirements are imposed, financial statements are usually prepared in accordance with South African GAAP.

USEFUL BUSINESS CONTACTS

When dialling from an international location, the international access number for South Africa, 27, must be used as a prefix and the 0 of the area code should be omitted. As most government departments have a large number of separate internal telefax lines, it is advisable to contact the relevant department by telephone to ascertain the correct telefax number before sending a telefax to such department.

Department	Physical Address	Postal Address	Telephone Fax	Internet
The Presidency	Union Buildings West Wing, Second Floor Government Ave Pretoria	Priv Bag X1000 Pretoria 0001	+27 (0)12 300 5200 +27 (0)12 323 8246	www.gov.za/president/index.php
Arbitration Foundation of Southern Africa	First Floor Maisels Chambers 4 Protea Place Sandown 2196	PO Box 653007 Benmore 2010 Sandton	+27 (0)11 320 0600 +27 (0)11 320 0533	www.arbitration.co.za info@arbitration.co.za
Bond Exchange of South Africa (BESA)	Mezzanine Level 30 Melrose Boulevard Melrose Arch 2196	PO Box 77 Melrose Arch 2076	+27 (0)11 215 4000 +27 (0)11 215 4100	www.bondex.co.za or www.besa.za.com bondex@besa.za.com
Business Partners Limited (formerly Small Business Development Corporation)	5 Wellington Road Parktown 2193	PO Box 7780 Johannesburg 2000	+27 (0)11 480 8700 +27 (0)11 642 2791	www.businesspartners.co.za enquiries@businesspartners.co.za
Companies and Intellectual Property Registration Office	Zanza Building 116 Proes Street Pretoria 0002	PO Box 429 Pretoria 0001	0861 843 384 (local) +27 11 254 9405 (international) 0861 843 888	www.cipro.gov.za cipro@e-centric.co.za

Council for Scientific and Industrial Research (CSIR)	Meiring Naude Rd Brummeria Pretoria 0002	P O Box 395 Pretoria 0001	+27 (0)12 841-2911 +27 (0)12 349 1153	http://www.csir.co.za/ csir@co.za
Credit Bureau Association	First Floor 376B, Atlas Office Park 376 Oak Avenue Randburg	P O Box 2146 JPinegowrie 2123	+27 (0)11 886 8519 +27 (0)11 789 6080	www.cba.co.za enquiries@cba.co.za
Credit Guarantee Insurance Corporation of Africa Limited	Credit Guarantee House 31 Dover Street Randburg	PO Box 125 Randburg 2125	+27 (011) 889 7000 +27 (011) 886 1027	http://www.creditguarantee.co.za/ info@cgic.co.za
Department of Foreign Affairs	East Wing Union Building Government Avenue Arcadia 0083	Private Bag X152 Pretoria 0001	+27 (0)12 351-1000	http://www.dfa.gov.za/
Department of Home Affairs (Immigration and Work Permits)	Civitas Building 242 Struben Street Pretoria 0002	Private Bag X114 Pretoria 0001	+27 (0)12 314-8911	http://www.home-affairs.gov.za/
Department of Home Affairs (Jhb regional office)	New Government Building Corner of Harrison and Plein Streets Johannesburg, 2001	Private Bag X11 Johannesburg 2000	+27 (0)11 836-3228 +27 (0)11 834-6623	
Department of Labour	Laboria House Cnr Schoeman / Paul Kruger Streets Pretoria 0002	Private Bag X117 Pretoria 0001	+27 (0)12 309-4000 +27 (0)12 320-2059	http://www.labour.gov.za/
Department of Transport	Forum Building Cnr Bosman / Struben Streets Pretoria 0002	Private Bag X193 Pretoria 0001	+27 (0)12 309-3000	http://www.transport.gov.za/

Department of Trade & Industry	House of Trade and Industry Tenth floor 226 Prinsloo Street Pretoria 0002	Private Bag X84 Pretoria 0001	0861 84 33 84 (local) +27 11 254 9405 (international) 0861 843 888 (local fax) +27 11 254 9406 (international fax)	http://www.dti.gov.za/ contactus@thedti.gov.za
Development Bank of Southern Africa Limited	1258 Lever Road Headway Hill Midrand 1685	PO Box 1234 Halfway House 1685	+27 (0)11 313 3911 +27 (0)11 318 2487	
Industrial Development Corporation Ltd (IDC)	19 Fredman Drive Sandton 2146	P O Box 784055 Sandton 2146	+27 (0)11 269-3000 or 0860 693 888 +27 (0)11 269-3116	http://www.idc.co.za callcentre@idc.co.za
Khula Enterprise Finance Limited	Mellis Park Bradenham Hall 7 Mellis Road Rivonia Ext. 20 2128	P O Box 4197 Rivonia 2128	+27 (0)11 807 8464 or 0800 118 815 +27 (0)11 807 8471	http://www.khula.org.za/ helpline@khula.org.za
Land and Agricultural Development Bank of Southern Africa (Land Bank)	192 Visagie Street Pretoria 0001	PO Box 375 Pretoria 0001	0800 00 52 59	www.landbank.co.za info@landbank.co.za
National Empowerment Fund	23 Melrose Boulevard Melrose North Johannesburg	PO Box 31 Melrose Arch Melrose North 2076	+27 (0)11 772 8000 +27 (0)11 772 8100	enquiries@nefcorp.co.za
Ntsika Enterprise Promotion Agency	Fifth Floor Pencardia 1 Building 501 Pretorius Street Arcadia Pretoria	PO Box 56714 Arcadia 0007	+27 (0)12 483 2000 Or 0800 11 38 57 +27 (0)12 483 2054	http://www.ntsika.org.za/ helpline@nepa.org.za
South African Futures Exchange (SAFEX)	One Exchange Square Gwen Lane Sandown	Private Bag X991174 Sandton 2146	+27 (0)11 520 7000 +27 (0)11 520 7458	www.safex.co.za

South African Revenue Service Head Office	299 Bronkhorst Street Nieuw Muckleneuk Pretoria 0181	Private Bag X923 or PO Box 402 Pretoria 0001	+27 (0)12 422 4000 +27 (0)12 422 5181	http://www.sars.gov.za/
South African Bureau of Standards (SABS)	1 Dr Lategan Road Groenkloof Pretoria	Private Bag X191 Pretoria 0001	+27 (0)12 428-7911 +27 (0)12 344-1568	http://www.sabs.co.za/ info@sabs.co.za
The South African Reserve Bank	370 Church Street Pretoria 0002	P O Box 427 Pretoria 0001	+27 (0)12 313 3911 +27 (0)12 313 3197/929	http://www.reservebank.co.za/
South African Chamber of Business (SACOB)	24 Sturdee Avenue Rosebank Johannesburg	PO Box 213 Saxonwold 2132	+27 (0)11 446 3800 +27 (0)11 446 3847/9	http://www.sacob.co.za info@sacob.co.za

SOUTH AFRICA TAX SYSTEM: PRACTICAL INFORMATION

TAX AMNESTY FOR BUSINESS FAQ

JUSTIFICATION FOR AMNESTY

1. Why is it necessary to grant a tax amnesty?

Small businesses play a vital role in stimulating economic activity, job creation, poverty alleviation and the general improvement of living standards. Many small businesses operate informally, were historically marginalised and were excluded from the economic mainstream, thus remaining outside of the tax system. These small businesses are now keen to regularise their tax affairs but an obstacle is their past non-compliance and the resultant potential tax liabilities, penalties and interest.

SARS's tax-base broadening efforts and "walkabouts" in informal business areas have shown that numerous small businesses not on register or that have not made full disclosure to SARS would like the opportunity to "come clean" without fear of hefty tax liabilities arising out of past non-compliance. This also includes taxi operators who wish to participate in the taxi recapitalisation programme.

Helping these businesses to become compliant has benefits for everyone: it helps small businesses to continue making an important economic contribution and to grow further; and it helps all taxpayers by increasing the tax register and ensuring the sustainable growth in revenue in the future.

2. Is the amnesty fair to persons who have been tax compliant?

Persons who are currently tax compliant will benefit from the increased number of persons who will register with SARS on the basis that the tax base will grow and contribute to additional revenue collections, i.e. the broader the tax base the lower the tax burden per taxpayer. This could enable the Minister of Finance to allocate additional funds to public services and infrastructure, further reduce the tax burden on taxpayers in future years, or both. The tax compliance culture in the country will also be improved.

3. What benefits are there for me to join the tax system?

Becoming tax compliant has a number of benefits to businesses. No longer do they have to live in fear of SARS's enforcement actions and possible criminal prosecution. And they can now access additional business (including tendering for government tenders) and finance because they will have a tax clearance certificate. Taxi operators can participate in the taxi recapitalisation programme. And, of course, you will be contributing your fair share to the growth and development of South Africa.

4. Why can't there be a simplified tax regime for small businesses?

Although generally the same tax rules apply to all taxpayers, the tax system does provide special concessions to small businesses to help ease the burden of compliance. For example

- Below R300 000 turnover VAT registration is optional;
- Where taxable supplies are less than R1,2 million VAT returns need only be submitted 4-monthly;
- Individuals whose taxable supplies are less than R2,5 million may account for VAT on a cash basis; and
- A VAT retail schemes has been introduced for small businesses.

Small business help desks have also been introduced at selected SARS offices.

5. What benefits are there in the current tax system for small businesses?

Unincorporated businesses already benefit from the progressive tax rates for income tax purposes with no tax payable on the first R40 000 of taxable income . Small business corporations

- pay no tax on the first R40 000 of taxable income;
- are taxed at lower rates than other companies up to a taxable income of R300 000 per annum;
- may deduct expenditure on manufacturing assets in full in the year it is brought into use; and
- get an accelerated wear and tear allowance over a 3 year period (50/30/20).

Contact your nearest SARS office to find out more about the special tax rates and products available for small businesses and to find out if your business qualifies.

6. Will there be another amnesty?

There are no plans for any further tax amnesties. This is a once-off chance for small businesses to come clean without fear of heavy penalties

Applicants who qualify

1. Who may apply for amnesty?

Any individual, close corporation, unlisted company, trust, body corporate, association of persons, co-operative, insolvent estate or deceased estate meeting certain requirements may apply for amnesty.

The requirements are that -

- the individual or entity must have carried out a business;
- the gross income (turnover) of the business during the 2006 tax year was not more than R10 million; and
- in the case of a company or close corporation all the shares or members' interests were held directly by individuals throughout the 2006 tax year.

Small businesses which are unregistered for tax purposes at the end of the 2006 tax year or which are registered but whose income from small business activities has not been declared or has been understated, will benefit from the amnesty.

2. Will a "stokvel" qualify for amnesty?

A stokvel is not necessarily a separate juristic person and also would not be conducting business activities with persons who are not members of the stokvel. Based on these criteria it is not likely that the stokvel would qualify for amnesty. But contact your nearest SARS office for advice concerning your specific case.

3. I am already registered for tax. Do I qualify for the amnesty?

Taxpayers who are already registered can also make use of the amnesty window. If you have not been completely honest about your business income in previous returns you can use this opportunity to come clean. If you don't then you can be prosecuted for previous non-compliance.

4. What are the implications if you were fully compliant for income tax but never registered for VAT or the payroll taxes?

You may apply for amnesty in respect of VAT, PAYE, skills development levies and unemployment insurance contributions. You will have to pay the amnesty levy of between 2 & 5% on your taxable business income for 2006. You will further forfeit an assessed loss and assessed capital losses brought forward from the 2005 tax year. You will have to submit returns for VAT, PAYE, skills development levies and unemployment insurance contributions as from 1 March 2006.

5. Why are persons who are being investigated or audited being excluded from the amnesty?

Persons under investigation are excluded because the purpose of the amnesty is to reward persons for voluntary compliance. If a person's tax affairs are already under investigation, that person has done nothing to merit amnesty.

6. Can you apply for amnesty if your business activities ceased before the 2006 tax year?

Yes. The business turnover for the 2006 tax year will be zero and would therefore be below the R10m threshold.

7. Why is the turnover threshold only R10 million?

The amnesty is specifically aimed at small businesses. As such, the R10 million turnover threshold for the 2006 tax year is considered sufficient to cover all small and informal businesses targeted in the amnesty.

8. Is the turnover threshold inclusive or exclusive of VAT?

The threshold is exclusive of VAT. This should, however, be seen in the context that the income of persons who are not registered for VAT is simply turnover and VAT does not come into the equation.

9. What if I conducted more than one business and would like to apply for tax amnesty in respect of both businesses?

If both businesses where conducted by a natural person the total gross income (turnover) of both businesses must not exceed R10 million. If the businesses were conducted as separate legal entities then each entity in itself will be able to apply for tax amnesty provided all the other requirements in the legislation are met. Each entity's total gross income from carrying on business must not exceed R10 million.

10. Do partners in a partnership qualify for amnesty and, if so, how would they go about submitting the application?

Partners in a partnership do qualify for amnesty, provided that such partner's gross income from the partnership in the 2006 tax year does not exceed R 10 million. Each partner in the partnership would need to apply in his own name, as the partnership is not a separate legal entity for tax purposes. Any amnesty levy would be calculated on the individual profit share of the partner in question for the 2006 tax year (as defined).

11. Because the amnesty does not extend beyond the applicant itself, such as a company or CC , the shareholders or members may be reluctant to apply for their company or CC for fear that this will expose them personally in respect of under-declarations by such company or CC where the amounts in question have accrued to them. Does the amnesty provide for exemption of such persons from the tax consequences of such prior under-declarations by the company or CC?

To the extent that small business income is understated and appropriated to the shareholders or members these amounts are treated as dividends declared for STC purposes under current law. As dividend income is not taxable income in the hands of the shareholder or member, the issue of personal tax consequences does not arise in such instances.

12. What is the position of business trusts who distribute their profits in full to the beneficiaries during the 2006 tax year, with the result that the taxable income of the trust is nil for that year? Would any levy be payable?

The trust will qualify for amnesty provided that all vested or contingent beneficiaries in the 2006 tax year are private individuals. In the circumstances described, where all the profits have been distributed to beneficiaries during the year, the trust would have Nil taxable income for the 2006 tax year and would not be liable for an amnesty levy due to the fact that their taxable income for the year is below R 35 000. What needs to be borne in mind is that the business income distributed to the beneficiaries retains its nature and is thus classified as business income in the hands of those beneficiaries. The beneficiaries may well be advised to apply for amnesty in their own names in such circumstances and if their share of the distribution exceeds R 35 000 will be liable for an amnesty levy on such amount.

13. Section 5(2) of the Act excludes persons from amnesty if a notice has been delivered to them advising of an audit, investigation or other enforcement action. Do demands or summonses for outstanding returns fall within this category, and thus result in the exclusion of the taxpayer from applying for amnesty.

No, such action will not be treated as an exclusion from amnesty. In such circumstances, if the taxpayer can show that he has applied for amnesty or is in the process of applying for amnesty, the follow-up action (and even summons, if appropriate) will be withdrawn by SARS.

SCOPE OF AMNESTY

1. What is business income?

Any form of income generated through a business conducted by the taxpayer. To determine whether a person is carrying on a business will depend on the specific circumstances of the case. However, factors which may influence the determination are, for example -

- The purpose to make a profit;
- The continuity of the activities; and
- The scope of the activities.

The income must be directly related to the business activities conducted by the taxpayer.

Independent contractors, commission agents and rental income may qualify as business income.

To find out if your activities qualify, contact your nearest SARS branch.

2. Can I apply for amnesty for only one tax?
The tax amnesty application covers all the qualifying taxes. If the taxpayer wishes to obtain tax amnesty in respect of any one of these taxes their application will also include all the other taxes even if the taxpayer has been fully compliant in respect of those other taxes. The applicant will still have to pay the amnesty levy on the taxable income of his business for the 2006 tax year.

3. Why are salary and other income not covered by the amnesty?
The objective of the amnesty is to assist small businesses to regularise their tax affairs as a growth point in the economy. Extending the amnesty to others will cause the ambit of the tax amnesty to become too wide and the true purpose and objective of the tax amnesty relief as contained in the legislation will not be achieved.

4. What is remuneration?

Remuneration is defined in the Fourth Schedule to the Income Tax Act and means income paid to a person as, for example, salary, leave pay, wages, overtime pay, bonus, commission, whether in cash or otherwise. It also includes fringe benefits, allowances, advances and gains on share schemes.

5. What is gross income?

This is the total amount, whether in cash or otherwise, received by or accrued (or deemed to have been received by or accrued) to a resident taxpayer, during any particular year of assessment, excluding amounts of a capital nature. From a practical perspective it is similar to the accounting concept of turnover.

6. What does the 2006 tax year mean?

The 2006 tax year for individuals and trusts is the period from 1 March 2005 to 28 February 2006. For other entities such as companies and close corporations the 2006 tax year is the financial year which ends during the period 1 April 2005 to 31 March 2006.

7. Why does a company held by another company not qualify for amnesty?

Groups of companies do not fall within the target market for which the tax amnesty has been designed. This is a sophisticated structure that does not normally correspond with small businesses. This exclusion also prevents multiplication in income splitting.

8. What does relief from interest and penalties cover?

A successful applicant will not be liable to pay any additional tax, penalty or interest to the extent that it relates to any amount for which tax amnesty has been granted to that applicant.

9. Why are tax debt, penalties and interest imposed by SARS in respect of taxes already assessed not also covered under the amnesty?

Although this aspect is not covered at this stage, the Minister may by regulation prescribe the circumstances upon which the Commissioner may waive, in whole or in part, any additional tax, penalty, or interest payable in respect of any year of assessment, dividend cycle, tax period or month ending during the qualifying period. Draft regulations in this regard must still be published in the Government Gazette.

10. Does the amnesty cover all offences and potential prosecution under any law of South Africa?

No. A person with approval under the tax amnesty is only deemed not to have committed any offence in terms of any Act to which the tax amnesty relates, hence it only covers tax offences committed in respect of income tax, STC, PAYE, withholding tax on royalties, VAT, SDL and UIF. Customs and Excise and indirect taxes such as transfer duties are not covered.

11. What is the scope of the tax amnesty relief?

Successful applicants will be granted relief from the payment of -

• Income Tax in respect of all amounts received or accrued or deemed to have been received or accrued by the small business for all tax years preceding the 2006 tax year;
• Secondary Tax on Companies (STC) in respect of any dividend declared or deemed to be declared for periods preceding the 2006 tax year;
• Value-added tax (VAT) in respect of the taxable supply of goods or services or the importation of any goods or the supply of imported services during any tax period ending on or before 28 February 2006;
• Employees' tax (PAYE) in respect of any remuneration paid to employees during any period or month ending on or before 28 February 2006
• Unemployment insurance contributions (UIF) in respect of any remuneration paid during any period or month ending on or before
28 February 2006; and
• Skills Development Levies (SDL) in respect of levies payable on any leviable amounts during any period or month ending on or before
28 February 2006;
• Withholding tax on Royalties in respect of any amounts paid to a non-resident for the period ending on or before 28 February 2006.

The relief also covers additional taxes, interest and penalties which relate to the above undisclosed amounts.

A successful applicant will not be subjected to any criminal prosecution relating to the non-disclosure of amounts for which amnesty is granted, which non-disclosure would otherwise have constituted an offence.

12. What is excluded from the tax amnesty relief?

The tax amnesty does not apply in respect of any tax, levy, contribution, interest, penalty or additional tax which -
• had already been paid by the applicant before the date of the application; or
• becomes payable as a result of any return, declaration or information submitted to SARS before the date of the application.

13. If no tax returns have been submitted for years prior to 2006, but provisional tax has been paid for those years, will the taxpayer be given credit for these payments?
The Act provides that the amnesty does not apply in regard to any tax already paid by the applicant. The provisional tax payments will therefore be dealt with as full settlement of tax liabilities for the years in question. No tax refunds will be made and no such credits will be offset against 2006 and subsequent tax liabilities.

14. Does the amnesty also apply in regard to capital gains?

Capital gains form part of taxable income although it is taxed at a different level. The Act provides income tax relief in respect of any amount received by or accrued to a person during the qualifying period from carrying on of any business. Capital gain events occurring during the qualifying period would therefore qualify for relief. However, if the capital gain event occurs during or after the 2006 tax year then it will be subject to capital gains tax in the normal course.

15. What will be the Secondary Tax on Companies (STC) implications where a company/CC applies for amnesty and there was a debit loan account as at the commencement of the 2006 year of assessment?
In terms of the Act, the qualifying period for STC purposes is defined as being any dividend cycle that ends prior to the 2006 year of assessment. Following from this, any debit loan that existed as at the commencement of the 2006 tax year will have been deemed to be distributed in the qualifying period and thus will qualify for amnesty in regard to STC. All distributions or deemed distributions during or after the 2006 year of assessment will be subject to STC in the normal course.

16. Will Farming Development Expenditure (FDE) carried forward from a previous year be disallowed in a similar way to the disallowance of previous years' tax losses upon the granting of amnesty?
Farming capital expenditure does not form part of "assessed loss" as defined. The rules in the First Schedule provide for the excess over taxable income to again qualify as expenditure incurred in the following tax year. Thus the FDE will not be disallowed, but may be carried forward in the normal course.

DECLARATION OF INFORMATION

1. What information is required in the application?

The applicant must:

- disclose the taxable income of all amounts received from carrying on business during the 2006 tax year;
- furnish an income tax return for the 2006 tax year and a statement of all assets (at cost) and liabilities as at 28 February 2006; and
- provide reasonable estimates of income if it is not possible to provide full particulars of any actual amounts

2. Must I declare the amounts of income received in years prior to 2006 which were not previously declared to SARS?
The only requirement is to make full disclosure of business income for the 2006 year of assessment. The income not declared for previous years is subject to amnesty and does not need to be reported.
3. If VAT and PAYE returns have not been lodged for the period prior to 1 March 2006, must I include these with my amnesty application?
There is no requirement to lodge returns for VAT, PAYE or other payroll taxes where these have not been lodged in the past. Amnesty will be granted in respect of any taxes in these categories for the period up until 28 February 2006, provided that the 2006 income tax return is lodged.

4. What if a person does not have accounting records or documentary proof on which to base the taxable income?
If it is not possible for the applicant to provide full particulars of any amounts declared in a return, the applicant may provide a reasonable estimate of the amounts.
Factors taken into account to determine the "reasonable estimate" may include:

- a person's possessions and lifestyle, or

- daily cash takings less daily expenses multiplied by the number of days traded, or
- obtaining confirmatory information from third parties, e.g. banks.

5. When would an estimate be materially incorrect and disqualify a person from getting amnesty?
Significant understatements when compared to other sources of information which SARS may access will disqualify a person from getting amnesty.

6. What values must be used in the statement of assets and liabilities?
The legislation requires that assets must be reflected at cost price. If this is not possible the taxpayer may have to reflect the asset at the estimated cost price on date of acquisition. As regards the liabilities this will be the outstanding liabilities as at the end of the 2006 year of assessment.

7. Must your personal assets and liabilities also be reflected in the statement of assets and liabilities?
Yes – the statement should reflect all assets and liabilities of the applicant and not only, for example, the business assets and liabilities.

8. At which date must the statement of assets and liabilities be compiled?
The legislation requires that the statement of assets at cost and liabilities must be as at the end of the 2006 tax year.

9. Must the values of assets be sworn valuations?
A sworn valuation of assets is not required. An applicant should be able to substantiate and give reasons for using the estimated values for the cost of assets in the statement of assets and liabilities if called upon by SARS to do so.

10. Certain taxpayers will have difficulty in having Financial Statements drawn up for the 2006 year of assessment due to the time constraints under which their accountants are operating. Will it be acceptable to submit an amnesty application at this point, to be followed up by the relevant Financial Statements and Statement of Assets and Liabilities at a later state? This would serve the purpose of indicating a desire to apply for amnesty and would effectively get a "foot in the door" to the amnesty process.

We will accept applications at this stage on the strength of application forms only, subject to the fact that the applicant is to submit the full documentation at a later stage. However, as the end of the window period approaches it will be necessary to tighten these rules in order to prevent an inadvertent and unofficial extension of the window period. Applicants are encouraged to submit full documentation at the earliest opportunity to prevent any difficulties in relation to late submission.

11. If a business has in previous years under-declared income via the mechanism of understating assets (eg. cash, debtors or stock) how can this be rectified to ensure full declaration in the 2006 tax year without creating an inexplicable increase in the retained income / capital account of the shareholders / members / business owner?

The correct way to do this would be to re-state the opening balances on the 2006 Financial Statements of the business to reflect the correct position as opposed to the understated balances previously recorded. This may call for a note to the accounts to explain the changes in the comparative figures as compared with the figures reflected in the previous set of Financial Statements lodged. The fact of amnesty will ensure that this does not result in any additional tax liability for the applicant.

AMNESTY LEVY

1. Why must I pay a levy?

Non-compliance with any provision of any of the tax acts administered by the Commissioner usually has a consequence in that the taxpayer will be required to pay additional tax, penalties and interest as a result of the taxpayer's non-compliance. Some of these penalties could be as high as 200 per cent of the actual tax debt. These mechanisms are in essence aimed at improving the compliance culture of taxpayers in South Africa in general by penalising non-compliance and thereby serving as a deterrent not to break the law. In the case of the tax amnesty the normal provisions of the tax acts relating to additional tax, penalties and interest do not apply. The tax amnesty levy is the only penalty paid by the taxpayer who was guilty of non-compliance with any of the tax acts to which the amnesty provisions apply. The amnesty levy, based on the 2006 taxable income, is the price to be paid to benefit from the amnesty from payment of unpaid taxes, duties and levies before the 2006 tax year and from prosecution for tax contraventions before the 2006 tax year. In comparison to the total arrear taxes a person would normally have to pay to regularise his/her affairs, the amnesty levy is a small amount.

2. Does an applicant have to pay taxes for the 2006 tax year if the amnesty levy is payable for that year?

Yes. For the 2006 tax year the taxpayer must make full disclosure and comply with the amnesty provisions. The tax amnesty levy is, therefore, payable in addition to the taxes payable in respect of the 2006 tax year.

3. How is the amnesty levy calculated?

An amnesty levy not exceeding 5% as in the table below is calculated on the taxable business income determined for the 2006 year of assessment. In determining the amount of the levy, losses brought forward from a previous year must be ignored.

From	To	Levy
R -	R 35,000	No levy payable
R 35,000	R 100,000	2% of the amount above R 35 000
R 100,000	R 250,000	R1 300 + 3% of the amount above R 100 000
R 250,000	R 500,000	R5 800 + 4% of the amount above R 250 000
R 500,000	and above	R15 800 + 5% of the amount above R 500 000

4. When must the amnesty levy be paid?

The tax amnesty levy must be paid within 12 months after the date on which the notice of approval of the tax amnesty application was delivered to the successful applicant, or such longer period as the Commissioner may allow subject to such conditions as the Commissioner may impose.

5. Is any levy payable in regard to VAT, PAYE, etc., that was not declared in the past?
No, the only levy payable is the levy calculated on the basis of the 2006 taxable income. This one levy covers the amnesty for all forms of tax.

6. Will I still have to pay a levy if I apply for amnesty only in regard to VAT and PAYE contraventions? My income tax has always been properly declared.
Yes. The amnesty levy applies to all the taxes, although it is calculated on the basis of the taxable income for the 2006 tax year. If amnesty is to be granted in respect of any tax contraventions then the levy will be applicable in all cases where the taxable income exceeds R 35 000.

PROCEDURE

1. Will there be an audit to check the correctness of the 2006 tax return?

Not necessarily, but the normal risk processes will be used to select taxpayers for audit. However in the event of the taxpayer not being able to provide full particulars of the actual amounts, the taxpayer may provide reasonable estimates of the amounts and disclose to the Commissioner that the amounts provided are estimates. In such instances the Commissioner may want to verify the facts and information and the basis upon which the estimates provided by the taxpayer have been made.

2. Is there a phased approach as announced in the Budget where taxi businesses can apply first?

No. Any type of small business that complies with the criteria as set out in the legislation can apply from 1 August 2006 until 31 May 2007. It became clear that the two phases for the taxi industry and other small businesses announced in the Budget are inseparable and the amnesty would be more successful if all small businesses could apply concurrently.

3. Why are applications processed by SARS and not a separate amnesty unit?

A separate amnesty unit was set up for the foreign exchange control and tax amnesty, since both the SA Reserve Bank and SARS were involved in administering the amnesty. The current amnesty only involves SARS and will be administered by SARS as was the case for the 1995 and 1996 tax amnesties.

4. How will SARS evaluate your application?

A separate unit within SARS, with regional presence, has been established to process all applications on a confidential basis.

5. When will an application form be available?

The final version will be available electronically from the SARS Website at www.sars.gov.za; or a hard copy thereof can be collected at any SARS office from 01 August 2006.

6. Where can the applications be submitted or delivered?

Applications on the prescribed application form with the required attachments should be -

- o hand delivered to any SARS office;
- o posted to :P O Box 292, Groenkloof, 0027
- o faxed to 011 602 5502.

7. Why can't the application be sent via e-mail?

As the applications will require attachments consisting of information relating thereto, it would be not practical to submit these applications electronically.

8. How long will the evaluation process take?

This will depend on the volume of applications received. It is envisaged that the applicant will be informed of the outcome of the evaluation of an application within a reasonable period from the date of receipt of the application by SARS.

9. Who will perform the evaluation of the amnesty applications?

In each office of SARS (excluding an office which deals solely with matters relating to customs and excise) there will be specifically designated employees who will be responsible for the receipt of the amnesty applications. A separate unit within SARS with a regional presence will be responsible for the evaluation and processing of applications.

10. What will happen if the amnesty application is turned down?

The Commissioner will deliver to the applicant a notice of the decision to deny the application for tax amnesty and will set out the reasons for the decision.

11. How do I get tax returns for the various taxes if I am not yet registered for all or any of the taxes covered by the amnesty?

Copies of the returns are obtainable on application from any office of SARS, other than an office which deals solely with matters relating to customs and/or excise.

12. What should you do if you are not happy that you have been denied amnesty?

If an unsuccessful applicant is aggrieved by a decision of SARS not to approve the application for tax amnesty, the applicant may object and appeal against that decision. In these instances the normal dispute resolution procedures as contained in the Income Tax Act, 1962, will apply.

Prior year losses and deductions

1. If you had an assessed loss for the 2005 tax year, can it be set off against the taxable income for the 2006 tax year?

No. An applicant with approval under the tax amnesty provisions may not claim any assessed loss arising in any year of assessment preceding the 2006 tax year. Any assessed loss that arose in the 2006 year of assessment will however be allowed for purposes of determining that applicant's taxable income for the 2006 tax year and for any subsequent tax year.

2. Why are losses and deductions during the 2005 and earlier tax years forfeited if you were fully compliant for income tax purposes?

As the successful applicant's tax liability for income tax and STC will be waived for the tax years preceding the 2006 tax year and for the periods or months ending up to 28 February 2006 for PAYE, VAT, withholding tax on royalties paid to non-residents, unemployment insurance contributions and skills development levies, the applicant should not be able to still claim any deductions, allowances, assessed loss, assessed capital loss or input tax incurred during the tax years for which the tax amnesty is granted. This also includes the set-off of any excess dividends which accrued to the applicant during any dividend cycle ending during the period for which tax amnesty is granted against any dividends declared by the applicant during any dividend cycle ending thereafter.

3. Explain the loss disallowance rule?

Example

A taxpayer conducted business since 1996 and fully complied with his income tax obligations. His business was struggling in 2004 and he had an assessed loss of R150 000 for the 2005 tax year. The business is not registered for VAT although the annual turnover exceeds R1 million.

The taxpayer applies for and is granted amnesty for his VAT contraventions for periods ending up to 28 February 2006. The assessed loss of R150 000 will be forfeited and the amnesty levy will be payable on the taxable business income for 2006.

CENTRAL GOVERNMENT TAXES

CORPORATE INCOME TAX

Corporations are taxed on a progressive system on income sourced in South Africa, excluding capital gains.

PERSONAL INCOME TAX

There is a system of individual deductions, corporate fringe benefits and capital allowances used to determine taxable income.

Taxable income Rs.	Tax Rs.
0- 5,000	17% of each rand
5,000-10,000	850 + 18% Of amount over 5,000
10,000-15,000	1750 + 19% of amount over 10,000
15,000-20,000	2700 + 20% of amount over 15,000
20,000-30,000	3700 + 21% of amount over 20,000
30,000-40,000	5800 + 31% of amount over 30,000
40,000-50,000	8900 + 42% of amount over 40,000
50,000-70,000	13100 + 43% of amount over 50,000
70,000-80,000	21700 + 44% of amount over 70,000
80,000 and above	26100 + 45% of amount over 80,000

VALUE ADDED TAX (VAT)

There is a 14% value added tax (VAT) on all goods and services (certain foodstuffs excluded).

RATES OF INCOME TAXATION

Individuals : Individuals pay tax at progressive rates which reach a marginal rate of 45 per cent at R 100 000 of taxable income per annum.

Companies : A flat rate of 35 per cent on taxable income derived from a source within South Africa. The rate for companies also includes close corporations.

Dividends : Tax on dividends is exempt in the hands of the recipient. A secondary tax on companies (STC) of 12.5 per cent is levied on companies on dividends distributed. The implementation of the Katz Commission recommendations during the 1996 Budget means that retirement funds now bear a 17 per cent tax on interest income and net rentals.

The Income Tax Act : The Act grants various special allowances to taxpayers as incentives to encourage particular economic activities and there are certain non-taxable financial incentive.

Branches of Foreign Companies : STC will be abolished on dividends declared by foreign companies out of their South African sourced income, in respect of all such dividends declared from the commencement of years of assessment ending on or after 1 April 1996.

In view of the removal of STC on foreign companies operating branches in the Republic it has been proposed that income tax be imposed at a rate of 40 per cent in respect of South African sourced income derived by such branches from the commencement of years of assessment ending on or after 1 April 1996.

Value Added Tax (VAT) : Levied at 14 per cent on the supply of goods and services at all stages of the production and distribution chain. It is also charged on the importation of certain goods and services. Certain supplies are zero rated for VAT purpose (e.g. certain basic foodstuffs & export of goods) whilst certain supplies are exempt (e.g. residential rentals).

All fee based financial services (with the exception of certain premiums on life policies and contributions to retirements funds as well as compulsory charges in respect of unit trust schemes) are subjected to VAT from October 1, 1996.

LOCAL TAXES

ESTATE DUTY

A 25 per cent tax is levied on the taxable value of the estate. Only the first R 1000 000 is exempt from estate duties.

TRANSFER DUTY

Payable by purchasers of fixed property. Companies pay a flat rate of 10 per cent. Individuals pay 1 per cent on the first R 60,000, 5 per cent on R 60,001 to R 250,000 and 8 percent on the excess over R 250,000.

REGIONAL SERVICES LEVY

There are two RSC levies: A regional establishment levy based on turnover, the rate of which is usually from 0.10 to 0.15 % & a levy based on payroll of 0.25 to 0.35 percent.

Donations

A 25 per cent tax on the value of the donation, subject to a tax free R 25,000 grant per annum. This tax is payable by the donor.

Marketable securities tax and stamp duty

The rate of marketable securities tax and stamp duty on the registration of transfer of share certificates has been reduced from 1 per cent to 0.5 per cent with effect from April 1,1996. Consideration will aslo be given to the imposition of marketable securities tax on transactions where a broker acts as a principal.

Property Taxes

Municipalities assess rates based on the rateable value of land and / or buildings. The levies are set by the municipalities and therefore vary across the country as is indicated below. In some cases a single levy is applied to the total valuation of the land and buildings. In other cases separate levies are applied to the land and/or building valuations.

Rates are payable by the land owner who may recover a prokrata share from each tenant in a multi-tenanted building. The figures below are the rates in the Rand for 1995/96 and are applied to the valuation of the land and/or buildings:

BLOEMFONTEIN	:	Land	6.837 cents
	:	Buildings	0.498 cents
CAPE TOWN	:	Land & Buildings	10.573 cents
DURBAN	:	Land	5.916 cents
	:	Building	0.493 cents
JOHANNESBURG	:	Land Only	6.427 cents
SANDTON	:	Land Only	2.65 cents
PRETORIA	:	Land Only	5.715 cents
PORT FLIZABETH	:	Land & Buildings	4.249 cents

SA REVENUE SERVICE

SARS CHARTERS

OUR VISION

To become an innovative revenue and customs agency that enhances economic growth and social development, and supports our integration into the global economy in a way that benefits all South Africans.

OUR MISSION

To optimise revenue yield, facilitate trade and enlist new tax contributors by promoting awareness of the obligation to voluntarily comply with South African tax and customs laws, and providing a quality and responsive service to the public.

OUR VALUES

We are committed to providing excellent service to the public. Our relationships, business processes and conduct are based on:

- Mutual Trust and Respect
- Equity and Fairness
- Integrity and Honesty
- Transparency and Openness
- Courtesy and Commitment

COMPREHENSIVE TREATIES IN FORCE

Country	PUBLISHED in Government Gazette	Date of Entry into Force
	AFRICA	
Algeria	(See GG No 21303 dd 2000-06-21)	12 June 2000
Botswana	(See GG No 5912 dd 1978-03-10)	21 September 1978
Egypt	(See GG No 19706 dd 1999-01-22)	16 December 1998
Lesotho	(See GG No 17948 dd 1997-04-22)	9 January 1997
Malawi	(See GG No 1479 dd 13/08/1971)	2 September 1971
Mauritius	(See GG No 18111 dd 1997-07-02)	20 June 1997
Namibia	(See GG No 19780 dd 1999-02-19)	11 April 1999
Seychelles	GG No ……….. dated ……………..	
Swaziland	(See GG No 3814 dd 1973-03-23)	23 August 1973
Tunisia	(See GG No 20728 dd 1999-12-15)	10 December 1999

Uganda	(See GG No 22313 dd 2001/05/24	9 April 2001
Zambia	(See Proclamations No. 174 of 1956 and 60 of 1960)	31 August 1956
Zimbabwe	(See GG No 1234 dd 1965/09/24)	3 September 1965
REST OF WORLD		
Australia	(See GG No 20761 dd 1999-12-24)	21 December 1999
Austria	(See GG No 17965 dd 1997-04-30)	6 February 1997
Belgium	(See GG No 19437 dd 1998-11-02)	10 October 1998
Canada	(See GG No 17985 dd 1997-05-07)	30 April 1997
China (People's Republic of)	(See GG No 22041 dd 2001-02-02)	7 January 2001
Croatia	(See GG No 18460 dd 1997-11-21)	7 November 1997
Cyprus	(See GG No 19638 dd 1998-12-22)	8 December 1998
Czech Republic	(See GG No 18603 dd 1998-01-07)	3 December 1997
Denmark	(See GG No 16891 dd 1995-12-22)	21 December 1995
Finland	(See GG No 16862 dd 1995-12-01)	12 December 1995
France	(See GG No 16681 dd 1995-09-27)	1 November 1995
Germany	(See GG No 3898 dd1973-05-25)	28 February 1975
Hungary	(See GG No 17438 dd 1996-09-13)	5 May 1996
India	(See GG No 18545 dd 1997-12-12)	28 November 1997
Indonesia	(See GG No 19766 dd 1999-02-16)	23 November 1998
Iran	(See GG No 19637 dd 1998-12-22)	23 November 1998
Ireland	(See GG No 18552 dd 1997-12-15)	5 December 1997
Israel	(See GG No 6577 dd 1973-05-25)	27 May 1980
Italy	(See GG No 19823 dd 1999-03-08)	2 March 1999
Japan	(See GG No 18391 dd 1997-10-27)	5 November 1997
Korea	(See GG No 16918 dd 1996-01-26)	7 January 1996
Luxembourg	(See GG No 21852 dd 2000/12/06)	8 September 2000
Malta	(See GG No 18461 dd 1997-11-21)	12 November 1997
Netherlands	(See GG No 3153 dd 1971-06-18)	20 January 1972
Norway	(See GG No 17504 dd 1996-10-15)	12 September 1996
Pakistan	(See GG No 19849 dd 1999-03-17)	9 March 1999
Poland	(See GG No 17201 dd 1996-05-16)	5 December 1995
Greece	(See GG No 24996 dd 2003-03-03)	14 February 2003
Romania	(See GG No 16680 dd 1995-09-27)	21 October 1995
Russian Federation	(See GG No 21395 dd 2000-07-20)	26 June 2000
Singapore	(See GG No 18599 dd 1998-01-02)	5 December 1997
Slovak Republic	(See GG No 20409 dd 1999-08-25)	30 June 1999
Sweden	(See GG No 16890 dd 1995-12-27)	25 December 1995

Switzerland	(See GG No 2157 dd 1968-09-06)	11 July 1968
Taiwan	(See GG No 17408 dd 1996-09-03)	12 September 1996
Thailand	(See GG No 17409 dd 1996-09-03)	27 August 1996
United Kingdom	(See GG No 24335 dd 2003-01-31)	17 December 2002
United States of America (USA)	(See GG No 18553 dd 1997-12-15)	28 December 1997
NOTE: The Agreement with the United Kingdom, signed at London on 14 October 1946 (Proclamation 229 of 1946), was extended to Grenada and Sierra Leone). The above-mentioned Agreement must be read together with the Supplementary Protocol (Proclamation 271 of 1954) and Proclamation 32 of 1961.		

IMPORTANT INFORMATION ON SA TAXES

FIXING OF RATE PER KILOMETRE IN RESPECT OF MOTOR VEHICLES FOR THE PURPOSES OF SECTION 8*(B)*(II) AND (III) OF THE INCOME TAX ACT, 1962

Section 8(1) of the Income Tax Act, 1962, makes provision for the taxation of that portion of an allowance or advance paid to any person to defray travelling expenses for business purposes, which was not actually expended by the person on such travelling.

Where the person has kept accurate data of the portion of the allowance expended by him or her during the year of assessment for business purposes, the taxable portion of the allowance or advance is calculated based on the data furnished by him or her. However, if no accurate data was kept, the deductible expenditure against the allowance or advance is calculated by applying the rate per kilometre prescribed by the Minister of Finance by notice in the *Gazette* for the category of vehicle used, to the distance travelled during the year for business purposes.

The Minister may also fix a specific rate per kilometre which may be applied where a reimbursive allowance is paid to the recipient which is based on the actual distance travelled for business purposes.

These rates per kilometre were last fixed by the Minister in 1996. In view of the steady increase in the fuel price and the fact that more than 3 years have lapsed, the table setting out the rates has been adjusted with effect from years of assessment commencing on or after 1 March 2000:

Where the value of the vehicle¾	Fixed Cost R	Fuel Cost c	Maintenance Cost c
does not exceed R30 000	16 916	23.1	17.1
exceeds R30 000 but does not exceed R35 000	18 984	23.5	17.3
exceeds R35 000 but does not exceed R40 000	21 051	23.8	17.8
exceeds R40 000 but does not exceed R45 000	23 116	24.3	18.5
exceeds R45 000 but does not exceed R50 000	25 197	24.8	19.2

exceeds R50 000 but does not exceed R55 000	27 670	25.3	19.9
exceeds R55 000 but does not exceed R60 000	29 778	25.5	20.6
exceeds R60 000 but does not exceed R70 000	33 873	25.9	21.3
exceeds R70 000 but does not exceed R80 000	38 102	26.1	22.2
exceeds R80 000 but does not exceed R90 000	40 538	26.3	22.7
exceeds R90 000 but does not exceed R100 000	44 535	26.5	23.4
exceeds R100 000 but does not exceed R110 000	48 533	26.8	24.1
exceeds R110 000 but does not exceed R120 000	51 110	27.5	24.8
exceeds R120 000 but does not exceed R130 000	54 990	28.1	25.5
exceeds R130 000 but does not exceed R140 000	58 803	28.9	26.2
exceeds R140 000 but does not exceed R150 000	62 677	29.4	26.9

Where the value of the vehicle exceeds R150 000—

(a) the fixed cost shall be the sum of R62 677 plus an amount of R3 874 for every R10 000 or part thereof by which the value of the vehicle exceeds R150 000;

(b) the fuel cost shall be 29.4 cents per kilometre; and

(c) the maintenance cost shall be 26.9 cents per kilometre.

Where a reimbursive allowance is paid to the recipient and the distance travelled in the vehicle for business purposes during the year of assessment does not exceed 8 000 kilometres and provided that no other compensation in the form of an allowance or reimbursement is payable by the employer to the employee in respect of the vehicle, the rate per kilometre shall at the option of the recipient be determined at a rate of 153 cents per kilometre.

INCOME TAX: PROVISION FOR SHIP REPAIRS IN TERMS OF SECTION (1)(C) OF THE INCOME TAX ACT

1. Section 14(1)(c) of the Income Tax Act (the Act) provides for a deduction from the income of a person referred to in section 9(1)(c) of the Act in respect of any expenditure which such person can satisfy the Commissioner for Inland Revenue he is likely to incur within five years from the end of the year of assessment in question on repairs to any ship used by him for the purpose of his trade. The allowance is additional to the normal annual expenditure incurred in keeping the ship in running repair and is designed to cover the cost of heavy repairs in overhauling and refitting which at the time the allowance was introduced was understood normally to be effected about once in every five years.
2. Practice Note No. 26 dated 18 August 1994 was issued with a view of clarifying the Commissioner's practice regarding the provision for ship repairs in terms of section

14(1)(c) of the Act. It has come to the attention of this office that the practice note is being interpreted in a manner which results in an allowance being claimed which exceeds that which was intended. Practice Note No.26 is, therefore, hereby withdrawn and replaced by this practice note with effect from 4 April 1996.

3. It is evident that the allowance contemplated in section 14(1)(c) of the Act cannot be compartmentalised into fixed cycles of five years. In the determination of the allowance at the end of any particular year of assessment regard must be had to the expenditure likely to be incurred during the next five years. In other words, the allowance must be recalculated at the end of each year of assessment in relation to the expenditure likely to be incurred during the next five years, the estimation being subject to revision from year to year.
4. The accepted method for the calculation of the expenditure to be allowed as a deduction from income is the following:

4.1 In the current year of assessment the expenditure likely to be incurred on heavy (extraordinary) repairs in each of the next five years must be estimated. The total amount to be allowed in the current year of assessment (year 0) of the estimated expenditure will be:

- 100% of the estimated expenditure to be incurred in year one
- 50% of the estimated expenditure to be incurred in year two
- 33.3% of the estimated expenditure to be incurred in year three
- 25% of the estimated expenditure to be incurred in year four
- 20% of the estimated expenditure to be incurred in year five

5. The following examples illustrate the calculation of the allowance:

5.1 Year 0: Estimated expenditure likely to be incurred on heavy (extraordinary) repairs during the period ending five years after the current year (year 0).

Vessel	Y1	Y2	Y3	Y4	Y5
No 1 (Estimated expenditure)	R25 000		R300 000		R50 000
No 2 (Estimated expenditure)		R150 000	R72 000		
No 3 (Estimated expenditure)	R75 000		R28 000	R150 000	
Total estimated expenditure	R100 000	R150 000	R400 000	R150 000	R50 000
Percentage to be allowed	100%	50%	33.3%	25%	20%
Allowance	R100 000	R75 000	R133 200	R37 500	R10 000

5.1.1 The allowance deductible in year 0 amounts to R355 700 (R100 000 + R75 000 + R133 200 + R37 500 + R10 000).

5.2. Year 1: Estimated expenditure likely to be incurred on heavy (extraordinary) repairs during the period ending five years after the current year (year 1)

Vessel	Y2	Y3	Y4	Y5	Y6

No 1 (Estimated expenditure)		R300 000		R50 000	R10 000
No 2 (Estimated expenditure)		R150 000	R20 000		R70 000
No 3 (Estimated expenditure)	R28 000		R15 000		R20 000
Total estimated expenditure	R28 000	R450 000	R35 000	R50 000	R100 000
Percentage to be allowed	100%	50%	33.3%	25%	20%
Allowance	R28 000	R225 000	R11 656	R12 500	R20 000

5.2.1 The allowance deductible in the current year (year 1) amounts to R297 156 (R28 000 + R225 000 + R11 656 + R12 500 + R20 000 The allowance of R355 700 (see par 5.1.1) deducted in the preceding year (year 0) must be included in the income of the taxpayer in the current year (year 1).

6. As the quantum of the allowance is at the discretion of the Commissioner, the taxpayer, if he wishes to claim it, will have to furnish the necessary information to the relevant Receiver of Revenue to enable him to calculate the allowance.

7. Since it is difficult to define "heavy repairs" (as the conditions relevant to, or the extent of, the repairs will vary from ship to ship), a useful guideline would be to distinguish between "ordinary running repairs", which are normally incurred every year, and "extraordinary repairs", which are expected to occur at intervals of more than a year.

INCOME TAX : DETERMINATION OF TAXABLE INCOME WHERE FINANCIAL ASSISTANCE HAS BEEN GRANTED BY A NON-RESIDENT OF THE REPUBLIC TO A RESIDENT OF THE REPUBLIC

1. INTRODUCTION

1.1. In anticipation of a possible relaxation in exchange controls, the Commission of Inquiry into certain aspects of the Tax structure of South Africa (under the Chairmanship of Prof. M M Katz) recommended in its first and second interim reports that transfer pricing provisions be introduced into the Income Tax Act, 1962 (the Act), inter alia to counter thin capitalisation practices which may have adverse tax implications for the South African fiscus.

Transfer pricing provisions are normally applied to adjust the prices of goods and services in terms of certain transactions concluded between related parties to reflect an arm's length price which would have applied had the transaction been concluded on normal commercial grounds between unrelated parties. The effect of the application of transfer pricing provisions is to neutralise the tax benefit arising from such transactions. On the other hand, thin capitalisation provisions are applied to limit the deductibility of interest where there is a disproportionate ratio between the loan capital and equity employed in, for example, a company.

In order to counter such practices, section 23 of the Income Tax Act, 1995 (Act No. 21 of 1995), substituted section 31 of the Act. Such section consists of a combination of transfer pricing and thin capitalisation provisions, which may, for instance, be applied where financial assistance is granted in respect of international transactions.

1.2 Measures to counter transfer pricing schemes are in essence contained in section 31(1) and (2). Although these provisions may also, in certain circumstances, be applied to combat thin capitalisation, the provisions of subsection (3) are mare specifically aimed at countering thin capitalisation schemes.

Once the excessive portion of financial assistance has been determined in accordance with the guidelines as set out in paragraph 4 of this Practice Note, the provisions of section 31(2) must be applied to determine whether the interest calculated on that portion of the financial assistance falling within the 3 1 guideline provided in the aforementioned paragraph, is based on an arm's length price (interest rate). In this regard consideration should be given to the guidelines provided in paragraph 2.2.

On a literal interpretation of section 31 the concept of financial assistance would include not only interest-bearing financial assistance, but also interest-free financial assistance. As the purpose of subsection (3) is in essence to enable the Commissioner for Inland Revenue to determine an acceptable debt/equity ratio in order to disallow a deduction in respect of interest relating to the excessive portion of loan capital, the application of subsection (3) will be limited to interest-bearing financial assistance. This will, however, not have the effect that financial assistance which is not interest bearing, will be regarded as permanent owners' capital.

On the same basis only, interest-bearing financial assistance will be taken into account in the application of the transfer pricing provisions of subsection (2) in cases where it is applied in conjunction with the provisions of subsection (3) in order to determine whether the interest calculated on that portion of the financial assistance falling within the 3 1 guideline, is based on an arm's length price (interest rate). However, where the application of the thin capitalisation provisions is not necessary because the financial assistance granted falls within the prescribed guidelines, financial assistance may include financial assistance, which is not interest- bearing in the application of the provisions of subsection (2).

1.3 EXAMPLE

A profitable South African company, TPS (Pty) Ltd, was capitalised in Rand by its shareholder who is a non-resident. The company's financial year ends on 31 August. The RSA prime rate was 18.5% throughout the 1995/6 year of assessment. The following further information is relevant for the application of section 31:

Fixed capital

Shareholder R1 000 000

Loans R4 000 000

- Shareholder granted loan # 1 on 1/9/95 @ 24% pa - R2000 000
- Shareholder granted loan # 2 on 26/1/96 @ 0% pa - R2000 000

Interest

- Loan # 1: R2 000 000 at 24% R480 000
- Section 31(3) is not applicable as the interest-bearing financial assistance granted falls within the 3 : 1 guideline.

Calculation of excessive interest in terms of section 31(2)

- Interest falling within the 3 : 1 guideline = R480 000
- Weighted average of financial assistance:
- R2 000 000 for 147 days 294 000 000
- R4 000 000 for 219 days 876 000 000
- 1 170 000 000 ¸ 366 = R3 196 721

Effective interest rate of acceptable financial assistance = R480 000 + `U 196 721 = 15%

Excessive interest relating to the 1995/6 year of assessment is Rnil as the 20.5% (18.5% + 2% (see 2.2 below)) limit has not been exceeded.

2. SECTION 31(1) AND (2)

2.1 The scope of subsections (1) and (2) is limited to an "international agreement" as defined. A transaction, operation or scheme qualifies as an international agreement where such agreement has been entered into between – * a natural person ordinarily resident in the Republic or a person other than a natural person managed or controlled in the Republic (hereinafter referred to as a resident); and * a natural person not ordinarily resident in the Republic or a person other than a natural person managed or controlled outside the Republic (hereinafter referred to as a non-resident). Furthermore, paragraph (c) of the definition of "services" in section 31(1) encompasses the granting of financial assistance, including a loan, advance or debt and the provision of any security or guarantee.

2.2 Where in terms of section 31(2) a service, specifically the granting of financial assistance, is provided by a non-resident to a resident who is a connected person in relation to the non-resident and the consideration relating to the financial assistance is excessive in the sense that the consideration does not reflect an arm's length price, the Commissioner may, in the determination of the taxable income of the resident, adjust the consideration in the hands of the resident to reflect an arm's length consideration in relation to the financial assistance granted. Consideration, in the context of financial assistance, will be interpreted to include not only interest or related finance charges, but also a discount or premium. where the loan, advance or debt is denominated in rand, a rate not exceeding the weighted average of the South African prime rate plus 2 percentage points will be an acceptable nominal annual interest rate. Where the loan, advance or debt is denominated in a foreign currency, a rate not exceeding the weighted average of the relevant inter bank rate plus 4 percentage points will be an acceptable nominal annual interest rate. Any interest exceeding the above mentioned prescribed rates will be regarded as excessive interest and will consequently not be allowed as a deduction for income tax purposes.

3. SECTION 31(3)

Section 31(3) was introduced specifically to address thin capitalisation transactions between certain related parties. The provisions of this section will apply where financial assistance is granted directly or indirectly by a non-resident of the Republic (the investor) to - (a) a resident (the resident) of the Republic who is a connected person in relation to the investor; or (b) a person other than a natural person who is managed or controlled in the Republic (the recipient) in whom the investor has a direct or indirect interest by virtue of which the investor is entitled to participate in 25% or more of the dividends, profits or capital of the recipient or is entitled to exercise, directly or indirectly, 25% or more of the voting rights of the recipient.

Where in terms of such an arrangement the Commissioner is satisfied that the financial assistance granted by the investor to the resident or the recipient is excessive in relation to the fixed capital of the resident or recipient, any interest relating to the excessive portion of the financial assistance shall be disallowed as a deduction in the hands of the resident or recipient.

4. DETERMINATION OF "DISALLOWABLE INTEREST" RELATING TO EXCESSWE FINANCIAL ASSISTANCE

4.1 As a general guideline, the Commissioner will not apply the thin capitalisation provisions contained in section 31(3) where the financial assistance/fixed capital ratio does not exceed 3:1. The excessive portion of financial assistance granted by an investor will, therefore, be that portion of the financial assistance which exceeds an amount equal to three times the fixed capital of the resident or recipient of the financial assistance. This approach will ensure a degree of continuity as it will, to some extent, correspond with the current practice of the Exchange Control Authorities. The interest (interest, finance charge or other consideration including inter alia a discount or premium) in relation to or in respect of financial assistance shall be apportioned between the amount of financial assistance which is considered to be acceptable and the amount of financial assistance which is regarded as excessive. In order to determine which portion of interest relates to excessive financial assistance in relation to an investor in respect of a year of assessment, the following formula will be applied: A = B x in which formula - "A" represents the disallowable interest, limited to interest incurred during such year in respect of financial assistance granted on or after 19 July 1995; "B" represents the total interest incurred during such year in respect of all financial assistance, contemplated in subsection (3), in existence during such year (whether or not such financial assistance was granted before, on or after 19 July 1995); "C" represents the weighted average of al] interest-bearing financial assistance which was in existence during such year (whether or not such financial assistance was granted before, on or after 19 July 1995); and "D" represents the greater of - * three times the fixed capital of the resident or recipient as at the end of the relevant year of assessment; and * the weighted average of all interest-bearing financial assistance granted prior to 19 July 1995, which existed during such year.

4.2 The financial assistance contemplated in section 31 to be used in symbol C is a amount equal to the weighted average of the financial assistance in existence during the relevant year of assessment and includes interest-bearing financial assistance only. where no significant variation occurred in the level of financial assistance during the year of assessment, the amount of financial assistance as it exists at the end of the relevant year of assessment may be used. Trade credit which is interest- bearing must be included in the amount of financial assistance granted as contemplated in section 31(1). Furthermore, where a South African company is partially owned by an investor (e.g. 50%) and such investor is jointly and severally, together with all other shareholders, liable in terms of a security provided in respect of - * a foreign bank overdraft of the South African company; or * any other independent third party foreign loan to the South Africa company, a portion of the overdraft or loan, pro rata to the investor's interest in the company, will be regarded as financial assistance granted by such investor.

4.3 In determining the amount of fixed capital of the resident or recipient in the Republic, the following items are to be taken into account on a pro rata basis in accordance with the investors' interest in the South African entity:

- share capital;
- share premium;
- accumulated profits of a capital and revenue nature; and

- permanent owners' capital (excluding any financial assistance) in circumstances where there is no share capital.

Fixed capital will be reduced by any reserves and increased by any losses, resulting from the revaluation of assets. The amount of fixed capital to be used when calculating symbol "D" of the formula is an amount equal to the fixed capital at the end of the relevant year of assessment. However, the annual net trading losses sustained during the current and immediately preceding two years of assessment, limited to losses sustained for years of assessment during which the investor has granted financial assistance to the resident or recipient, may be added back to fixed capital to be used in symbol "D" of the formula.

4.4 In determining the fixed capita] relating to investors, the calculation should not be done on the basis of what the investors invested, but rather on such investors' pro rata share of the total fixed capital. Furthermore, fixed capital will exclude deferred tax as determined for accounting purposes.

4.5 Where financial assistance is granted to a resident of the Republic by more than one investor as contemplated in subsection (3), the rules of section 31 will be applied to such investors, without reference to any person other than an investor having an interest in the fixed capital of the resident or recipient.

5 EXAMPLE

A profitable South African company, TCS (Pty) Ltd, was capitalised in rand by its shareholders, all of them being non-residents. Only X is an investor. The company's financial year ends on 31 August. The RSA prime rate was 18.5% throughout the 199516 year of assessment. The following further information is relevant for the application of section 31:

Fixed capital R15 000 000

Shareholder X - (2/3) R10 000 000

Various other shareholders - (1/3) R 5 000 000

Loans R40 000 000

Shareholder X granted loan # 1 on 1/9/95 ® 24% pa R30 000 000

Shareholder X granted loan # 2 on 26/1/96 @ 18% pa R10 000 000

Interest R 8 277 049

Loan # 1: 1130 000 000 at 24% for 366 days R 7 200 000

Loan # 2: R1O 000 000 at 18% for 219 days R 1 077 049

Calculation of disallowable interest in respect of shareholder X in terms of section 31(3)

B = R8277049

C = R30 000 000 for 147 days 4 410 000 000

R40 000 000 for 219 days 8 760 000 000

R13 170 000 000 ¸ 366 = R35 983 606

D = The greater of (R10 000 000 x 3) or Rnil = R30 000 000

A = 8 277 049 x (35 983 606 - 30 000 000)

1 35 983 606

= R1 376 365 (disallowable interest for the 1995/6 year of assessment)

Calculation of excessive interest in respect of shareholder X in terms of section 31(2)

Interest falling within the 3 1 guideline = R8 277 049 – R1 376 365 = R6 900 684

Effective interest rate of acceptable financial assistance = R6 900 684 ¸ R30 000 000 = 23%

Excessive interest relating to the 1995/6 year of assessment = R6 900 684 x (23 - 20.5) + 23 = R750 074

6 COMMISSIONER'S DISCRETION

6.1 Notwithstanding the guideline of the 3 1 ratio and the interest rates referred to in paragraph 2.2, with regard to the application of section 31, it is acknowledged that a higher level of financial assistance in contrast with the guideline ratio of financial assistance to fixed capital or a higher interest rate may be applicable as a result of transactions and agreements entered into for commercial and economic reasons rather than to obtain tax advantages.

6.2 where a taxpayer, therefore, can justify a higher level of financial assistance in contrast with the guideline ratio of financial assistance to fixed capital or a higher interest rate under particular or special circumstances, he may approach the

Commissioner, to exercise his discretion in terms of section 31. This will, generally be of a temporary nature and a period may be specified within which the 3 1 ratio should be restored or the interest rate be reduced.

6.3 Taxpayers falling within the 3 :1 ratio will not be required to justify their ratio. They must, however, submit the information requested in the annual income tax return.

7 FINANCIAL ASSISTANCE IN CURRENCY OTHER THAN RAND

Where financial assistance is denominated in a currency other than the currency of the Republic, the equivalent currency value of the Republic must be determined by applying the spot or relevant forward rate, as the case may be, on the date the amount of financial assistance is to be determined. However, where there is an increase in the rand value of the financial assistance as a result of a weakening of the rand against the relevant foreign currency, the rand value of the financial assistance may be determined with reference to the spot or relevant forward rate, as the case may be, on the following dates: In the case of a loan owing by a person, the date on which the amount payable in respect of the loan was received by such person and in the case of a debt owing by a person, the date on which the debt was actually incurred.

8 BACK-TO-BACK ARRANGEMENTS

In the application of section 31(3), the term `financial assistance granted includes back-to-back arrangements through independent parties or co-investors. where a foreign parent company, therefore, makes a loan to a South African bank, a foreign bank or any other person on condition that the bank or other person on-lends the funds to the South African subsidiary of the parent company, the loan will be treated as financial assistance. where the foreign parent company provides a guarantee to a foreign bank or any other non-resident as security for a loan to the local subsidiary, the bank debt will be treated as financial assistance. where, however, the foreign parent company provides a guarantee to a South African bank as security for a loan to the local subsidiary, the bank loan will not be treated as financial assistance as the foreign company will not receive any interest and the recipient of the interest will be taxed thereon.

9. EXCESSIVE (see par.2.2) AND DISALLOWABLE (see par.4) INTEREST SUBJECT TO SECONDARY TAX ON COMPANIES (STC)

In the case of companies the total amount of the excessive and disallowable interest will be deemed to be a dividend declared in terms of section 64C(3)(e) of the Act and STC will be payable on the excessive and disallowable interest. As the determination of the excessive and disallowable portions of interest and the exercising of the Commissioner's discretion are to be made at the time the relevant assessment is raised, the dividend cycle in respect of such deemed dividend will, for purposes of the definition of "dividend cycle" in section 64B(1), be regarded to end on the date of assessment in respect of the year of assessment to which the excessive and disallowable interest relates. Where, however the taxpayer has been notified in writing by the Commissioner of the amount of the excessive and disallowable interest prior to such date of assessment, the dividend cycle will be regarded to end one month after the date of such notification.

10. APPLICATION

The provisions of section 31 shall inter alia only apply to any services supplied on or after 19 July 1995. As already mentioned, the supply of services includes the granting of financial assistance. Interest incurred after that date

VALUE-ADDED TAX

7. IMPOSITION OF VALUE-ADDED TAX[1]

1) Subject to the exemptions, exceptions, deductions and adjustments provided for in this Act, there shall be levied and paid for the benefit of the National Revenue Fund a tax, to be known as the value-added tax-

[1] Selected Chapters for the VA Act

a) on the supply by any vendor of goods or services supplied by him on or after the commencement date in the course or furtherance of any enterprise carried on by him;

b) on the importation of any goods into the Republic by any person on or after the commencement date; and

c) on the supply of any imported services by any person on or after the commencement date,

calculated at the rate of 14 per cent on the value of the supply concerned or the importation, as the case may be.

2) Except as otherwise provided in this Act, the tax payable in terms of paragraph (a) of subsection (1) shall be paid by the vendor referred to in that paragraph, the tax payable in terms of paragraph (b) of that subsection shall be paid by the person referred to in that paragraph and the tax payable in terms of paragraph (c) of that subsection shall be paid by the recipient of the imported services.

3)

a) Where any goods manufactured in the Republic, being of a class or kind subject to excise duty under Part 2 of Schedule No. 1 to the Customs and Excise Act, have been supplied at a price which does not include such excise duty and tax has become payable in respect of the supply in terms of subsection (1)(a), value-added tax shall be levied and paid at the rate of 14 per cent for the benefit of the National Revenue Fund on an amount equal to the amount of such excise duty which, subject to any rebate of such excise duty under the said Act is paid.

b) The tax payable in terms of paragraph (a) shall be paid by the person liable in terms of the Customs and Excise Act for the payment of the said excise duty.

c) Deleted by Act 34 of 1997

d) Subject to this Act, the provisions of the Customs and Excise Act relating to the clearance of goods subject to excise duty and the payment of such excise duty shall *mutatis mutandis* have effect as if enacted in this Act.

CERTAIN SUPPLIES OF GOODS OR SERVICES DEEMED TO BE MADE OR NOT MADE

1) For the purposes of this Act, where-

a) goods acquired, manufactured, assembled, constructed or produced by a person are sold, under a power exercisable by another person, in or towards satisfaction of a debt owed by the person whose goods are sold; and

b) the person whose goods are sold has not furnished, to the person exercising the power of sale, a statement in writing that the supply of those goods would not be a taxable supply if those goods were sold by the person whose goods are sold, and stating fully the reasons why that supply would not be a taxable supply, those goods shall be deemed to be supplied in the course of an enterprise.

2) For the purposes of this Act, where a person ceases to be a vendor, any goods (other than any goods in respect of the acquisition of which by the vendor a deduction of input tax under section 16(3) was denied in terms of section 17(2) or would have been denied if those sections had been applicable prior to the commencement date) or right capable of assignment, cession or surrender which in either case then forms part of the assets of his enterprise, shall be deemed to be supplied by him in the course of his enterprise immediately before he ceased to be a vendor, unless the enterprise is carried on by another person who in terms of section 53 is deemed to be a vendor: Provided that-

i) where such right is so deemed to be supplied that supply shall be deemed to be a supply of a service;

ii) this subsection shall not apply to any such goods or right to the extent that a deduction in terms of section 16(3) has not been allowed or will not be allowed, in respect of the acquisition or use by such vendor, where such vendor on or before 30 June 2000-

aa) ceases to be a vendor for the sole reason that the total value of taxable supplies made by that vendor in the preceding period of 12 months has not exceeded R20 000; or

bb) ceases to be a vendor in respect of a commercial rental establishment or a residential rental establishment for the sole reason that the total receipts and accruals derived from that commercial rental establishment or residential rental establishment in the preceding period of 12 months have not exceeded R48 000;

iii) this subsection shall not apply to fixed property to the extent that a deduction in terms of section 16(3) has not been allowed or will not be allowed in respect of that fixed property or any improvements thereto, where such vendor, on or before 30 June 2000, requests the Commissioner in writing, in the circumstances contemplated in section 24(2), to cancel his registration.

2A) Where a supply is deemed to have been made by a vendor in terms of subsection (2) and that vendor ceases to be a vendor solely as a consequence of the circumstances contemplated in paragraph (ii) of the proviso to subsection (2), the tax payable to the Commissioner in respect of that deemed supply shall, if the amount thereof is in excess of R3 000, be paid to the Commissioner in so many equal monthly instalments as the Commissioner may allow, the last of which shall not be paid later than 28 February 2001.

3) For the purposes of this Act, a credit agreement to which section 13 of the Credit Agreements Act, 1980(Act No. 75 of 1980), applies shall be deemed not to be a supply of

goods or services unless the credit receiver has failed to exercise the right under that section to terminate the agreement within the period available to him under that section.

4)

a) For the purposes of this Act, any lay-by agreement (as defined in Government Notice No. R 1234 of 13 June 1980, as amended by Government Notice No. R 1814 of 29 August 1980, issued in terms of section 9 of the Sale and Service Matters Act, 1964 (Act No. 25 of 1964)), whereby goods are sold for a consideration not exceeding R10 000 and are reserved by deposit for delivery when the purchase price or a determined portion thereof is paid shall not be deemed to be a supply of goods or services unless and until the goods are delivered to the purchaser.

b) Where such agreement is cancelled or terminates for any other reason and the seller retains any amount paid by the purchaser or recovers any amount owing by the purchaser under such agreement, the seller shall for the purposes of this Act be deemed to have supplied a service in respect of such agreement.

5) For the purposes of this Act a vendor shall be deemed to supply services to any public authority or local authority to the extent of any payment made by the authority concerned to or on behalf of the vendor in respect of the taxable supply of goods or services by the vendor to any person.

6) For the purposes of this Act-

a) where a local authority makes any supply to any person of goods or services contemplated in paragraph (c)(i), (ii) or (iii) of the definition of "enterprise" in section 1 and no consideration relating specifically to such supply is payable to such local authority by such person, the local authority shall be deemed to make such supply to that person where any amount of rates on the value of fixed property is payable by that person to such local authority;

b) a regional services council, joint services board or transitional metropolitan council shall be deemed to supply services to a person in respect of the other activities of that council or board referred to in paragraph (c) of the said definition where any amount of any levy is payable by that person to such council or board in terms of the Regional Services Councils Act, 1985 (Act No. 109 of 1985), or the KwaZulu and Natal Joint Services Act, 1990 (Act No. 84 of 1990), as the case may be, or where any amount of such levy may in terms of the Local Government Transition Act, 1993, be levied and claimed by a transitional metropolitan council; and

c) the transfer of all its assets and liabilities by an administrative unit of a local authority that is separately registered under subsection (2) of section 50, to the vendor intended in subsection (1) of that section, shall be deemed not to be a supply.

7) The disposal of an enterprise as a going concern, or a part thereof which is capable of separate operation, shall for the purposes of this Act be deemed to be a supply of goods made in the course or furtherance of such enterprise.

8) For the purposes of this Act, except section 16(3), where a vendor receives any indemnity payment under a contract of insurance or is indemnified under a contract of insurance by

the payment of an amount of money to another person, that payment or indemnification, as the case may be, shall, to the extent that it relates to a loss incurred in the course of carrying on an enterprise, be deemed to be consideration received for a supply of services performed on the day of receipt of that payment or on the date of payment to such other person, as the case may be, by that vendor in the course or furtherance of his enterprise: Provided that this subsection shall not apply in respect of any indemnity payment received or indemnification under a contract of insurance where the supply of services contemplated by that contract is not a supply subject to tax under section 7(1)(a): Provided further that this subsection shall not apply in respect of any indemnity payment received by a vendor under a contract of insurance to the extent that such payment relates to the total reinstatement of goods, stolen or damaged beyond economic repair, in respect of the acquisition of which by the vendor a deduction of input tax under section 16(3) was denied in terms of section 17(2) or would have been denied if these sections had been applicable prior to the commencement date.

9) For the purposes of this Act, where any vendor in carrying on an enterprise in the Republic transfers goods or provides any service to or for the purposes of his branch or main business in respect of which the provisions of paragraph (ii) of the proviso to the definition of "enterprise" in section 1 are applicable, the vendor shall be deemed to supply such goods or service in the course or furtherance of his enterprise.

10) For the purposes of this Act, where any goods are repossessed under an instalment credit agreement, a supply of such goods shall be deemed to be made by the debtor under such instalment credit agreement to the person exercising his right of possession, and where such debtor is a vendor the supply shall be deemed to be made in the course or furtherance of his enterprise unless such goods did not form part of the assets held or used by him for the purposes of his enterprise.

11) For the purposes of this Act a supply of the use or right to use or the grant of permission to use any goods (whether with or without a driver, pilot, crew or operator) under any rental agreement, instalment credit agreement, charter party, agreement for charter or any other agreement under which such use or permission to use is granted, shall be deemed to be a supply of goods.

12) Deleted by Act 136 of 1992

13) For the purposes of this Act, where any person bets an amount on the outcome of a race or on any other event or occurrence, the person with whom the bet is placed shall be deemed to supply a service to such first-mentioned person.

13A) For the purposes of this Act, except section 16(3), where any vendor who makes taxable supplies of services contemplated in subsection (13) of this section, receives any amount paid by any other vendor as a prize or winnings in consequence of a supply of such services made by the last-mentioned vendor to the first-mentioned vendor, the first-mentioned vendor shall be deemed to supply a service to the last-mentioned vendor.

14) For the purposes of this Act, where any goods are supplied by a vendor to a person otherwise than in the circumstances contemplated in paragraph 2(b) of the Seventh Schedule to the Income Tax Act, and a deduction under section 16(3) in respect of the acquisition by the vendor of such goods was denied in terms of section 17(2) or would have been denied if section 7 of this Act had been applicable prior to the commencement

date, the vendor shall be deemed to have supplied the goods otherwise than in the course or furtherance of his enterprise.

15) For the purposes of this Act, where a single supply of goods or services or of goods and services would, if separate considerations had been payable, have been charged with tax in part at the rate applicable under section 11, each part of the supply concerned shall be deemed to be a separate supply.

16)

a) The supply by a vendor-

i) of any goods (other than fixed property acquired prior to the commencement date by a vendor who is a natural person if such property was used by him mainly as his private residence and no deduction of any amount has been made by him under section 16(3) in respect of such property); or

ii) of services,

where such goods or services were acquired or imported by him partly for the purpose of consumption, use or supply in the course of making taxable supplies (including supplies which would have been taxable supplies if section 7 of this Act had been applicable prior to the commencement date) and were held or utilized by him partly for the said purpose immediately prior to the supply by him of such goods or services, shall be deemed to be made wholly in the course or furtherance of his enterprise.

b) The supply by any vendor of fixed property acquired prior to the commencement date by such vendor, being a natural person, shall be deemed to be made otherwise than in the course or furtherance of his enterprise provided-

i) such property was used by him prior to such supply mainly as his private residence; and

ii) no deduction of any amount has been made by him under section 16(3) in respect of such property.

17)

a) For the purposes of this Act, where, together with the supply of a share referred to in the definition of "fixed property" in section 1, any amount of the loan obligation, as defined in section 1 of the Share Blocks Control Act, of the share block company is allocated as contemplated in section 14 of that Act, or any amount of the loan obligation thus allocated is delegated, or any interest in or right to be paid money that is, or is to be, owing by the share block company under its loan obligation is transferred to any person who is or will be a shareholder of such share block company, such allocation, delegation or transfer, as the case may be, shall be deemed to form part of the supply of such share.

b) For the purposes of this Act, where any allocation, delegation or transfer as contemplated in paragraph (a) is made without the supply of a share referred to in the definition of "fixed property" in section 1 and otherwise than in the circumstances contemplated in that paragraph, such allocation, delegation or transfer shall be deemed to constitute the supply of a share referred to in the said definition.

18) For the purposes of the definition of "input tax" in section 1 and section 18(4) and (5), as applicable to any share block company, any taxable supply of a share referred to in subsection (17) made on or after a date fixed by the Minister by notice in the *Gazette* by a share block developer where such share is a share in a share block scheme in respect of which that developer is a share block developer as contemplated in section 1 of the Share Blocks Control Act, shall be deemed to have been made by the share block company in relation to which that developer is a share block developer, to the extent that-

a) the supply of such share to such developer was not a taxable supply by such company to such developer; or

b) such developer was not or will not in terms of section 16(3) be entitled to make a deduction of input tax referred to in paragraph (b) of the definition of "input tax" in section 1 in respect of the supply of such share to him.

19) For the purposes of this Act, where any supply of-

a) goods consisting of a unit is made by a share block company; or

b) services comprising the waiving of rights against a share block company is made to that share block company,

in the circumstances referred to in Item 8 of Schedule 1 to the Share Blocks Control Act, such supply shall be deemed to have been made otherwise than in the course or furtherance of an enterprise.

20) For the purposes of this Act, where an importation of goods is deemed to have been made by an agent in the circumstances contemplated in section 54(2A)(b), such agent shall be deemed to make a supply of goods to the recipient of the supply by the principal, as contemplated in subparagraph (iii) of that section.

21) For the purposes of this Act, compensation or any other payment, other than an amount contemplated in section 12(a), received by a vendor in consequence of the expropriation of land, including an improvement thereto, is deemed to be received in respect of a supply of goods made in the course or furtherance of an enterprise unless that land or improvement thereto forms no part of the assets held or used by the vendor for the purposes of an enterprise.

VALUE OF SUPPLY OF GOODS OR SERVICES

) For the purposes of this Act the following provisions of this section shall apply for determining the value of any supply of goods or services.

2) The value to be placed on any supply of goods or services shall, save as is otherwise provided in this section, be the value of the consideration for such supply, as determined in accordance with the provisions of subsection (3), less so much of such value as represents tax: Provided that-

i) there shall be excluded from such consideration the value of any postage stamp as defined in section 1 of the Post Office Act, 1958 (Act No. 44 of 1958), when used in the payment of consideration for any service supplied by the postal company as defined in section 1 of the Post Office Act, 1958;

ii) where the portion of the value of the said consideration which represents tax is not accounted for separately by the vendor, the said portion shall be deemed to be an amount equal to the tax fraction of that consideration.

3) For the purposes of this Act the value of any consideration referred to in this section shall be-

a) to the extent that such consideration is a consideration in money, the amount of the money; and

b) to the extent that such consideration is not a consideration in money, the open market value of that consideration.

4) Where-

a) a supply is made by a person for no consideration or for a consideration in money which is less than the open market value of the supply; and

b) the supplier and recipient are connected persons in relation to each other; and

c) if a consideration for the supply equal to the open market value of the supply had been paid by the recipient, he would not have been entitled under section 16(3) to make a deduction of the full amount of tax in respect of that supply,

the consideration in money for the supply shall be deemed to be the open market value of the supply: Provided that this subsection shall not apply to the supply of a benefit or advantage of employment contemplated in section 18(3).

4A) For the purposes of this Act, where any share in a share block company is sup plied, the consideration in money for that supply shall include the amount of any allocation, delegation or transfer referred to in section 8(17).

5) Where goods or services are deemed to be supplied by a vendor in terms of section 8(2) or (9), the supply shall be deemed to be made for a consideration in money equal to the lesser of-

a) the cost to the vendor of the acquisition, manufacture, assembly, construction or production of such goods or services, including-

i) any tax charged in respect of the supply to the vendor of such goods or services or of any components, materials or services utilized by him in such manufacture, assembly, construction or production;

ii) where such goods or any right referred to in section 8(2), when held by the vendor, constituted trading stock as defined in section 1 of the Income Tax Act, any further costs (including tax) incurred by him in respect of such goods or right as contemplated in section 22(3)(a) of that Act;

iii) any costs (including tax) incurred by the vendor in respect of the transportation or delivery of such goods or the provision of such services in connection with the transfer of such goods or the provision of such services as contemplated in section 8(9); and

iv) where such goods or services were acquired under a supply in respect of which the consideration in money was in terms of section 10(4) deemed to be the open market value of the supply or would in terms of that section have been deemed to be the open market value of the supply were it not for the fact that the recipient would have been entitled under section 16(3) to make a deduction of the full amount of tax in respect of that supply, such open market value to the extent that it exceeds the consideration in money for that supply; or

b) the open market value of such supply.

6) For the purposes of this Act, where goods are supplied under an instalment credit agreement, the consideration in money for the supply shall be deemed to be the cash value of that supply.

7) Where goods or services are deemed by section 18(1) to be supplied by a vendor, the supply shall, subject to the provisions of subsection (8), be deemed to be made for a consideration in money equal to the open market value of such supply.

8) Where any repairs, maintenance or insurance in respect of a motor vehicle is deemed to be supplied by a vendor by section 18(1), such supply shall be deemed to made for a consideration in money equal to the cost (including tax) to such vendor of acquiring such repairs, maintenance or insurance: Provided that where such vendor does not maintain accurate data for the purposes of calculating such consideration in money, such supply shall be deemed to be made for a consideration in money equal to the amount determined in the manner prescribed by the Minister in the *Gazette* for the category of motor vehicle concerned.

9) Where goods or services are deemed by section 18(2) to be supplied by a vendor, the supply shall be deemed to be made for a consideration in money determined in accordance with the formula

$$A \times (B - C)$$

in which formula-

"A" represents the lesser of-

i)

aa) the cost (including any tax forming part of such cost) to the vendor of the acquisition, manufacture, assembly, construction or production of those goods or services: Provided that where the goods or services were acquired under a supply in respect of which the consideration in money was in terms of section 10(4) deemed to be the open market value of the supply or would in terms of that section have been deemed to be the open market value of the supply were it not for the fact that the recipient would have been entitled under section 16(3) to make a deduction of the full amount of tax in respect of that supply, the cost of those goods or services shall be deemed to include such open market value to the extent that it exceeds the consideration in money for that supply;

bb) where the vendor was at some time after the acquisition of such goods or services deemed by section 18(4) to have been supplied with such goods or services, the amount which was represented by "B" in the formula contemplated in section 18(4) when such goods or services were deemed to be supplied to the vendor; or

cc) where the vendor was at some time after the acquisition of the goods or Services required to make an adjustment contemplated in section 18(2) or (5), the amounts then represented by "A" in the said formula or by "B" in the formula contemplated in section 18(5) respectively, in the most recent adjustment made under section 18(2) or (5) by the vendor prior to such deemed supply of goods or services; and

ii) the open market value of the supply of those goods or services at the time any reduction in the extent of the consumption or use of the goods is deemed by section 18(6) to take place;

"B" represents the percentage that the use or application of the goods or services for the purposes of making taxable supplies was of the total use or application of such goods or services determined under section 17(1), section 18(4) or (5) or this subsection, whichever was applicable in the period immediately preceding the 12 month period contemplated in "C"; and

"C" represents the percentage that, during the 12 month period during which the decrease in use or application of the goods or services is deemed to take place, the use or application of the goods or services for the purposes of making taxable supplies (in respect of which, if such goods or services had been acquired at the time of such use or application, a deduction of input tax would not have been denied in terms of section 17(2)(a)), was of the total use or application of the goods: Provided that where the percentage contemplated in "B" does not exceed the said percentage by more than 10 per cent of the total use or application, the said percentage shall be deemed to be the percentage determined in "B".

10) Where domestic goods and services are supplied at an all-inclusive charge in any enterprise supplying commercial accommodation for an unbroken period exceeding 28 days the consideration in money is deemed to be 60 per cent of the all-inclusive charge.

11) Where a service is under section 8(4)(b) deemed to be supplied, the consideration in money for the supply shall be deemed to be an amount equal to the amount retained or recovered as contemplated in that section.

12) Where any supply of goods is a supply which would, but for the proviso to section 11(1), be charged with tax at the rate of zero per cent, the consideration in money for that supply shall be deemed to be an amount equal to the purchase price of those goods to the supplier: Provided that in any case where the deduction of input tax referred to in that proviso has been made by any other person (where that supplier and that other person are connected persons), the consideration in money for that supply shall be deemed to be an amount equal to the greater of the purchase price of those goods to that supplier and the purchase price of those goods to that other person: Provided further that for the purposes of this subsection, the purchase price of any goods shall not be reduced by any amount of input tax deducted under section 16(3) by the supplier or, as the case may be, any other person where the supplier and that other person are connected persons.

13) Where goods or services are deemed to be supplied by a vendor under section 18(3), the consideration in money for the supply shall be deemed to be an amount equal to the cash equivalent of the benefit or advantage granted to the employee or office holder, as contemplated in section 9(7): Provided that where such benefit or advantage consists of the right to use a motor vehicle as contemplated in paragraph 2(b) of the Seventh Schedule to the Income Tax Act, the consideration in money for the supply shall be deemed to be the amount determined in the manner prescribed by the Minister in the *Gazette* for the category of motor vehicle used.

14) Where services are or are deemed by section 8(5) to be supplied to any public authority or local authority by any vendor the consideration in money for such supply shall be deemed to be the amount of any payment made from time to time by the authority concerned to or on behalf of the vendor as contemplated in the said section.

15) Where a supply of goods or services is deemed by section 8(6) to be made to any person by any local authority the consideration in money for such supply shall be deemed to be the amount of any payment (together with tax) made from time to time by such person in respect of the rates referred to in section 8(6)(a) or in respect of the levy referred to in section 8(6)(b), as the case may be.

16) Where by reason of the repossession of goods from a debtor under an instalment credit agreement a supply of such goods is deemed by section 8(10) to be made by that debtor, the consideration in money for that supply shall be deemed to be an amount equal to the balance of the cash value of the goods (being the cash value thereof applied under subsection (6) in respect of the supply of the goods to the debtor under the said agreement) which has not been recovered on the date on which the supply of the goods by the debtor is deemed by section 9(8) to be made: Provided that the said balance shall be deemed to be the amount remaining after deducting from the cash value so much of the sum of the payments made by the debtor under the said agreement as, on the basis of an apportionment in accordance with the rights and obligations of the parties to the said instalment credit agreement, may properly be regarded as having been made in respect of the cash value.

17) Where a service is deemed by section 8(13) to be supplied to any person, the consideration in money for such supply shall be deemed to be the amount that is received in respect of the bet.

17A) Where a service is deemed by section 8(13A) to be supplied to any vendor, the consideration in money for such supply shall be deemed to be the amount that is received as a prize or winnings.

18) Where a right to receive goods or services to the extent of a monetary value stated on any token, voucher or stamp (other than a postage stamp as defined in section 1 of the Postal Services Act, 1998, and any token, voucher or stamp contemplated in subsection (19)) is granted for a consideration in money, the supply of such token, voucher or stamp is disregarded for the purposes of this Act, except to the extent (if any) that such consideration exceeds such monetary value.

19) Where any token, voucher or stamp (other than a postage stamp as defined in section 1 of the Postal Services Act, 1998) is issued for a consideration in money and the holder thereof is entitled on the surrender thereof to receive goods or services specified on such token, voucher or stamp or which by usage or arrangement entitles the holder to specified goods or services, without any further charge, the value of the supply of the goods or services made upon the surrender of such token, voucher or stamp is regarded as nil.

20) Where any token, voucher or stamp is issued by any vendor for no consideration and the holder thereof is entitled on surrender thereof to another person, being the supplier of goods or services, to a discount on the price of goods or services supplied to the holder, the consideration in money for the supply of such goods or services shall be deemed to include the monetary value stated on such token, voucher or stamp: Provided that such monetary value shall be deemed to include tax.

21) Where any supply of entertainment is made by a vendor and in terms of section 17 no deduction of input tax was made in terms of section 16(3) in respect of the acquisition by the vendor of goods or services for the purpose of such entertainment, the value of such supply shall be deemed to be nil.

21A) A Where any supply of medical or dental services or other goods or services is made as contemplated in section 17(2)(d) by a scheme referred to in that section, the value of such supply shall be deemed to be nil.

22) Where a taxable supply is not the only matter to which a consideration relates, the supply shall be deemed to be for such part of the consideration as is properly attributable to it.

22A) Where any supply is made which comprises the management of a superannuation scheme as contemplated in section 2(1)(i), the consideration in money for such supply shall be deemed to be the greater of the cost of making such supply or any consideration for such supply.

22B) Where any supply of goods is deemed to be made as contemplated in section 8(20), the consideration in money for such supply shall be deemed to be the total amount of the value placed on the importation in terms of section 7(1)(b).

23) Save as otherwise provided in this section, where any supply is made for no consideration the value of that supply shall be deemed to be nil.

INCENTIVES FOR INVESTORS

Several investment incentives have been created for the potential investor in South Africa. Foreign investment is welcomed - all business sectors are open to investors, no government approval is required, and there are almost no restrictions on the form or extent of foreign investment.

The current tariff reform programme is specifically aimed at lowering input costs for the producer, while import controls have been relaxed in line with South Africa's GATT and World Trade Organisation obligations.

Exporters are granted incentives such as export marketing assistance, zero rating for value added tax (VAT) on exports of goods and services and relief from various customs and excise duties.

In his February 2001 budget speech, Finance Minister Trevor Manuel announced a R3-billion incentive package for inventors in strategic industrial projects for the next four years. This will entail tax allowances of either 50% or 100% of an approved investment, and will be managed through the Strategic Industrial Project (SIP) programme.

The trade and industry department announced in April 2002 that the SIP programme had come on stream after finalising the criteria for the evaluation of projects. See:

REGIONAL INCENTIVES

To encourage investors to establish or relocate industry and business to areas throughout South Africa, the country's various regions (provinces) have development bodies that offer incentives. These incentives, which vary from area to area, include reduced interest rates, reduced rentals for land and buildings, cash grants for relocation of plant and employees, reduced rates for basic facilities, railage and other transport rebates and assistance in the provision of housing.

Industrial, technology and agro-tourism strategic development initiatives have been planned in various provinces and include the Maputo Corridor in Mpumalanga, the Gauteng special economic zone and the Wild Coast and Fish River areas in the Eastern Cape.

STATE FINANCING BODIES

Industrial Development Corporation of South Africa Limited (IDC)

The state-owned Industrial Development Council promotes investment by funding viable projects with development impact. It operates throughout South Africa and offers a range of financing services for small, medium and large scale industries, so as to assist businesses in the establishment of manufacturing concerns in South Africa and the Southern African region. The most common form of financing given by the IDC is a medium to long-term low interest rate loan. The IDC has in certain cases taken equity stakes in industrial entities.

Department of Trade and Industry

The Department of Trade and Industry (DTI) has developed a package of incentives, which include the following schemes:

- Small and medium enterprise development programme
- Skills support programme
- Critical infrastructure programme
- Industrial Development Zone programmes

CASH INCENTIVES FOR NEW FIRMS

The government's Small and Medium Enterprise Development Programme (SMEDP) offers cash incentive for new industries as well as the expansion of existing industries.

People planning new business projects or the expansion of existing projects in manufacturing, tourism, certain business services, information and communication technology investments, high-value agricultural projects, agro-processing, recycling, bio-technology industries, aqua-culture and cultural industries may apply for assistance.

The SMEDP replaces the former SMMDP (Small Medium Manufacturing Development Programme).

SMEDP is an excellent investment incentive:

- Initial quarterly payments contribute towards positive cash flow;
- Tax-free;
- Easy-to-understand application and claim procedures; and
- User-friendly procedures.

The SMEDP incentive package aims to:

- Create wealth;
- Generate employment;
- Develop entrepreneurship;
- Promote empowerment;
- Utilise local raw material;
- Ensure sustainability of projects receiving incentives in the long run;
- Reduce investment lost for small and medium investors;
- Encourage greater investment in training;
- Improve industrial training systems;
- Create opportunities for the introduction of new and advanced skills in South Africa; and
- Promote foreign investment.

SMEDP PROGRAMMES

Establishment Grant
Assistance in the form of a tax-free establishment grant for the first two years, calculated on qualifying investment per year as follows:

- First R5-million investment - 10% per annum

- Next R10-million investment - 6% per annum.
- Next R15-million investment - 4% per annum.
- Next R20-million investment - 3% per annum.
- Next R25-million investment - 2% per annum.
- Next R25-million investment - 1% per annum.

Note: The establishment grant can be awarded for an additional year (ie, a third year) if the labour remuneration to the value-added ratio is 30% or bigger.

Skills Support Programme (SSP)
A three-year cash grant to the value of 50% of the cost of training new staff (through an approved training programme) resulting from a new or expansion project:

- Grant capped at 30% of annual wage bill.
- Grant paid on a performance basis.

NUMBER OF TAX INCENTIVES

The Income Tax Act, 1962 (as amended) contains several specific tax incentives, including:

- double taxation avoidance agreements are presently in place to avoid the full taxation of same income of certain persons, enterprises and property under the laws of two countries have been entered into by South Africa with Algeria, Austria, Australia, Belgium, Botswana, Canada, Croatia, Cyprus, Czech Republic, Denmark, Egypt, Finland, France, Germany, Hungary, India, Indonesia, Iran, Ireland, Italy, Israel, Japan, Korea, Lesotho, Luxembourg, Malawi, Malta, Mauritius, Namibia, Netherlands, Norway, Pakistan, Peoples Republic of China, Poland, Republic of China, Romania, Russian Federation, Singapore, Slovak Republic Swaziland, Sweden, Switzerland, Thailand, Tunisia, United Kingdom, USA, Zambia and Zimbabwe. Sea and air transport agreements have also been entered into by South Africa with Belgium, Brazil, Republic of China (Taiwan), Denmark, Finland, France, Greece, Ireland, Italy, Japan, Norway, Portugal and Spain.
- depreciation may be claimed in respect of the cost of plant and machinery, implements, utensils and other articles used for the purpose of trade. The allowance generally consists of the amount by which the value of the asset has diminished by reason of wear and tear or depreciation during the year and is calculated according to the declining balance method;
- capital allowance write-off over 5 years at 20% per annum on a straight line basis in respect of machinery and equipment used for the first time in a manufacturing or similar process.
- wear-and-tear allowance is available annually for machinery and equipment, which do not qualify for the 20% capital allowance. Rates are not prescribed and are subject to the tax authorities that favour the diminishing balance method of calculating wear and tear. However, in respect of non manufacturing plant and machinery, office equipment, furniture and motor vehicles the following rates are normally granted: office equipment - 10%, office furniture - 10% and motor vehicles - 20%;

- 5% depreciation allowance is allowed annually on cost of buildings (and improvements) where the building is used in a manufacturing or similar process and the building or improvement is commenced after 1 January 1989;
    - initial and annual depreciation allowances on ships and aircraft;
    - special depreciation allowances on hotel buildings and equipment;
    - patents, copyright, trademarks, designs and other intellectual property acquiring and developing costs incurred before 29 October 1999 may be written off over the expected life of such assets or 25 years, whichever is the shorter or if incurred after 29 October 1999 the allowance per year shall amount to 5% of the amount of the expenditure connected with the use of an invention, patent trade mark, or copyright or 10% of the amount of the expenditure connected to the use of any design;
    - CSIR (Council for Scientific and Industrial Research) approved capital investment on buildings and equipment used exclusively for scientific research, may be written off, on a straight line basis, at the rate of 25% per year;
- employee housing may result in special deductions and allowances being available for the cost of erecting same;

lease premiums paid for the use of land or buildings, plant and machinery, film recordings or advertising matter connected therewith, patent, design, copyright or similar property and any know-how connected with all of the above may be written off over periods for which the right of use has been granted or 25 years, whichever is shorter;

Tax incentives fall under the jurisdiction of the South African Revenue Services (SARS).

Capital grant for training equipment and course materials.

IMPORTANT LAWS AN REGULATIONS ON TAXATION

INCOME TAX ACT[2]

CHAPTER I ADMINISTRATION

2. Act to be administered by Commissioner

1) The Commissioner shall be responsible for carrying out the provisions of this Act.

3. EXERCISE OF POWERS AND PERFORMANCE OF DUTIES

1) The powers conferred and the duties imposed upon the Commissioner by or under the provisions of this Act or any amendment thereof may be exercised or performed by the Commissioner personally, or by any officer engaged in carrying out the said provisions under the control, direction or supervision of the Commissioner.

2) Any decision made and any notice or communication issued or signed by any such officer may be withdrawn or amended by the Commissioner or by the officer concerned, and shall for the purposes of the said provisions, until it has been so withdrawn, be deemed to have been made, issued or signed by the Commissioner: Provided that a decision made by any such officer in the exercise of any discretionary power under the provisions of this Act or of any previous Income Tax Act shall not be withdrawn or amended after the expiration of three years from the date of the written notification of such decision or of the notice of assessment giving effect thereto, if all the material facts were known to the said officer when he made his decision.

3) Any written decision made by the Commissioner personally in the exercise of any discretionary power under the provisions of this Act or of any previous Income Tax Act shall not be withdrawn or amended by the Commissioner if all the material facts were known to him when he made his decision.

4) Any decision of the Commissioner under the definitions of 'benefit fund ', 'pension fund ', 'provident fund ', 'retirement annuity fund ' and 'spouse ' in section 1, section 6, section 8(4)(b), (c), (d) and (e), section 9D, section 9E, section 9F, section 10(1)(cH), (cK), (e), (iA), (j) and (nB), section 11(e), (f), (g), (gA), (j), (l), (t), (u) and (w), section 12C, section 12E, section 12G, section 13, section 14, section 15, section 22(1), (3) and (5), section 24(2), section 24A(6), section 24C, section 24D, section 24I, section 25D, section 27, section 30, section 31, section 35(2), section 38(4), section 41(4), section 57, paragraphs 6, 7, 9, 13, 13A, 14, 19 and 20 of the First Schedule, paragraph (b) of the definition of 'formula A' in paragraph 1 and paragraph 4 of the Second Schedule, paragraphs 18, 19(1), 20, 21, 22, 24 and 27 of the Fourth Schedule, paragraphs 2, 3, 6, 9 and 11 of the Seventh Schedule and paragraphs 29(2A), 29(7), 31(2), 65(1)(d) and 66(1)(c) of the Eighth Schedule, shall be subject to objection and appeal.

4. PRESERVATION OF SECRECY

[2] Selected sections. For a complete test, please contact Global Investment & Business Center, USA at (202) 546-2103. Fax: (202) 546-3275. E-mail: rusric@erols.com

) Every person employed in carrying out the provisions of this Act shall preserve and aid in preserving secrecy with regard to all matters that may come to his knowledge in the performance of his duties in connection with those provisions, and shall not communicate any such matter to any person whatsoever other than the taxpayer concerned or his lawful representative nor suffer or permit any such person to have access to any records in the possession or custody of the Commissioner except in the performance of his duties under this Act or by order of a competent court: Provided that--

a) any information obtained by the Commissioner in the performance of his duties under the provisions of this Act or any previous Income Tax Act may be used by him for the purposes of the provisions of any other fiscal law administered by him;

b) the Auditor-General shall in the performance of his duties in terms of section 3 of the Auditor-General Act, 1995 (Act No. 12 of 1995), have access to documents in the possession or custody of the Commissioner;

c) the provisions of this subsection shall not be construed as preventing the Commissioner from--

i) disclosing to the Statistician-General such information in relation to any person as may be required by such Statistician-General in connection with the collection of statistics in complying with the provisions of the Statistics Act, 1999 (Act No. 6 of 1999), or any rule made thereunder; or

ii) publishing a list of approved public benefit organisations for the purposes of the provisions of sections 18A and 30.

d) the provisins of this subsection shall not be construed as preventing the Commissioner from disclosing to the Board administering the National Student Financial Aid Scheme, any information relating to the name and address of the employer of any borrower or bursar to whom any loan or bursary has been granted in terms of such scheme.

e) the Commissioner shall disclose information in respect of any class of taxpayers to the Director-General of the National Treasury, to the extent necessary for the purposes of tax policy design or revenue estimation.

1A) The Staticticain-General or any person acting under the direction and control of such Statistician-General, shall not disclose any information supplied under subsection (1)(c) to any person or permit any person to have access thereto, except in the exercise of his powers or the carrying out of his duties to publish statistics in any anonymous form.

1B) The Commissioner may apply *ex parte* to a judge in chambers for an order allowing him or her to disclose to the National Commissioner of the South African Police Service, contemplated in section 6(1) of the South African Police Services Act, 1995 (Act No. 68 og 1995), or the National Director of public prosecutions, contemplated in section 5(2)(a) of the National Prosecuting Authority Act, 1998 (Act No. 32 of 1998), such information, which may reveal evidence-

a) that an offence, other than an offence in terms of this Act or any other Act administered by the Commissioner or any other offence in respect of which the commissioner is a complainant, has been or may be committed, or where such information may be relevant to the investigation or prosecution of such an offence, and such offence is a serious offence in respect of which a court may impose a sentence of imprisonment exceeding five years; or

b) of an imminent and serious public safety or environmental risk, and where the public interest in the disclosure of the information outweighs any potential harm to the taxpayer concerned should such information be disclosed: Provided that any information, document or thing provided by a taxpayer in any return or document, or obtained from a taxpayer in terms of section 74A, 74B or 74C, which is disclosed in terms of this subsection, shall not, unless a competent court otherwise directs, be admissible in any criminal proceedings against such taxpayer, to the extent that such information, document or thing constitutes an admission by such taxpayer of the commission of an offence contemplated in paragraph (a).

1C) For the purposes of subsection 1(b), the Commissioner may delegate the powers vested in him or her by that subsection, to any other officer.

1D) The Director-General or any peson acting under the direction and control of such Director-General shall not disclose any information supplied under subsection (1)(e) to any other person or permit any other person to have access thereto, except in the performance of any function contemplated in subsection (1) (e).

1E) The National Police Commissioner or the National Director of Public Prosecutions or any person acting under the direction and control of such National Police Commissioner or National Director of Public Prosecutions, shall not disclose any information supplied under subsection (1B) to any other person or permit any other person to have access thereto, except in the exercise of his or her powers or the carrying out of his or her duties –

a for purposes of any investigation of, or prosecution for, an offence contemplated in subsection (1B); or

b to combat any public safety or environmental risk contemplated in subsection (1B).

2)

a) Every person so employed shall, before acting under this Act, take and subscribe before a magistrate or justice of the peace or a commissioner of oaths, such oath or solemn declaration, as the case may be, of fidelity or secrecy as may be prescribed.

b) Any oath of secrecy taken and subscribed under the provisions of any previous Income Tax Act by any person who is employed in carrying out the provisions of this Act shall be deemed to be an oath taken and subscribed in terms of this sub-section.

c) The Director-General of the National Treasury, and any person acting under the direction and control of that Director-General, who performs any function as contemplated in subsection (1)(e), shall take and subscribe before a magistrate or justice of the peace or a commissioner of oaths, such oath or solemn declaration, as the case may be, of fidelity or secrecy as may be prescribed.

2A) No person shall in any manner publish or make known to any other person (not being an officer carrying out his duties under the control, direction or supervision of the Commissioner) the contents or tenor of any instruction or communication given or made by the Commissioner or any such officer in the performance of his or their duties under this Act for or concerning the examination or investigation of the affairs of any taxpayer or class of taxpayers or the fact that such instruction or communication has been given or made, or any information concerning the tax matters of a taxpayer or class of taxpayers: Provided that the provisions of this subsection shall not be construed--

i) as preventing any taxpayer or his representative who is or may be affected by any such examination, investigation or furnishing of information from publishing or making known information concerning his own tax matters; or

ii) subject to the provisions of subsection (1). as in any way limiting the duties powers of the Commissioner or any such officer; or

iii) as preventing any person from publishing or making known anything which has been published or made known by the taxpayer or his representative as contemplated in paragraph (i) or by the Commissioner or any such officer in the exercise of his duties or powers.

2B) The provisions of this section shall not apply in respect of any information relating to any person, where that person has consented that such information may be published or made known to any other person.

3) Any person who contravenes the provisions of subsection (1), (1A), (1D), (1E) or (2A), shall be guilty of an offence and liable on conviction to a fine or to imprisonment for a period not exceeding two years.

4) Any person who acts in the execution of his office before he has taken the prescribed oath or solemn declaration shall be guilty of an offence and liable on conviction to a fine not exceeding fifty rand.

CHAPTER II: THE TAXES

PART I: NORMAL TAX

5. Levy of normal tax and rates thereof

1) Subject to the provisions of the Fourth Schedule there shall be paid annually for the benefit of the National Revenue Fund, an income tax (in this Act referred to as the normal tax) in respect of the taxable income received by or accrued to or in favour of--

a) [deleted by the Taxation Laws Amendment Act, 2002];

b) any person carrying on farming, fishing or diamond digging operations whose last year of assessment ended on 30 June 2002, during the period of eight months ending on the last day of February 2003;

c) any person (other than a person in respect of whom paragraph (b) applies or a company) during the year of assessment ended the last day of February, each year; and

d) any company during every financial year of such company.

1A) Notwithstanding the provisions of subsection (1)(c)--

a) where the income of any person for any year of assessment includes any net remuneration as defined in paragraph 11B of the Fourth Schedule, the normal tax payable by such person in respect of such year shall not be less than the sum of the amounts of Standard Income Tax on Employees required to be determined in relation to such net remuneration under the provisions of the said paragraph; and

b) where the taxable income of any person for any year of assessment was derived solely from such net remuneration and the employees tax required to be deducted or withheld from such net remuneration under the said Schedule consisted solely of such Standard Income Tax on Employees, the normal tax payable by him in respect of such year shall be an amount equal to the sum of the amounts of such Standard Income Tax on Employees required to be so determined.

2) Subject to the provisions of subsections (2A) and (3) to (7), inclusive, and the provisions of the Fourth Schedule, the rates of tax chargeable in respect of taxable income shall be fixed annually by Parliament, but the rates fixed by Parliament in respect of any year of assessment or financial year or, if the rates so fixed have been varied by the Minister of Finance by way of an amendment made under subsection (3) which is still in force, the rates as so varied, shall be deemed to continue in force until the next such determination or variation of rates and shall be applied for the purposes of calculating the tax payable in respect of any such taxable income received by or accrued to or in favour of any person during the next succeeding year of assessment or financial year, as the case may be, if in the opinion of the Commissioner the calculation and collection of the tax chargeable in respect of such taxable income cannot without risk of loss of revenue be postponed until after the rates for that year have been determined.

2A)

a) In the case of any company which derives taxable income from mining for natural oil, the normal tax payable in respect of such taxable income shall be determined in accordance with the rates referred to in subsection (2) which are in force in respect of the year of assessment in question, and in addition thereto there shall, in respect of such taxable income, be paid by such company, by way of additional normal tax, an amount equal to 40 per cent of the amount remaining after deducting the said amount of normal tax from such taxable income.

b) The normal tax and the additional normal tax chargeable in respect of taxable income referred to in paragraph (a), shall be reduced to or by such an amount, and on such conditions, as the Minister of Mineral and Energy Affairs may with the concurrence of the Minister of Finance determine.

c) For the purposes of this subsection where sulphur, salt or any other mineral is won by any company in the course of mining for natural oil, the income derived from the mining of such sulphur, salt or other mineral shall be deemed to be derived from the mining for natural oil.

2B)

a) Notwithstanding the provisions of subsection (1), any portion of the normal tax which in terms of paragraph (b) of this subsection, the Income Tax Act, 1970, or any subsequent Income Tax Act is a loan portion of such tax and has been paid by the person concerned, shall be repayable to such person in the manner and at the time provided in the Fifth Schedule.

b) The portions of the normal tax determined in accordance with the provisions of paragraph 1 (g) or (h) of the Schedule to the Income Tax Act, 1965 (Act No. 88 of 1965), paragraph 1 (g) or (h) of the Schedule to the Income Tax Act, 1966 (Act No. 55 of 1966), paragraph 1 (h) or (i) of the Schedule to the Income Tax Act, 1967 (Act No. 95 of 1967), paragraph 1 (h) or (i) of the Schedule to the Income Tax Act, 1968 (Act No. 76 of 1968), and paragraph 2 (h) or (i) of the Schedule to the Income Tax Act, 1969 (Act No. 89 of 1969), shall be loan portions of the normal tax.

3) After the promulgation of any Act of Parliament fixing rates of normal tax for years of assessment specified therein, before the date mentioned in subsection (6) and when Parliament is not in session the Minister of Finance may from time to time by notice in the *Gazette* amend the provisions of such Act so as to effect a variation or further variation of the said rates--

a) by increasing or reducing the rate at which any loan portion of the normal tax is payable in terms of the said Act; or

b) where no loan portion of the normal tax is in terms of the said Act payable by taxpayers of any category, by imposing a charge in respect of the normal tax payable by such taxpayers which shall be a loan portion of such tax and be payable in addition to the tax chargeable under the said Act:

Provided that the rates fixed under the said Act shall not be varied under this subsection so as to impose upon any taxpayer, in addition to the tax payable by him under the said Act. any charge or charges to tax in excess of ten per cent of the basic tax payable by him under that Act.

4) For the purposes of subsection (3) the basic tax payable by any taxpayer in respect of any year of assessment referred to in that subsection shall be deemed to be the normal tax payable by him for such year in terms of the Act referred to in the said subsection before the addition of any loan portion contemplated in the said subsection and before the deduction of any discount provided for in the said Act but after the deduction of any rebate provided for in section 6 of this Act.

5) Any amendment made in terms of subsection (3)--

a) may be made so as to apply only to persons other than companies or only to companies or both to such persons and to companies, and may differentiate between such persons and companies; or

b) may, subject to the provisions of the proviso to subsection (3). be made so as to provide that the loan portion of the normal tax payable by companies shall be calculated at rates which differ according to the various categories of taxable income in respect of which rates of normal tax have been enacted in the Act referred to in subsection (3).

6) Any amendment made under subsection (3) which is in force immediately before the date of promulgation of the Act of Parliament fixing rates of normal tax for years of assessment succeeding the years of assessment referred to in subsection (3), shall, unless Parliament otherwise provides, lapse on that date, and in such case it shall as from that date cease to have the force of law.

7) Subject to the provisions of sections 79 and 102 and the provisions of the Fourth Schedule. where a taxpayer has been assessed for normal tax in respect of any year of assessment and the rate of the tax payable by him has been subsequently fixed or varied, his assessment for such year shall be adjusted, any amounts paid in excess being refundable to him and amounts shortpaid being recoverable from him.

8) Deleted by section 5 of Act 65 of 1973

9) For the purposes of subsection (10) "special remuneration" means any amount received by or accrued to any mineworker over and above his normal remuneration and any regular allowance, in respect of special services rendered by him (otherwise than in the course of his normal duties) in combating any fire, flood, subsidence or other disaster in a mine or in rescuing persons trapped in a mine or in performing any hazardous task during any emergency in a mine, if such services are rendered by him as a member of a team recognized by the management of the mine and the members of such team have been appointed for the purpose of rendering such services.

10) Where any taxpayer's income includes any special remuneration, or where the provisions of section 7A(4A) or paragraph 15(3) or 17 or 19(1) of the First Schedule or paragraph 7 of the Second Schedule are applicable in the case of the taxpayer in respect of any year of assessment, the normal tax payable by the taxpayer in respect of such year (as determined before the deduction of any rebate) shall be determined in accordance with the formula--

$$Y = \frac{A}{B + D - (C + L)} \times (B - L) + (L \times R)$$

in which formula--

a) "Y" represents the amount of normal tax to be determined;

b) "A" represents the amount of normal tax (as determined before the deduction of any rebate) calculated at the full rate of tax chargeable for the said year in respect of a taxable income equal to the amount represented by the expression "B + D -- (C + L)" in the formula;

c) "B" represents the taxpayer's taxable income for the said year;

d) "C" represents an amount equal to the sum of--

i) the amount of any special remuneration (as defined in subsection (9)) which is included in the taxpayer's income for the said year;

ii) where the provisions of paragraph 15 (3) of the First Schedule are in the case of the taxpayer applicable in respect of the said year, an amount determined in accordance with those provisions as being the amount, if any, by which the taxable income derived by the taxpayer during the said year from the disposal of plantations and forest produce exceeds the annual average taxable income derived by him from that source over the three years of assessment immediately preceding the said year;

iii) where the provisions of paragraph 17 of the First Schedule are in the case of the taxpayer applicable in respect of the said year, an amount equal to so much of the taxable income of the taxpayer for such year as has been derived from the disposal of sugar cane as a result of fire in his cane fields and but for such fire would not have been derived by him in that year;

iiiA) where the provisions of subparagraph (1) of paragraph 19 of the First Schedule are in the case of the taxpayer applicable in respect of the said year, the amount by which his taxable income derived from farming for that year exceeds his average taxable income from farming as determined in relation to that year in accordance with subparagraph (2) of the said paragraph;and

e) "D" represents an amount equal to so much of any current contribution to a retirement annuity fund as is allowable as a deduction in terms of section 11(n)(aa)(A) solely by reason of the inclusion in the taxpayer's income of any amount contemplated in paragraph (d) (i), (ii), (iii) and (iiiA) and paragraph (f);

f) "L" represents an amount equal to the sum of--

i) in relation to any amount which accrued to the taxpayer on or after 1 September 1995 to which the provisions of section 7A (4A) are applicable in respect of the said year, the lesser of--

aa) that amount; or

bb) an amount equal to three times the annual average of the amounts derived by such taxpayer during the three years of assessment which immediately preceded the year of assessment under Charge by way of remuneration as defined in paragraph 1 of the Fourth Schedule, including any amount referred to in paragraph (vii) of that definition but excluding so much of the sum of any other amounts contemplated in the said section 7A (4A) as were included in the amounts represented by the symbols "C" and "L" in respect of the said year and any previous year of assessment; and

ii) in relation to any amount which accrued to the taxpayer on or after 1September 1995 to which the provisions of paragraph 7 of the Second Schedule are applicable, any amount determined in accordance with the provisions of that Schedule and included in his income for the said year; and

g) "R" represents the greater of the amounts determined by applying the formula--

$$R = \frac{F}{B + D - (C + L + G)}$$

in respect of the said year and the preceding year of assessment, in which formula the amounts represented by the symbols 'B', 'C', 'D', and 'L' shall be determined in accordance with the aforegoing provisions of this subsection as applicable in the said year or in the said preceding year, as the case may be;

Provided that

a) where, as a result of the death or insolvency of the taxpayer, the period assessed is less than 12 months, the symbol "R" shall be determined with reference to the said year only; and

b) where the said preceding year ended on 28 February, 1995, the symbols 'D' and 'L' in the formula shall be disregarded:

Provided that in no case shall the amount of normal tax so payable be less than the amount of normal tax which would be chargeable at the relevant rate fixed in terms of subsection (2) in respect of the first rand of taxable income, and nothing in this section contained shall be construed as relieving any person from liability for taxation under this Act upon any portion of his taxable income: Provided further that where the sum of the amounts included in symbol "L" exceed the taxpayer's taxable income for the said year, the amount of normal tax so payable shall be calculated on the taxpayer's total taxable income for the said year, at the greater of the relevant rate contemplated in the preceding proviso and the amount determined as symbol "R" in relation to the preceding year only.

6. Normal tax rebates

1) There shall be deducted from the normal tax payable by any natural person an amount equal to the sum of the amounts allowed to the taxpayer by way of rebates under subsection (2).

2) In the case of a natural person there shall, subject to the provisions of subsection (4), be allowed by way of--

a) a primary rebate, an amount of R4 860; and

b) a secondary rebate, if the taxpayer was or, had he lived, would have been over the age of 65 years on the last day of the year of assessment, an amount of R3 000.

3) Deleted by section 5 of Act 21 of 1995

4) Where the period assessed is less than 12 months, the amount to be allowed by way of a rebate under subsection (2) shall be such amount as bears to the full amount of such rebate, the same ratio as the period assessed bears to 12 months unless, where such period terminates at the death of the taxpayer or commences at the death of the spouse of the taxpayer, the Commissioner in the special circumstances of the case otherwise directs.

6quat. Rebate in respect of foreign taxes on income

) Subject to the provisions of subsection (2),a rebate determined in accordance with this section shall be deducted from the normal tax payable by any resident in whose taxable income there is included--

a) any income received by or accrued to such resident from any source outside the Republic other than any foreign dividend contemplated in paragraph (d); which is :

i) not deemed to be from a source within the Republic; or

ii) deleted by the Revenue Laws Amendment Act, 74 of 2002

b) any proportional amount contemplated in section 9D; or

c) deleted by section 4 of Act 59 of 2000 or

d) any foreign dividend contemplated in section 9E, or

e) any taxable capital gain contemplated in section 26A, from a source outside the Republic which is not deemed to be from a source in the Republic; or

f) any amount –

i) contemplated in paragraphs (a), (b) or (d) which is received by or accrued to any other person and which is deemed to have been received by or accrued to such resident in terms of section 7;

ii) of capital gain of any other person from a source outside the Republic which is not deemed to be from a source in the Republic and which is attributed to that resident in terms of paragraph 68, 69, 70, 71, 72 or 80 of the Eighth Schedule; or

iii) contemplated in paragraphs (a), (b), (d) or (e) which represents capital of a trust, and which is included in the income of that resident in terms of section 25B(2A) or taken into account in determining the aggregate capital gain or aggregate capital loss of that resident in terms of paragraph 80(3) of the Eighth Schedule,

1A) For the purposes of subsection (1), the rebate shall be an amount equal to the sum of any taxes on income proved to be payable to any sphere of government of any country other than the Republic, without any right of recovery by any person (other than a right of recovery in terms of any entitlement to carry back losses arising during any year of assessment to any year of assessment prior to such year of assessment), by--

a) such resident in respect of

i) any income contemplated in subsection (1)(a); or

ii) any dividend contemplated in subsection (1)(d); or

iii) any amount of taxable capital gain as contemplated in subsection (1)(e); and

b) any controlled foreign company, in respect of such proportional amount contemplated in subsection (1)(b); or

c) any company in respect of any profits from which any dividend contemplated in subsection (1)(d) is declared or deemed to have been declared; or

d) any company in respect of the proportional amount of any profits from which any dividend is declared or deemed to have been declared to a controlled foreign company, and which dividend relates to any proportional amount equal to the amount which was included in the income of that resident as contemplated in subsection (1)(b); or

e) any portfolio of a collective investment scheme in respect of the amount of any foreign dividend which is deemed to have been declared to such resident in terms of section 9E(5) and included in the taxable income of that resident; or

f) any other person contemplated in subsection (21)(f)(i) or (ii) or any trust contemplated in subsection (1)(f)(iii), in respect of the amount included in the taxable income of that resident as contemplated in subsection (1)(f).

which is so included in that resident's taxable income: Provided that where such resident is a member of any partnership or a beneficiary of any trust and such partnership or trust is liable for tax as a separate entity in such other country, a proportional amount of any tax payable by such entity, which is attributable to the interest of such resident in such partnership or trust, shall be deemed to have been payable by such resident.

1B) Notwithstanding the provisions of subsection (1A)—

a) the rebate or rebates of any tax proved to be payable to the government of any other country or countries as contemplated in subsection (1A), shall not in aggregate exceed an amount which bears to the total normal tax payable the same ratio as the total taxable income attributable to the income, proportional amount, foreign dividend, taxable capital gain or amount, as the case may be, which is included as contemplated in subsection (1), bears to the total taxable income : Provided that—

i) in determining the amount of the taxable income that is attributable to that income, proportional amount, foreign dividend, taxable capital gain or amount, any allowable deductions contemplated in sections 11(n), 18 and 18A must be deemed to have been incurred proportionately in respect of income derived from sources within and outside the Republic;

ii) where the sum of any such taxes payable to the government of any such other country or countries exceeds the rebate as so determined (hereinafter referred to as the excess amount), excess amount may—

(aa) be carried forward to the immediately succeeding year of assessment and shall be deemed to be a tax on income paid to the government of any other country in that year; and

(bb) be set off against the amount of any normal tax payable by that resident during that year of assessment in respect of any amount derived from any other country which is included in the taxable income of that resident during that year, as contemplated in subsection (1), after any tax payable to the government of any other country in respect of any amount so included during such year of assessment which may be deducted in terms of subsection (1) and (1A) has been deducted from the amount of such normal tax payable in respect of such amount so included; and

iii) the excess amount shall not be allowed to be carried forward for more than seven years reckoned from the year of assessment when such excess amount was for the first time carried forward;

b) deleted by section 4 of Act 59 of 2000

c) the amount of any tax which—

i) becomes payable to the government of any other country in respect of any amount which is declared to anyresident as a foreign dividend which is exempt from tax in terms of section 9E(7)(e); and

ii) has not been taken into account as a rebate against any normal tax payable by such resident in respect of such amount previously included in his taxable income in terms of section 9D,
may be deducted from any normal tax which becomes payable by such resident during any year of assessmentthat anyincome is derived by way of dividends declared to such resident by any controlled foreign entity from profits relating to any amount so previously included;

d) may be deducted from any normal tax which becomes payable by that resident during any year of assessment that any income is derived by way of dividends declared to that resident by any controlled foreign company from profits relating to any amount so previously included;

i) Any company distributing any dividend to such resident, if such resident together with any connected person in relation to that resident holds for their own benefit less than ten persent of the equity share capital in such comapny or

ii) any company in respect of any profits from which the dividend is declared or deemed to have been declared, if such resident does not hold a qualifying interest in such company; and

e) no rebate shall be allowed in respect of any tax payable on any amount contemplated in subsection (1)(d), if the resident has made an election as contemplated in section 9E(6).

2) The rebate under subsection (1) shall not be granted in addition to any relief to which the resident is entitled under any agreement between the governments of the Republic and the said other country for the prevention of or relief from double taxation, but may be granted in substitution for the relief to which the resident would be so entitled.

3) '**qualifying interest**' means any qualifying interest as defined in section 9E;
'**taxes on income**' does not include any compulsory payment to the government of any other country which constitutes a consideration for the right to extract any mineral or natural oil

4) For the purposes of this section the amount of any foreign tax proved to be payable as contemplated in subsection (1A) in respect of any amount which is included in the taxable income of any resident during any year of assessment, shall be converted to the currency of the Republic on the last day of that year of assessment by applying the average exchange rate for that year of assessment.

5) Where a rebate was allowed in terms of this section against the normal tax payable by any resident in any previous year of assessment in respect of any amount of tax which was which was proved to be payable to the government of any other country, and -

a) it is proved by that resident that the amount of the tax actually payable to such government exceeds the amount of tax in respect of which the rebate was so allowed; or

b) the Commissioner is satisfied that the amount of the tax actually payable to such government is less than the amount of tax in respect of which the rebate was so allowed

the Commissioner may, notwithstanding the provisions of section 79 or section 81(5), but subject to subsection (1B)(a) issue a reduced or additional assessment, as the case may be, reflecting the amount of the rebate in respect of that amount of tax actually payable in that other currency translated to the currency of the Republic at the average exchange rate applicable for that previous year of assessment, which shall be allowed against normal tax:

7. When income is deemed to have accrued or to have been received

1) Income shall be deemed to have accrued to a person notwithstanding that such income has been invested, accumulated or otherwise capitalized by him or that such income has not been actually paid over to him but remains due and payable to him or has been credited in account or reinvested or accumulated or capitalized or otherwise dealt with in his name or on his behalf, and a complete statement of all such income shall be included by any person in the returns rendered by him under this Act.

2) Any income received by or accrued to any person married with or without community of property (hereinafter referred to as the recipient) shall be deemed for the purposes of this Act to be income accrued to such person's spouse hereinafter referred to as the donor) if--

a) such income was derived by the recipient in consequence of a donation, settlement or other disposition made by the donor on or after 20 March 1991 or of a transaction, operation or scheme entered into or carried out by the donor on or after that date, and the sole or main purpose of such donation, settlement or other disposition or of such transaction, operation or scheme was the reduction, postponement or avoidance of the donor's liability for any tax, levy or duty which, but for such donation, settlement, other disposition, transaction, operation or scheme, would have become payable by the donor under this Act or any other Act administered by the Commissioner; or

b) income was received by or accrued to the recipient--

i) from any trade carried on by the recipient in partnership or association with the donor or which is in any way connected with any trade carried on by the donor; or

ii) from the donor or any partnership of which the donor was at the time of such receipt or accrual a member or any private company of which the donor was at such time the sole or main shareholder or one of the principal shareholders,

and such income represents the whole or any portion of the total income so received by or accrued to the recipient which exceeds the amount of income to which the recipient would reasonably be entitled having regard to the nature of the relevant trade, the extent of the recipient's participation therein, the services rendered by the recipient or any other relevant factor; or

2A) In the case of spouses who are married in community of property--

a) any income (other than income derived from the letting of fixed property which has been derived from the carrying on of any trade shall, if such trade is carried on--

i) by only one of the spouses, be deemed to have accrued to that spouse; or

ii) jointly by both spouses, be deemed, subject to the provisions of subsection (2) (b), to have accrued to both spouses in the proportions determined by them in terms of the agreement that regulates their joint trade or, if there is no such agreement, in the proportion to which each spouse would reasonably be entitled having regard to the nature of the relevant trade, the extent of each spouse's participation therein, the services rendered by each spouse or any other relevant factor; and

b) any income derived from the letting of fixed property and any income derived otherwise than from the carrying on of any trade shall be deemed to have accrued in equal shares to both spouses: Provided that any such income which does not fall into the joint estate of the spouses shall be deemed to be income accrued to the spouse who is entitled thereto.

2B) So much of any deduction or allowance which may be made under the provisions of this Act in the determination of the taxable income derived from any income referred to in subsections (2) and (2A) as relates to any portion of such income which is under the provisions of that subsection deemed to be income accrued to a spouse shall be deemed to be a deduction or allowance which may be made in the determination of the taxable income of such spouse.

2C) For the purposes of subsection (2A)--

a) any benefit paid or payable to a spouse in his capacity as a member or past member of a pension fund, provident fund, benefit fund, retirement annuity fund or any other fund of a similar nature shall be deemed to be income derived by such spouse from a trade carried on by him;

b) any annuity amount (as defined in section 10A) paid or payable to a spouse shall be deemed to be income derived by such spouse from a trade carried on by him; and

c) where any spouse is the--

i) registered holder of a patent as defined in the Patents Act, 1978 (Act No. 57 of 1978), or any design as defined in the Designs Act, 1993 (Act No. 195 of 1993), or any trade mark as defined in the Trade Marks Act, 1993 (Act No. 194 of 1993);

ii) author of a work on which copyright has been conferred in terms of the Copyright Act, 1978 (Act No. 98 of 1978), or the owner of such a copyright by reason of assignment, testamentary disposition or operation of law;

iii) holder of any other property or right of a similar nature, any income derived from the grant of the right of use of such patent, design, trade mark, copyright or other property or right shall be deemed to be income derived by such spouse from a trade carried on by him.

3) Income shall be deemed to have been received by the parent of any minor child, if by reason of any donation, settlement or other disposition made by that parent of that child--

a) it has been received by or has accrued to or in favour of that child or has been expended for the maintenance, education or benefit of that child; or

b) it has been accumulated for the benefit of that child.

4) Any income received by or accrued to or in favour of any minor child of any person, by reason of any donation, settlement or other disposition made by any other person, shall be deemed to be the income of the parent of such minor child, if such parent or his spouse

has made a donation, settlement or other disposition or given some other consideration in favour directly or indirectly of the said other person or his family.

5) If any person has made any donation, settlement or other disposition which is subject to a stipulation or condition, whether made or imposed by such person or anybody else, to the effect that the beneficiaries thereof or some of them shall not receive the income or some portion of the income thereunder until the happening of some event, whether fixed or contingent, so much of any income as would, but for such stipulation or condition, in consequence of the donation, settlement or other disposition be received by or accrue to or in favour of the beneficiaries, shall, until the happening of that event or the death of that person, whichever first takes place, be deemed to be the income of that person.

6) If any deed of donation, settlement or other disposition contains any stipulation that the right to receive any income thereby conferred may, under powers retained by the person by whom that right is conferred, be revoked or conferred upon another, so much of any income as in consequence of the donation, settlement or other disposition is received by or accrues to or in favour of the person on whom that right is conferred, shall be deemed to be the income of the person by whom it is conferred, so long as he retains those powers.

7) If by reason of any donation, settlement or other disposition made, whether before or after the commencement of this Act, by any person (hereinafter referred to as the donor)--

a) the donor's right to receive or have paid to him or for his benefit any amount by way of rent, dividend, interest, royalty or similar income in respect of any movable or immovable property (including without limiting the foregoing any lease, company share, marketable security, deposit, loan, copyright, design or trade mark) or in respect of the use of, or the granting of permission to use, such property, is ceded or otherwise made over to any other person or to a third party for that other person's benefit in such manner that the donor remains the owner of or retains an interest in the said property or if the said property or interest is transferred, delivered or made over to the said other person or to a third party for the said other person's benefit, in such manner that the donor is or will at a fixed or determinable time be entitled to regain ownership of or the interest in the said property; or

b) the donor's right to receive or have paid to him or for his benefit any income that is or may become due to him by any other person acting in a fiduciary capacity is ceded or otherwise made over to any other person or to a third part for that other person's benefit in such manner that the donor is or will at a determinable time be entitled to regain the said right, any such rent, dividend, interest, royalty or income (including any amount which, but for this subsection, would have been exempt from tax in the hands of the said other person) as is received by or accrues to or for the benefit of the said other person on or after 1 July 1983 and which would otherwise, but for the said donation, settlement or other disposition, have been received by or have accrued to or for the benefit of the donor, shall be deemed to have been received by or to have accrued to the donor.

8) Where by reason of or in consequence of any donation, settlement or other disposition (other than a donation, settlement or other disposition to an entity which is not a resident and which is similar to a public benefit organisation contemplated in section 30) made by any resident, income is received by or accrued to any person who is not a resident (other than a controlled foreign company in relation to such resident), there shall be included in the income of that resident so much of the amount of any income as is attributable to that

donation, settlement or other disposition: Provided that any amount of income received by or accrued to that person by way of foreign dividends, shall for the purposes of this section be determined in accordance with the provisions of section 9E, as if that person had been a shareholder who is a resident.

9) Where any asset has been disposed of for a consideration which is less than the market value of such asset, the amount by which such market value exceeds such consideration shall for the purposes of this section be deemed to be a donation.

10) Any resident who, at any time during any year of assessment makes any donation, settlement or other disposition as contemplated in this section, shall disclose such fact to the Commissioner in writing when submitting his return of income for such year and at the same time fumish such information as may be required by the Commissioner for the purposes of this section.

7A. Date of receipt or accrual of antedated salaries or pensions and of certain retirement gratuities

1) For the purposes of this section--

"antedated salary or pension" means an amount of salary or pension which has become payable to any person under a permanent grant, made with retrospective effect, of a salary or pension or of an increase in a salary or pension, and which in terms of such grant is payable in respect of a period ending on or before the date on which the grant has become effective.

"pension" means an annuity payable under any law or under the rules of a pension fund or provident fund or by an employer to a former employee of that employer or to the widow, child or dependant of a deceased person who was employed by such employer.

"salary" means salary, wages or similar remuneration payable by an employer to an employee. but does not include any bonus or any amount referred to in subsection (4)

2) Where any antedated salary or pension has been received by or has accrued to any person during any period of assessment and the period in respect of which such antedated salary or pension has become payable (herinafter referred to as the accrual period) commenced before the commencement of the said year or period of assessment, such antedated salary or pension shall at the option of the taxpayer be deemed--

a) if the accrual period commenced not more than two years before the commencement of the said year or period of assessment, to have been received by or to have accrued to the said person in part during each of the years or periods of assessment in which any portion of the accrual period falls (the part of the said amount relating to any such year or period of assessment being determined on the basis of a reasonable apportionment of the whole of the said amount between all the said years or periods of assessment); or

b) if the accrual period commenced more than two years before the commencement of the first-mentioned year or period of assessment, to have been received by or to have accrued to the said person in three equal annual instalments (the first and second instalments two years and one year respectively before the date on which the said amount accrued to the said person and the third instalment on the said date).

3) Where any member of the citizen force or of the commandos has bound himself to serve in such force or the commandos for a continuous period of service of at least eighteen months as contemplated in section 22(6A) or 44(5A) of the Defence Act, 1957 (Act No. 44 of 1957), the provisions of subsection (2) shall *mutatis mutandis* apply in respect of any gratuity which has become payable to him by the State upon and by reason of the completion of such period of service, as though such gratuity were antedated salary or pension granted permanently and with retrospective effect, in respect of the said period of service.

4A) Where the taxable income of any taxpayer for any year of assessment includes any amount (other than an amount contemplated in paragraph (e) of the definition of "gross income" in section 1) received by or accrued to him as an employee or the holder of any office by way of bonus, gratuity or compensation upon or because of the termination of his services or because of the impending termination of his services within five years (or such longer period as the Commissioner may approve) From the date of actual receipt or accrual of such amount, and--

a) the taxpayer has attained the age of 55 years; or

b) the termination or impending termination of the taxpayer's services is due to superannuation, ill-health or other infirmity; or

c) Deleted by section 7 of Act 21 of 1995; or

d) the Commissioner is satisfied that--

i) the termination or impending termination of the taxpayer's services is due to his employer having ceased to carry on or intending to cease carrying on the trade in respect of which the taxpayer was employed or to the taxpayer having become redundant in consequence of his employer having effected a general reduction in personnelor a reduction in personnel of a particular class; and

ii) the circumstances of the case warrant this concession,

the normal tax payable by the taxpayer in respect of such year shall, subject to the provisions of section 5, be determined in accordance with the provisions of section 5(10), but nothing herein contained shall be construed as relieving any person from liability for taxation under this Act upon any portion of his taxable income.

8. Certain amounts to be included in income or taxable income

1)

a)

i) There shall be included in the taxable income of any person (hereinafter referred to as the 'recipient') for any year of assessment any amount which has been paid or granted during that year by his or her principal as an allowance or advance, excluding any portion of any allowance or advance actually expended by that recipient-

aa) on travelling on business, as contemplated in paragraph (b);

bb) on any accommodation, meals and other incidental costs, as contemplated in paragraph (c), while such recipient is by reason of the duties of his or her office or employment obliged to spend at least one night away from his or her usual place of residence in the Republic; or

cc) by reason of the duties attendant upon his or her office, as contemplated in paragraph (d).

ii) There shall not be included in the taxable income of a person in terms of the provisions of paragraph (a)(i), any amount paid or granted by a principal in reimbursement of, or as an advance for, any expenditure incurred or to be incurred by the recipient-

aa) on the instruction of his or her principal in the furtherance of the trade of that principal; and

bb) where that recipient must produce proof to that principal that such expenditure was wholly incurred as aforesaid and must account to that principal for that expenditure:

Provided that where that expenditure was incurred to acquire any asset, the ownership in that asset must vest in that principal.

iii) For the purposes of this paragraph, 'principal' in relation to a recipient includes his or her employer or the authority, company, body or other organisation in relation to which any office is held, or any associated institution, as defined in the Seventh Schedule, in relation to such employer, authority, company, body or organisation.

iv) The provisions of this paragraph shall not apply in respect of any allowance or advance received by or accrued to a person contemplated in section 9(1)(e) stationed outside the Republic which is attributable to that person's services rendered outside the Republic.

b) For the purposes of paragraph (a)(i)(aa)-

i) any allowance or advance in respect of transport expenses shall, to the extent to which such allowance or advance has been expended by the recipient on private travelling (including travelling between his place of residence and his place of employment or business or any other travelling done for his private or domestic purposes), be deemed not to have been actually expended on travelling on business;

ii) subject to the provisions of subparagraph (iii), where such allowance or advance has been paid to the recipient in order that it may be utilized for defraying expenditure in respect of any motor vehicle used by the recipient, the portion of the allowance expended by the recipient during the year of assessment for business purposes shall, unless an acceptable calculation based on accurate data is furnished by the recipient, be deemed to be an amount calculated by applying the rate per kilometre determined in the manner prescribed by the Minister of Finance by notice in the *Gazette* for the category of vehicle used, on a distance travelled during the said year for business purposes (other than private travelling as contemplated in subparagraph (i)): Provided that where an allowance or advance has been paid to a recipient in relation to a motor vehicle in respect of which he has been granted the right of use as contemplated in paragraph 7 of the Seventh Schedule, no regard shall be had to such rate per kilometre in order to determine the portion of such allowance or advance expended by the recipient for business purposes: Provided further that--

aa) the recipient shall, unless the contrary appears, be deemed to have used the vehicle during such year for such business purposes over a distance equal to the difference between the total number of kilometres travelled by him in such vehicle during such year (but not exceeding 32 000 kilometres) and a distance of 14 000 kilometres;

bb) where the vehicle has been used for business purposes during a period in such year which is less than the full period of such year, the reference in paragraph (aa) of this proviso to the distances of 32 000 kilometres and 12 000 kilometres shall be construed as a reference to the distances which bear to 32 000 kilometres and 12 000 kilometres, respectively, the same ratio as the period of use for business purposes bears to 12 months;

cc) where the recipient has during the whole or any portion of the year of assessment interchangeably used more than one vehicle for business purposes, the provisions of paragraphs (aa) and (bb) of this proviso shall be applied separately to each such vehicle;

iii) where such allowance or advance is based on the actual distance travelled by the recipient in using a motor vehicle on business (excluding the said private travelling), or such actual distance is proved to the satisfaction of the Commissioner to have been travelled by the recipient, the amount expended by the recipient on such business travelling shall, unless the contrary appears, be deemed to be an amount determined on such actual distance at the rate per kilometre fixed by the Minister of Finance by notice in the *Gazette* for the category of vehicle used;

iv) where any motor vehicle which is owned or leased by an employee, his spouse or his child, whether directly or indirectly by virtue of an interest in a company or trust or otherwise, has been let to the employer or any associated institution in relation to the employer, the sum of the rental paid by the employer or associated institution and any expenditure defrayed by the employer or associated institution in respect of the vehicle, shall be deemed to be an allowance paid to the employee in respect of transport expenses, and in such case the said rental shall for the purposes of this Act (excluding this paragraph) be deemed not to have been received by or to have accrued to the lessor of such motor vehicle, and for the purposes of paragraph 2 (b) of the Seventh Schedule such employee shall be deemed not to have been granted the right to use such motor vehicle.

c) A recipient shall, for the purposes of paragraph (a)(i)(bb), be deemed to have actually expended,-

i) where that recipient proves to the Commissioner the amount of the expenses incurred by him or her in respect of accommodation, meals or other incidental costs (other than any amount of expenditure borne by the employer otherwise than by way of payment or granting of the allowance), the amount so actually incurred but limited to the amount of the allowance or advance paid or granted to meet those expenses; or

ii) for each day or part of a day in the period during which that recipient is absent from his or her usual place of residence, an amount in respect of meals and other incidental costs, or incidental costs only, determined by the Minister for the relevant year of assessment by way of notice in the Gazette, but limited to the amount of the allowance paid or granted to meet those expenses :

Provided that this subparagraph does not apply to the extent that -

aa) the employer has borne the expenses (otherwise than by way of granting the allowance or advance) in respect of which the allowance was paid or granted for that day or part of that day; or

bb) the recipient has proved to the Commissioner any amount of actual expenditure in respect of meals or incidental costs for that day or part of that day, as contemplated in subparagraph (i)

d) Any allowance granted to the holder of any public office contemplated in paragraph (e) to enable him to defray expenditure incurred by him in connection with such office shall for the purposes of paragraph (a) be deemed to have been so expended by him to the extent that expenditure relevant to such allowance and not otherwise recoverable by him has actually been incurred by him for the purposes of his office in respect of--

i) secretarial services, duplicating services, stationery, postage, telephone calls, the hire of office accommodation and the maintenance of such accommodation;

ii) travelling;

iii) hospitality extended at any official or civic function which the holder of such office is by reason of the nature of such office normally expected to arrange;

iv) ***[deleted by the Taxation Laws Amendment Act 2002]***

v) subsistence and incidental costs incurred in the circumstances contemplated in paragraph (c).

e) For the purposes of paragraph (d) the holder of a public office includes--

i) the President, Deputy President, a Minister, Deputy Minister, a member of the National Assembly, a permanent delegate to the National Council of Provinces, a Premier, a member of an Executive Council or a member of a provincial legislature;

ii) any member of a municipal council, a traditional leader, a member of a provincial House of Traditional Leaders and a member of the Council of Traditional Leaders; and

iii) a person occupying the office of president, chairman or chief executive officer of any non-profit making organization which is organized on a national or regional basis to represent persons with common interests and the funds of which are derived wholly or mainly from subscriptions of members or donations from the general public.

f) Where it is expected of any person contemplated in paragraph (e)(i) to defray any expenditure referred to in paragraph (d) out of his salary received as the holder of any public office, an amount equal to a portion (which shall be determined by the National Assembly or the President, as the case may be, as provided for in the Remuneration of Public Office Bearers Act, 1998 (Act No. 20 of 1998)) of such salary shall for the purposes of paragraph (d) be deemed to be an allowance granted to such person.

g) Where, during any year of assessment, any person contemplated in paragraph (e) has held a public office for less than 12 months, the amount determined in terms of paragraph (f), shall be reduced to an amount which bears to the relevant amount, the same ratio as the number of months (in the determination of which a part of a month shall be reckoned as a full month), for which the office was held bears to 12 months.

4)

a) There shall be included in the taxpayer's income all amounts allowed to be deducted or set off under the provisions of sections 11 to 20, inclusive, section 24D, section 24F, section 24G and section 27(2)(b) and (d) of this Act, except section 11(k), (p) and (q), section 11quin, section 12(2) or section 12(2) as applied by section 12(3), section 12A(3), section 13(5), or section 13(5) as applied by section 13(8), or section 13bis(7), or section 15(a), section 15A, or under the corresponding provisions of any previous Income Tax Act, whether in the current or any previous year of assessment which have been recovered or recouped during the current year of assessment: Provided that the provisions of this paragraph shall not apply in respect of any such amount so recovered or recouped which has been included in the gross income of such taxpayer in terms of paragraph (eB) or (jA) of the definition of 'gross income'.

b) If any amount referred to in paragraph (a) of this subsection is an amount which has been recovered or recouped during any year of assessment by a resident who carries on any business as owner or charterer of any ship as a result of the loss, sale or disposal in any other manner by that person of a ship, and if that person satisfies the Commissioner that--

i) he will within a period of one year (or such longer period as the Commissioner in the circumstances of the case may allow) after the end of that year of assessment conclude a contract for the acquisition by him of a further ship to replace the aforesaid ship;

ii) such further ship will be used by him for the purposes of his trade for a period of not less than ten years or, if the said amount was recovered or recouped by him on or after the seventeenth day of August, 1966, for a period of not less than seven years; and

iii) such further ship will be a ship in relation to which the provisions of section 14(1) (b) will apply and will continue to apply for the said period of not less than ten years or, if the said amount was recovered or recouped by him on or after the seventeenth day of August, 1966, the further ship will be a ship in relation to which the provisions of section 14(1)(a) or (b) will apply and will continue to apply for the said period of not less than seven years,

the said amount shall, notwithstanding anything to the contrary contained in paragraph (a) of this subsection, but subject to the provisions of paragraphs (c), (d) and (dA) of this subsection--

(aa) if it was recovered or recouped before the seventeenth day of August, 1966, not be included in the income of that person for the aforesaid year of assessment, but shall be included in his income for the period of assessment ending on the date of his death, insolvency or liquidation (in the case of a company), as the case may be; or

(bb) if it was recovered or recouped on or after 17 August 1966, not be included in the income of that person for the aforesaid year of assessment except to the extent that such amount is not, in terms of the definition of "adjustable cost" or "adjustable cost price" in section 14(2), deductible from the cost or estimated cost price of such further ship:

Provided that the provisions of this paragraph shall not apply to any amount which has been recovered or recouped as a result of any such loss, sale or disposal which has taken or takes place on or after 1 April 1995.

c) Within three months after the end of the year of assessment during which any amount referred to in paragraph (b) has been recovered or recouped by the person concerned in respect of any ship of more than two hundred gross register tons, there shall be deposited by the said person with the Public Debt Commissioners for such period and on such conditions as may be approved by the Commissioner an amount equal to the amount to be excluded from such person's income in terms of that paragraph, less such amount, if any, as has in the meantime been paid by the said person in respect of the cost price of the further ship referred to in that paragraph.

d) If owing to any occurrence (other than the loss by the said person of the further ship referred to in paragraph (b)) or because of any circumstance arising during any year of assessment the Commissioner is no longer satisfied in regard to the matters in regard to which he is in terms of that paragraph of the corresponding provisions of any previous Income Tax Act required to be satisfied, the amount not included in the taxpayer's income in terms of that paragraph or the corresponding provisions of any previous Income Tax Act shall be included in the income of the taxpayer for the year of assessment during which such occurrence takes place or such circumstance arises.

dA) If as a result of the loss, sale or disposal in any other manner by the person concerned of the further ship referred to in paragraph (b) there has accrued to or has been received by the taxpayer an amount in excess of the cost thereof less the amount not included in the taxpayers income in terms of subparagraph (bb) of the said paragraph, so much of the excess as does not exceed such last-mentioned amount shall (unless such last-mentioned amount has been included in income in terms of paragraph (d)) be deemed to have been recovered or recouped and shall, in addition to any amount referred to in paragraph (a) which has been recovered or recouped, be included in the taxpayer's income for the year of assessment during which such further ship was so lost, sold or disposed of.

dB) For the purposes of paragraph (a), where any company which is or was a parent company contemplated in paragraph (b) of the definition of "South African ship" in section 14(2) has--

i) exercised the election in terms of section 14(1D) in relation to any other company which is or was a subsidiary company contemplated in the last-mentioned paragraph; and

ii) sold or disposed of in any other manner any shares held in such other company during any year of assessment, such company shall be deemed to have recovered or recouped during such year of assessment an amount equal to the lessor of--

(aa) the total of all amounts allowed to be deducted or set off under the provisions of sections 11(o), 12C and 14, whether in such or any previous year of assessment, in the determination of such company's taxable income in respect of any ship owned by such other company, at the date of sale or disposal of such shares; and

(bb) the market value of such ship as at the date of sale or disposal of such shares;

e) If any amount which was deducted--

i) under the provisions of section 11(e) or section 12(1) or section 12(1) as applied by section 12(3) or the corresponding provisions of any previous Income Tax Act or section 12B or section 12C or section 12E or section 12G or section 14 or section 14bis or section 27(2)(d), in respect of machinery or plant which was used by the taxpayer directly in a process of manufacture, or directly in any other process carried on by him on or after 15 March 1961, which in the opinion of the Commissioner was of a similar nature; or

ii) in respect of machinery or plant which was used by an agricultural co-operative (as defined in section 27(9)) directly for storing or packing pastoral, agricultural or other farm products or for subjecting such products to a primary process as defined in the said section 27(9); or

iii) in respect of a ship or aircraft used by him for purposes of his trade; or

iv) in respect of any pipeline, transmission line or cable or railway line as contemplated in section 12D, or

v) in respect of any aircraft hangar, apron, runway or taxiway as contemplated in section 12F;

has as a result of damage or destruction (hereinafter referred to as "the event") been recovered or recouped during any year of assessment, and if the taxpayer satisfies the Commissioner--

aa) that he has concluded or will within a period of one year (or such longer period as the Commissioner in the circumstances of the case may allow) from the date of the event conclude a contract for the acquisition by him of further new or unused machinery, plant, ship, aircraft, pipeline, transmission line or cable, railway line, aircraft hangar, apron, runway or taxiway (hereinafter referred to as the "further asset") to replace the aforesaid machinery, plant, ship, aircraft, pipeline, transmission line or cable, railway line; aircraft hangar, apron, runway or taxiway; and

bb) that the further asset has been or will be brought into use within a period of three years from the date of the event and will be used by him--

A) directly in a process of manufacture or any other process which in the opinion of the Commissioner is of a similar nature;

B) in the case of such co-operative, directly for storing or packing pastoral agricultural or other farm products or for subjecting such products to primary process, as defined in section 27(9);

C) in the case of a ship or aircraft, directly for the purposes of the taxpayer's trade; or

D) in the case of a pipeline, transmission line or cable or railway line in his sole business of the transporttation of persons, goods, things or natural oil as defined in section 12D or the transmission of electricity or any telecommunication signal, or

E) in the case of an aircraft hangar, apron, runway or taxiway in carrying on his sole business of airport operator as contemplated in section 12F; for a period of not less than five years or until the further asset is scrapped or disposed of in the ordinary course of the taxpayer's trade prior to the expiry of such period of five years, the said amount shall, notwithstanding the provisions of paragraph (a) of this subsection, not be included in the income of the taxpayer for the aforesaid year of assessment: Provided that if, owing to any occurrence or because of any circumstance arising during any year of assessment the Commissioner is no longer satisfied in regard to the matters in regard to which in terms of the preceding provisions of this paragraph he is required to be satisfied, the said amount shall be included in the income of the taxpayer for the year of assessment during which such occurrence takes place or such circumstance arises.

f) If as a result of the loss, sale or disposal in any other manner by the taxpayer of the further asset referred to in paragraph (e) there has accrued to or has been received by the taxpayer an amount in excess of the cost thereof less the amount referred to in the said paragraph, so much of the excess as does not exceed such last-mentioned amount shall (unless such last-mentioned amount has been included in income in terms of the proviso to the said paragraph) be deemed to have been recovered or recouped and shall be included in the taxpayer's income for the year of assessment during which such further asset was so lost, sold or disposed of in addition to any recovery or recoupment referred to in paragraph (a).

g) If any amount referred to in paragraph (a) of this subsection is an amount which has been recovered or recouped by any person during any year of assessment as a result of the loss, sale or disposal in any other manner by such person of an aircraft, and if that person satisfies the Commissioner that--

i) he will within a period of one year (or such longer period as the Commissioner in the circumstances of the case may allow) after the end of that year of assessment conclude a contract for the acquisition by him of a further aircraft to replace the aforesaid aircraft; and

ii) such further aircraft will be used by him for the purposes of his trade for a period of not less than three years, the said amount shall, notwithstanding anything to the contrary contained in paragraph (a), but subject to the provisions of paragraphs (h), (i) and (j), not be included in the income of that person for the aforesaid year of assessment, except to the extent that such amount is not in terms of paragraph (a) of subsection (2) of section 14bis deductible from the cost or estimated cost price of such further aircraft: Provided that the provisions of this paragraph shall not apply to any amount which has been recovered or recouped as a result of any such loss, sale or disposal which takes place on or after 1 August 1992.

h) Within three months after the end of the year of assessment during which any amount referred to in paragraph (g) has been recovered or recouped by the person concerned, there shall be deposited by the said person with the Public Debt Commissioners for such period and on such conditions as may be approved by the Commissioner an amount equal to the amount to be excluded from such person's income in terms of that paragraph, less such amount, if any, as has in the meantime been paid by the said person in respect of the cost price of the further aircraft referred to in that paragraph.

i) If owing to any occurrence (other than the loss by the person concerned of the further aircraft referred to in paragraph (g)) or because of any circumstance arising during any year of assessment, the Commissioner is no longer satisfied in regard to the matters to which he is in terms of that paragraph required to be satisfied, the amount not included in the taxpayer's income in terms of that paragraph shall be included in the income of the taxpayer for the year of assessment during which such occurrence takes place or such circumstance arises.

j) If as a result of the loss, sale or disposal in any other manner by the person concerned of the further aircraft referred to in paragraph (g) there has accrued to or has been received by the taxpayer an amount in excess of the cost thereof less the amount not included in the taxpayer's income in terms of the said paragraph, so much of the excess as does not exceed such last-mentioned amount shall (unless such last-mentioned amount has been included in income in terms of paragraph (i)) be deemed to have been recovered or recouped and shall; in addition to any amount referred to in paragraph (a) which has been recovered or recouped, be included in the taxpayer's income for the year of assessment during which such further aircraft was so lost, sold or disposed of.

k) For the purposes of paragraph (a), where during any year of assessment any person has

i) donated any asset;

ii) transferred in whatever manner or form any asset to any shareholder of that company; or; and

iii) disposed of any asset to a person who is a connected person in relation to aht person,

in respect of which a deduction or an allowance has been granted to such person in terms of any of the provisions referred to in that paragraph, such person shall be deemed to have recovered or recouped an amount equal to the market value of such asset as at the date of such donation, transfer or disposal.".

l) For purposes of paragraph (a), where--

i) any person was entitled to a deduction in respect of any interest or related finance changes (including a discount or premium), which was incurred or deemed to have been incurred by such person in relation to any financial arrangement during any year of assessment and such interest or related finance charges were allowed as a deduction in terms of the provisions of this Act during such year of assessment in the hands of such person;

ii) such person has transferred such financial arrangement during any year of assessment to any other person; and

iii) any obligation or part thereof in respect of such interest or related finance charges which such person is legally liable to pay has, as a result of such transfer, been transferred to such other person,

such person shall be deemed to have recovered or recouped an amount equal to the amount of such obligation or part thereof so transferred during the year of assessment in which such obligation or part thereof has been so transferred.

m) Subject to the provisions of section 20, where--

i) as a result of the cancellation, termination or variation of an agreement or due to the prescription, waiver or release of a claim for payment, any person was during any year of assessment relieved or partially relieved from the obligation to make payment of any expenditure actually incurred;

ii) such expenditure was at the date on which such person was so releived or partially relieved not paid; and

iii) such expenditure or any allowance in relation to such expenditure was in the current or any previous year of assessment allowed as a deduction from such person's income,

such person shall for the purposes of paragraph (a) be deemed to have recovered or recouped an amount equal to the amount of the obligation from which the person was so relieved or partially relieved during the year of assessment in which the person was so relieved or partially relieved.

n) Where a taxpayer disposes of an industrial asset contemplated in section 12G before completion of the write off period of that asset for purposes of section 11(e), 12C or 13, as applicable, there shall be included in the taxpayers income, all amounts allowed to be deducted in respect of that industrial asset under section 12G, whether in the current year or any previous year of assessment, which have been recovered or recouped during the current year of assessment, in addition to the inclusion of those amounts in terms of paragraph (a).

4A) The provisions of subsection (4)(a), (e), (f) or (k) shall not apply in respect of any amount which is deemed to have been allowed as a deduction in terms of subparagraph (ix) of the proviso to section 11(e), section 11(o)(bb). section 12B(4B), section 12C(4A), section 12D(3A), section 13(1A), section 13bis(3A) or section 13ter(6A).

5)

a) Any amount which has been paid, whether in the form of rent or otherwise, by any person for the right of use or occupation of any movable or immovable property and has been allowed as a deduction in the determination of such person's taxable income, and which or the equivalent of which is upon the subsequent acquisition of such property by that or any other person applied in reduction or towards settlement of the purchase price of such property, shall be included in the income of the person by whom the property is acquired as aforesaid for the year of assessment in which such person exercises the option or concludes the agreement, as the case may be, in consequence of which the property is acquired by him: Provided that the provisions of this subsection shall not apply in any case where, in consequence of the acquisition of such property, the person who has acquired the property or any other person has derived a taxable benefit the cash equivalent of which has been included in his gross income in terms of the provisions of paragraph (i) of the definition of "gross income" in section 1.

b) Where any amount has been paid by any person for the right of use or occupation of any property which is thereafter acquired by that or any other person for a consideration which in the opinion of the Commissioner is not an adequate consideration or for no consideration, it shall for the purposes of paragraph (a) be deemed, unless the Commissioner having regard to the circumstances of the case otherwise decides, that the said amount, or so much thereof as does not exceed the fair market value of such property as determined by the Commissioner less the amount of the consideration, if any, for which it has been acquired as aforesaid, has been applied in reduction or towards settlement of the purchase price of such property.

bA) If after the termination on or after 1 September 1983 by the effluxion of time or otherwise of a lease of property consisting of corporeal movable goods or of any machinery or plant in respect of which the lessor under such lease was entitled to any allowance under the provisions of this Act, the person who was the lessee under such lease (hereinafter referred to as the former lessee) is, with the express or implied consent or acquiescence of the person who was the lessor under such lease (hereinafter referred to as the former lessor) or of the owner of the property, allowed to use, enjoy or deal with the property as the former lessee may deem fit--

i) without the payment of any consideration; or

ii) in the case of a lease entered into on or after 1 September 1983, wiithout the payment of any rental or other consideration or subject to the payment of any consideration which is nominal in relation to the fair market value of the property,

the former lessee shall be deemed for the purposes of paragraph (b) to have acquired the property for no consideration and, if the property was owned by the former lessor, the fair market value thereof shall, unless and until that value is otherwise determined to the satisfaction of the Commissioner, be deemed for the said purposes to be the cost to the former lessor of the property (or, where the said lease was a financial lease as defined in section 1 of the Sales Tax Act, 1978 (Act No. 103 of 1978), the cash value of the property contemplated in paragraph 2 of Schedule 4 to the said Act), less a depreciation allowance calculated in accordance with paragraph (bB) (i) for the period from the commencement to the termination of the lease.

bB) For the purposes of paragraph (bA)--

i) the depreciation allowance shall be calculated as an aggregate of annual allowances for the years in the period for which the depreciation allowance may be made, the allowance for the first year in the said period being calculated at the rate of 20 per cent of the said cost or cash value, as the case may be, of the property in question and the allowance for each succeeding year in that period being calculated at the said rate on the balance of the said cost or cash value, as the case may be, remaining after the deduction therefrom of the allowance or allowances calculated for the year or years preceding such succeeding year;

ii) the former lessor of the property in question, or the owner thereof, as the case may be, shall, unless and until the contrary is proved, be deemed to have consented to the former lessee using, enjoying or dealing with the property as contemplated in the said paragraph if, at the end of a period of three months reckoned after the date on which the lease in question terminated, the former lessor has not instituted proceedings to compel the former lessee to return the property to the former lessor or to relinquish possession thereof or to dispose thereof in accordance with the terms of the least: Provided that if such lease terminated on or before 31 December 1983 the said period of three months shall be reckoned from that date;

iii) where any consideration is payable in respect of the property in question for the period after the termination of the lease in question, such consideration shall be deemed to be nominal in relation to the fair market value of the property if that consideration, in relation to the period for which it is payable, amounts to less than 10 per cent per annum of the said fair market value;

iv) if after the termination of a lease referred to in the said paragraph (bA) the former lessee is required to pay a consideration in respect of his right to use, enjoy or deal with the property in question but ceases to pay such consideration or, in the case of a lease referred to in subparagraph (ii) of the said paragraph (bA), pays a consideration in respect of such right which is nominal in relation to the fair market value of the property, the said lease shall be deemed to have been terminated on the date from which the former lessee is no longer required to pay such consideration or in the case of a lease referred to in the said subparagraph (ii), whereafter the consideration payable by him becomes nominal as aforesaid;

v) where in the circumstances contemplated in paragraph 3B of Schedule 4 to the Sales Tax Act, 1978, a lease is deemed to be part of a lease which has ceased to exist, the leases shall be deemed to be one lease.

bC) Any person who, as a former lessor of property referred to in paragraph (bA) or as the owner thereof, has after the termination of the lease of such property consented to the former lessee thereof using, enjoying or dealing with such property as contemplated in the said paragraph, or is deemed to have so consented under the provisions of paragraph (bB)(ii), shall not later than 14 days after the end of three months after the termination of the relevant lease advise the former lessee of the fair market value of such property as determined in accordance with paragraph (bA), and shall furnish the Commissioner with a copy of such advice.

c) Any decision of the Commissioner under paragraph (b) or (bA) shall be subject to objection and appeal.

8E. Dividends on certain shares deemed to be interest in relation to the recipient thereof

1) For the purposes of this section--

"affected instrument" means--

a) any redeemable preference share which the relevant company is obliged to redeem in whole or in part within a period of three years from the date of issue thereof, or which may at the option of the holder be redeemed in whole or in part within the said period, or in respect of which the holder has a right of acquisition which may be exercised within the said period; or

b) any other share, if--

i) the holder has a right of acquisition in respect of such share which may be exercised within a period of three years from the date of issue thereof and

ii) such share does not rank *pari passu* as regards its participation in dividends with all other ordinary shares in the capital of the relevant company or, where the ordinary shares in such company are divided into two or more classes, with the shares of at least one of such classes, or any dividend payable on such share is to be calculated with reference to any specified rate of interest or is otherwise to be calculated having regard to the amount of capital subscribed for such share.

"effective date" means 23 March 1989.

"right of acquisition" means a right which the holder of an affected instrument has to require any party--

a) to acquire such affected instrument from such holder; or

b) to procure, facilitate or assist with the redemption in whole or in part of such affected instrument or the repayment in whole or in part of the capital subscribed for such affected instrument or the conversion of such affected instrument into any other share which is redeemable in whole or in part within a period of three years from the date of issue thereof.

2) Subject to the provisions of subsections (3) and (4), any dividend declared by a company on an affected instrument shall for the purposes of this Act be deemed in relation to the recipient thereof only to be an amount of interest by him from a source within the Republic.

3) The provisions of subsection (2) shall apply--

a) to any dividend declared on an affected instrument issued on or after the effective date, and

b) in the case of any affected instrument issued before the effective date, to any dividend declared after the earliest date (being a date falling on or after the effective date) upon which, having regard to the terms attaching to such instrument as at the effective date or to the terms as at the effective date of any agreement relating to the holding of such instrument (including an agreement which confers a right of acquisition), such instrument--

i) became or would have become redeemable or repayable;

ii) could at the instance of the holder have been redeemed or repaid;

iii) could at the instance of the holder have been acquired by any party by reason of the exercise of a right of acquisition; or

iv) being an instrument which may by the exercise of a right of acquisition be converted into any other share, could at the instance of the holder have been so converted and such other share could at the instance of the holder have been redeemed,

other than any such dividend which the relevant company was in accordance with the said terms required to declare before the said earliest date.

4) The provisions of subsection (2) shall not apply--

a) where the holder of any affected instrument is for the purposes of any agreement concluded under section 108 or 109 between the Government of the Republic and the government of any other state a resident of such other state, if the rate or amount of tax which may be levied under this Act on any dividend accruing to such holder is subject to a limitation imposed under such agreement; and

b) to any dividend which, if such provisions were to be applied, would not be included in the taxable income of the recipient.

9. Circumstances in which amounts deemed to have accrued from sources within the Republic

1) An amount shall be deemed to have accrued to any person from a source within the Republic if it has been received by or has accrued to or in favour of such person by virtue of--

a) Deleted by section 7 of Act 59 of 2000;

b) the use or right of use in the Republic of, or the grant of permission to use in the Republic –

i) any patent, design, trade mark, copyright, model, pattern, plan, formula or process or any other property or right of a similar nature; or

ii) motion picture film, or any film or video tape or disc, any sound recording or advertising matter, contemplated in section 35;

bA) the imparting of or undertaking to impart any scientific, technical, industrial or commercial knowledge or information for use in the Republic or rendering or undertaking to render any assistance or service in connection with the application or utilization of such knowledge or information, as contemplated in section 35;

c) Deleted by section 7 of Act 59 of 2000;

cA) any contract made by such person for the disposal of any mineral (including natural oil) won by him in the course of mining operations carried on by him under any mining authorization granted under the Minerals Act, 1991 (Act No. 50 of 1991), wheresoever such contract was made or such mining operations were carried on;

d) Deleted by section 7 of Act 59 of 2000;

e)

i) any services rendered by such person to or work or labour done by such person for or on behalf of any employee in the national or provincial sphere of government, or any local authority in the Republic or any national or provincial public entity if not less than 80 per cent of the expenditure of such entity is defrayed directly or indirectly from funds voted by Parliament, notwithstanding that such services are rendered or that such work or labour is done outside the Republic, provided such services are rendered or such work or labour is done in accordance with a contract of employment entered into with the Government or local authority or national or provincial public entity; or

ii) the holding of a public office to which such person has been appointed or is deemed to have been appointed in terms of an Act of Parliament, notwithstanding that such public office is held outside the Republic :

(proviso deleted by the Revenue Laws Amendment Act, 74 of 2002)

f) Deleted by section 7 of Act 59 of 2000;

fA) any services rendered by such person to, or work or labour done by such person for, any other person upon, beneath or above the continental shelf referred to in section 8 of the Maritime Zones Act, 1994 (Act No. 15 of 1994), in the course of any operations connected with operations carried on by any person under any prospecting permit or mining authorization issued or which may be issued under the Minerals Act, 1991 (Act No. 50 of 1991), or any prospecting or mining lease granted under the Mining Rights Act, 1967 (Act No. 20 of 1967), or under any sublease granted or which may be granted under any such lease, wheresoever payment for such services or work or labour is or is to be made;

g) any pension or annuity granted to such person, wheresoever payment of that pension or annuity is made and wheresoever the funds from which payment is made are situate--

i) by the Government, any provincial administration, or by any local authority in the Republic; or

ii) by any person, whether residing or carrying on business in the Republic or not, if the services in respect of which that pension or annuity was granted were performed within the Republic for at least two years during the ten years immediately preceding the date from which the pension or annuity first became due: Provided that if the pension or annuity was granted in respect of services which were rendered partly within and partly outside the Republic, only so much of such pension or annuity as bears to the amount of such pension or annuity the same ratio as the period during which the services were rendered in the Republic bears to the total period during which the services were rendered, shall be deemed to be derived from a source within the Republic: Provided further that any services rendered in the territory of the former Republic of Transkei, Bophuthatswana, Venda or Ciskei shall be deemed to have been rendered within the Republic;

h) a judicial order or written agreement of separation or an order of divorce, if the taxable income of such person's spouse or former spouse has been reduced by such amount in terms of section 21, wheresoever such judicial order or order of divorce was granted or such agreement was made or such amount is paid or payable and whether such person's spouse or former spouse is resident in or out of the Republic.

1A) For the purposes of paragraph (g)(ii) the services referred to in paragraph (fA) shall be deemed to have been performed within the Republic.

2) The capital gain or capital loss from the disposal of an asset of a person shall be deemed to be from a source in the Republic, where –

a) in the case of immovable property held by that person or any interest or right of whatever nature of that person to or in immovable property, that property is situated in the Republic;

b) in the case of any asset other than immovable property or any interest or right to or in immovable property –

i) that person is a resident and that asset is not attributable to a permanent establishment of that person which is situated outside the Republic; or

ii) that person is not a resident, but that asset is attributable to a permanent establishment of that person which is situated in the Republic:

Provided that for the purpose of this subsection, an interest in immovable property held by a person includes any equity shares in a company or other entity, where –

aa) 80 per cent or more of the value of the net assets of that company or other entity, determined on the market value basis, is attributable directly or indirectly to immovable property, (other than immovable property held by that company or entity as trading stock); and

bb) that person (whether alone or together with any connected person in relation to that person) holds at least 20 per cent in the equity share capital of that company or other entity

3) Deleted by section 7 of Act 28 of 1997.

4) Deleted by section 7 of Act 28 of 1997.

5) Deleted by section 7 of Act 59 of 2000.

6) Any interest as defined in secion 24J shall for the purposes of this Act be deemed to have been recieved or accrued froma source within the Republic, where such interest was derived from the utilisation or application in the Republic by any person of any funds or credit obtained in terms of any form of interest-bearing arrangement.

7) For the purposes of sebsection (6) the place of utilisation or application shall, until the contrary is proved, be deemed to be, in the case where such funds are or credit is utilised or applied by--

a) a natural person, the place where such person is ordinarily residnet; or

b) a person other than a natural person, its place of effective management.

9A : Blocked foreign funds

) Where any amount, or any portion of any amount –

a) received by or accrued to any person which is required to be included in the gross income or taxable income of that person; or

b) of the net income of a controlled foreign company which is taken into account in determining an amount which is required to be included in the income of any resident in terms of the provisions of section 9D,

during any year of assessment, may not be remitted to the Republic during that year of assessment as a result of currency or other restrictions or limitations imposed in terms of the laws of the country where the amount arose, that amount or any portion thereof shall be deemed not to have been received or accrued to that person, or shall not be included in the income of that resident, as the case may be, during that year and that amount or portion thereof shall be included in the gross income or taxable income of that person or the income of that resident during the year of assessment during which that amount or portion thereof may be so remitted to the Republic.

9B. Circumstances in which certain amounts received or accrued in relation to disposal of listed shares are deemed to be of capital nature

1) For the purposes of this section--

"affected share", in relation to any taxpayer, means a share listed on a stock exchange as defined in the Stock Exchanges Control Act, 1985 (Act No. 1 of 1985), which has been disposed of by the taxpayer who immediately prior to such disposal had been the owner of such share as a listed share for a continuous period of at least five years: Provided that--

a) where the taxpayer is a company which acquired such share from any other company in the same "group of companies" as defined in section 48 of the Taxation Laws Amendment Act,1988 (Act No. 87 of 1988), and such company qualified for an exemption from stamp duty in respect of the registration of transfer of such share in terms of the said section, both such companies shall be deemed to be one and the same company;

b) where any other share or shares are issued to such taxpayer by the company in which he holds such share in substitution for any such share by reason of a subdivision of any such share or any similar arrangement, or any capitalization share in relation to such share is issued by such company to such taxpayer, such share and such other share or shares or such capitalization share shall be deemed to be one and the same share if--

   i) such taxpayer's participation rights and interests, whatsoever, in such company remain unaltered; and

   ii) no consideration whatsoever passes directly or indirectly from such taxpayer to such company in relation to the issue of such other share or shares or such capitalization share;

c) the taxpayer shall be deemed to have disposed of a share if the share has been cancelled or redeemed or if the relevant company has been liquidated or deregistered.

d) where the taxpayer is a registered insurer in terms of the insurance Act, 1943 (Act No. 27 of 1943), and has acquired a share in accordance with a transfer of insurance business as contemplated in section 25A of that Act from another insurer who carried on long-term and short-term insurance business, both such insurers shall be deemed to be one and the same insurer; and

e) where--

   i) any share has been lent by a lender to a borrower as contemplated in the definition of "lending arrangement" in section 23(1) of the Stamp Duties Act, 1968 (Act No 77 of 1968) such share shall for the purposes of the lender be deemed not to have been disposed of by the lender; and

   ii) any other share of the same kind and of the same or equivalent quantity and quality has been returned by the borrower to the lender, such share and such other share shall be deemed to be one and the same share in the hands of the lender.

2) Any taxpayer may elect that any amount received by or accrued to or in favour of him as a result of the disposal on or after 14 March 1990 of an affected share, be deemed to be of a capital nature for the purposes of the definition of "gross income" in section 1: Provided that where the taxpayer is a natural person who dies or is declared insolvent during his ownership in an affected share or is a company which is liquidated during its ownership in such share, the executor of such person's deceased estate or the curator of such person's insolvent estate or the liquidator of such company may exercise the election in terms of this subsection.

3) The election referred to in subsection (2) shall be exercised in respect of the first affected share disposed of by any taxpayer on or after 14 March 1990, and such election shall be made by such taxpayer in his return of income in respect of the relevant year of assessment in which he disposed of such affected share.

3A)

a) Any election made under subsection (2) in respect of an affected share disposed of prior to 18 March 1992, may be withdrawn by the taxpayer or the executor, curator or liquidator referred to in the proviso to the said subsection and be replaced by a new election which shall be exercised in respect of the first affected share disposed of by the taxpayer on or after that date.

b) The provisions of subsections (2), (3) and (4) shall *mutatis mutandis* apply to a new election made under paragraph (a).

4) An election made under subsection (2) shall be binding upon the taxpayer in respect of each succeeding disposal of an affected share during the year of assessment in which he exercised his election and every succeeding year of assessment.

5) The provisions of this section shall not apply to any affected shares where such shares constitute shares which were deemed to be trading stock of the taxpeyer in terms of section 24A(2)(a) of this Act.

6) If any taxpayer has elected that the provisions of this section shall apply to him, there shall in the year of assessment in which any affected share is disposed of by him, be included in his income any expenditure or losses (excluding so much of any such expenditure or losses as may be allowable as a deduction in the determination of the taxable income derived by the taxpayer from dividends) incurred in respect of such affected share and allowed as a deduction from the income of such taxpayer during such or any previous year of assessment, and any amount allowed to be deducted from the cost price of such affected share under the provisions of section 22(1) in any such year.

7) Where the taxpayer holds affected shares in any company which were acquired by him on different dates and he has disposed of any of those shares, he shall for the purposes of this section be deemed to have disposed of the affected shares held by him for the longest period of time.

8) For the purposes of this section any amount included in the income of any company in terms of the provisions of section 22(8)(b) as a result of the application, disposal or distribution of any affected share as contemplated in that section, shall be deemed to be an amount which has accrued to such company as a result of the disposal of such affected share.

9D Net income of controlled foreign companies

1) For the purposes of this section—

'business establishment', in relation to a controlled foreign company, means –

a) a place of business with an office, shop, factory, warehouse or other structure which is used or will continue to be used by the controlled foreign company for a period of not less than one year, whereby the business of such company is carried on, and where –

i) that place of business is suitably equipped with on-site operational management, employees, equipment and other facilities for the purposes of conducting the primary operations of that business; and

ii) that place of business is utilised outside the Republic for a bona fide business purpose (other than the avoidance, postponement or reduction of any liability for payment of any tax, duty or levy imposed by this Act or by any other Act administered by the Commissioner);

b) a mine, oil or gas well, a quarry or any other place of extraction of natural resources, where that controlled foreign company has a right to directly explore or extract those natural resources, or any area where that controlled foreign company has the right to carry on prospecting operations preliminary to the establishment of a mine, oil or gas well, quarry or other place of extraction, and where that controlled foreign company carries on those exploration, extraction or prospecting operations;

c) a site for the construction or installation of buildings, bridges, roads, pipelines, heavy machinery or other projects of comparable magnitude which lasts for a period of not less than six months, where that controlled foreign company carries on those construction or installation activities;

d) agricultural land used for bona fide farming activities directly carried on by that controlled foreign company; or

e) a vessel or an aircraft solely engaged in transportation within a single country, or a fishing vessel or a vessel used for prospecting, exploration or extraction, where that vessels or aircraft is operated directly by that controlled foreign company,

"controlled foreign company"means any foreign company where more than 50 per cent of the total participation rights in that foreign company are held by one or more residents whether directly or indirectly: Provided that a person who holds less than five per cent of the participation rights of a foreign company which is either a listed company or a scheme or arrangement contemplated in paragraph (e)(ii) of the definition of 'company' in section 1, shall be deemed not to be a resident in determining whether residents directly or indirectly hold more than 50 per cent of the participation rights in –

a) that foreign company; or

any other foreign company in which that person indirectly holds any participation rights as a result of the interest in that listed company or scheme or arrangement, unless more than 50 per cent of the participation rights of that foreign company or other foreign company are held by persons who are connected persons in relation to each other;

'foreign company' means any association, corporation, company, arrangement or scheme contemplated in paragraph (a), (b) or (e) of the definition of 'company' in section 1, which is not a resident, or which is a resident but where that association, corporation, company, arrangement or scheme is as a result of the application of the provisions of any agreement entered into by the Republic for the avoidance of double taxation treated as not being a resident;

'foreign financial instrument holding company' means any foreign company where more than 50 per cent of the market value or actual cost of all the assets of that company, together with any controlled group company in relation to that foreign company, consists of financial instruments, other than –

a) any financial instrument that constitutes a debt due to that foreign company, or a controlled group company in relation to that foreign company, in respect of goods sold or services rendered by that foreign company or controlled group company, as the case may be, where –

   i) the amount of that debt is or was included in the income of that foreign company or controlled group company, as the case may be; and

   ii) that debt is an integral part of a business conducted by that foreign company or controlled group company, as the case may be, as a continuing independent operation;

b) any financial instrument arising from the principal trading activities of any company that is a bank, insurer, dealer or broker with a licence or registration that allows that foreign company to operate in the same manner as a company that mainly conducts business with clients who are residents in the same country of residence as the foreign company and that foreign company either -

   i) regularly accepts deposits, premiums or effects transactions for the account of clients from the general public; or

   ii) derives more than 50 per cent of its income or gains arising from principal trading activities with respect to persons who are not connected persons in relation to that foreign company :

   Provided that in determining whether 50 per cent of the market value or actual cost of the assets of the company and controlled group company consist of financial instruments, the following assets must be wholly disregarded –

   i) any share in any other company in the same group of companies; and

   ii) any financial instrument which constitutes a loan, advance or debt if both the debtor and creditor companies form part of the same group of companies

'foreign tax year' in relation to a controlled foreign company means the year or period of reporting for foreign income tax purposes or, if that company is not subject to foreign income tax, the annual period of financial reporting by that company;

'participation rights' in relation to a foreign company means the right to participate directly or indirectly in the share capital, share premium, current or accumulated profits or reserves of that foreign company, whether or not of a capital nature.

2) There shall be included in the income for the year of assessment of any resident who holds any participation rights in a controlled foreign company –

a) on the last day of the foreign tax year of that controlled foreign company which ends during that year of assessment, an amount equal to –

i) where that foreign company was a controlled foreign company for the entire foreign tax year, the proportional amount of the net income of that controlled foreign company determined for that foreign tax year, which bears to the total net income of that company during that foreign tax year, the same ratio as the percentage of the participation rights of that resident in relation to that company bears to the total participation rights in relation to that company on that last day; or

ii) where that foreign company became a controlled foreign company at any stage during that foreign tax year, at the option of the resident, either –

aa) an amount which bears to the proportional amount determined in accordance with subparagraph (i), the same ratio as the number of days during that foreign tax year that the foreign company was a controlled foreign company bears to the total number of days in that foreign tax year; or

bb) the proportional amount determined in the manner contemplated in subparagraph (i) (as if the day that foreign entity commenced to be a controlled foreign entity was the first day of its foreign tax year), of the net income of that company for the period commencing on the day that the foreign company commenced to be a controlled foreign company and ending on the last day of that foreign tax year; or

b) immediately before that foreign company ceased to be a controlled foreign company at any stage during that year of assessment before the last day of the foreign tax year of that controlled foreign company, an amount which shall be equal to, at the option of the resident, either –

i) an amount determined in accordance with paragraph (a)(ii)(aa); or

ii) the proportional amount determined in the manner contemplated in paragraph (a)(i) (as if the day that foreign company ceased to be a controlled foreign company was the last day of its foreign tax year), of the net income of that company determined for the period commencing on the first day of that foreign tax year and ending on the date that the company so ceased to be a controlled foreign company :

Provided that this subsection shall not apply –

A) where that resident (together with any connected person in relation to that resident) –

i) at the end of the last day of the foreign tax year of the controlled foreign company; or

ii) in the case where that foreign company ceased to be a controlled foreign company during the relevant foreign tax year, immediately before that foreign company so ceased to be a controlled foreign company, in aggregate holds less than 10 per cent of the participation rights in that controlled foreign company; or

B) to the extent that the participation rights are held by that resident indirectly through any company which is a resident.

2A) For the purposes of this section, the 'net income' of a controlled foreign company in respect of a foreign tax year is an amount equal to the taxable income of that company determined in accordance with the provisions of this Act as if that controlled foreign company had been a taxpayer, and as if that company had been a resident for purposes of the definition of 'gross income', sections 7(8), 9E, 10(1)(h), 10(1)(hA), 25B and paragraphs 2(1)(a), 12, 24, 70, 71, 72 and 80 of the Eighth Schedule: Provided that -

a) any deductions or allowances which may be allowed, or any amounts which may be set off against, the income of that foreign company in terms of this Act shall be limited to the amount of that income;

b) any amount whereby such deductions or allowances or amounts exceed the amount of such income, shall be carried forward to the immediately succeeding foreign tax year and be deemed to be a balance of assessed loss which may be set off against the income of such company in such succeeding year for the purposes of section 20;

c) no deduction shall be allowed in respect of any interest, royalties, rental or income of a similar nature paid or payable or deemed to be paid or payable by that company to any other controlled foreign company in relation to the resident (including any similar amount adjusted in terms of section 31) or any exchange difference determined in terms of section 24I in respect of any exchange item to which that controlled foreign company and other foreign company are parties, as contemplated in subsection (9)(fA);";

d) deleted by section 13 of the Revenue Laws Amendment Act, 74 of 2002

e) where a foreign company becomes a controlled foreign company after 1 October 2001, the valuation date for purposes of the determination of any taxable capital gain or assessed capital loss in terms of the Eighth Schedule, shall be the date that such company becomes a controlled foreign company;

f) where the resident contemplated in subsection (2) is a natural person, special trust or an insurer in respect of its individual policyholder fund, the taxable capital gain of the controlled foreign company shall, for the purposes of paragraph 10 of the Eighth Schedule, be 25 per cent of that company's net capital gain for the relevant foreign tax year

g) deleted by section 13 of the Revenue Laws Amendment Act, 74 of 2002

h) or the purposes of section 241, 'local currency' in relation to an exchange item of a controlled foreign company which is not attributable to a permanent establishment of that company, means any currency used by that company for purposes of financial reporting;

i) for the purposes of section 31 –

(aa) any transaction, operation or scheme between that controlled foreign company and any connected person in relation to that controlled foreign company shall be deemed to be an international agreement as defined in that section; and

(bb) that controlled foreign company must for purposes of section 31(3)(a)(i) and (ii) be deemed to be a resident;

j) for the purposes of determining any capital gain or capital loss of that controlled foreign company from the disposal of any interest in any other foreign company (which is a controlled foreign company in relation to the resident contemplated in subsection (2)), the base cost of that interest shall be increased in terms of paragraph 20(1)(h)(iii) of the Eighth Schedule, by any amount derived by that other foreign company (or any other company in which that foreign company holds a direct or indirect interest which is also a controlled foreign company in relation to that resident), which was taken into account in determining the amount to be included in the income of that resident in terms of this section by virtue of that resident's shareholding in the controlled foreign company, reduced by the amount of any dividend distributed to that controlled foreign company by any such other foreign company from such income so taken into account; and

k) for the purposes of paragraph 43 of the Eighth Schedule, 'local currency' of a controlled foreign company otherwise than in relation to a permanent establishment of that controlled foreign company, means the currency used by that company for purposes of financial reporting.

3) Deleted by section 10 of Act 59 of 2000

4) Deleted by section 10 of Act 59 of 2000.

5) Deleted by section 10 of Act 59 of 2000.

6) The net income of a controlled foreign company, shall be determined in the currency used by that controlled foreign company for purposes of financial reporting and shall, for purposes of determining the amount to be included in the income of any resident during any year of assessment under the provisions of this section, be translated to the currency of the Republic by applying the average exchange rate for that year of assessment, as contemplated in section 25D: Provided that –

a) any capital gain or capital loss of that controlled foreign company shall, when applying paragraph 43(4) of the Eighth Schedule, be determined in the currency of the Republic and that capital gain or capital loss shall be translated to the currency used by that controlled foreign company for purposes of financial reporting by applying that average exchange rate; and

b) any amount to be taken into account in determining the net income of that controlled foreign company in respect of the disposal of any foreign equity instrument shall, when applying section 9G, be determined in the currency of the Republic and that amount shall be translated to the currency so used by that controlled foreign company by applying that average exchange rate.

7) Deleted by section 10 of Act 59 of 2000.

8) Deleted by section 10 of Act 59 of 2000.

9) The provisions of this section shall not apply to the extent that the net income of the controlled foreign company –

a) is attributable to amounts –

i) that have been or will be subject to tax on income in a designated country at a qualifying statutory rate

b) is attributable to any business establishment of [such] that controlled foreign company in any country other than the Republic: Provided that the provisions of this paragraph shall not apply to any net income that is attributable to any amounts –

i) derived from any transaction relating to the supply of goods or services by or to that controlled foreign company with any connected person (in relation to that controlled foreign company), who is a resident, unless the consideration in respect of that transaction reflects an arm's length price that is consistent with the provisions of section 31; or

ii) derived from –

aa) any sale of goods by that controlled foreign company to any connected person (in relation to that controlled foreign company) who is a resident, unless -

A) that controlled foreign company purchased those goods within the country of residence of that controlled foreign company from any person who is not a connected person in relation to that controlled foreign company;

B) the creation, extraction, production, assembly, repair or improvement of goods undertaken by that controlled foreign company amount to more than minor assembly or adjustment, packaging, repackaging and labeling; or

C) that controlled foreign company sells a significant quantity of goods of the same or a similar nature to persons who are not connected persons in relation to that controlled foreign company, at comparable prices (after accounting for the level of the market, volume discounts and costs of delivery); or bb) any sale of goods by that controlled foreign company to a person, other than a connected person (in relation to that controlled foreign company) who is a resident, where that controlled foreign company initially purchased those goods or any tangible intermediary inputs thereof from one or more connected persons (in relation to that controlled foreign company) who are residents, unless –

A) those goods or tangible intermediary inputs thereof purchased from connected persons (in relation to such controlled foreign company) who are residents amount to an insignificant portion of the total tangible intermediary inputs of those goods;

B) the creation, extraction, production, assembly, repair or improvement of goods undertaken by that controlled foreign company amount to more than minor assembly or adjustment, packaging, repackaging and labeling; or

C) the products are sold by that controlled foreign company to persons who are not connected persons in relation to that controlled foreign company, for delivery within the country of residence of that controlled foreign company; or

cc) any service performed by that controlled foreign company to a connected person (in relation to such controlled foreign company) who is a resident, unless the service is performed outside the Republic and –

A) such service relates directly to the creation, extraction, production, assembly, repair or improvement of goods utilised within one or more countries outside the Republic; or

B) such services relate directly to the sale or marketing of goods of a connected person (in relation to that controlled foreign company) who is a resident and those goods are sold to persons who are not connected persons in relation to that controlled foreign company for delivery within the country of residence of that controlled foreign company;

iii) in the form of dividends, interest, royalties, rental, annuities, insurance premiums or income of a similar nature, or any capital gain determined in respect of the disposal of any asset from which any such income is or could be earned, or any foreign currency gain determined in respect of any foreign equity instrument or any foreign currency gain determined in terms of section 241, except where those amounts –

aa) do not in total exceed five per cent of the sum of the amounts (other than those of a capital nature) and the amount of all capital gains and foreign currency gains of that controlled foreign company; or bb) arise from the principal trading activities of any banking or financial services, insurance or rental business, excluding any such amounts derived-

A) by a company which is a foreign financial instrument holding company at the time that the amounts are so derived;

B) from any connected person (in relation to that controlled foreign company) who is a resident or any resident who holds at least five per cent of the participation rights in that controlled foreign company; or

C) from any resident to the extent that those amounts are produced as part of a scheme for the purpose of avoiding the liability for any tax, duty or levy imposed in terms of this Act or any other law administered by the Commissioner;

e) is included in the taxable income of the company and has not been or will not be exempt or taxed at a reduced rate in the Republic, as a result of the application of any agreement for the avoidance of double taxation;

f) is attributable to any foreign dividend contemplated in section 9E declared to or deemed to have been declared to that controlled foreign company, by any other company from an amount which relates to an amount of income which has been or will be included in the income of the resident in terms of this section;

fA) is attributable to any interest, royalties, rental or income of a similar nature, which is paid or payable or deemed to be paid or payable to that company by any other foreign company (including any similar amount adjusted in terms of section 31), or any exchange difference determined in terms of section 24I in respect of any exchange item to which that controlled foreign company and that other foreign company are parties, where that controlled foreign company and that other foreign company form part of the same group of companies

fB) is attributable to any capital gain of that company, which is determined in respect of the disposal of any asset, as defined in the Eighth Schedule, (other than any financial instrument or intangible asset as defined in paragraph 16 of the Eighth Schedule), where that asset was attributable to any business establishment of that controlled foreign company or any other foreign company where that controlled foreign company and that other foreign company form part of the same group of companies; or

g) deleted by section 10 of Act 59 of 2000

h) is attributable to any amount received by or accrued to that controlled foreign company

i) from the disposal of any interest in the equity share capital of any other foreign company; or

ii) by way of a dividend declared to that controlled foreign company by any other foreign company, if that controlled foreign company immediately before that disposal or at the time of the declaration of dividend –

(aa) held more than 25 per cent of the equity share capital in that other foreign company; and

(bb) in the case of any disposal contemplated in subparagraph (i), held such interest contemplated in item (aa) for a period of at least 18 months prior to that disposal, unless that interest was acquired by the controlled foreign company from any other foreign company, where that controlled foreign company and that other foreign company form part of the same group of companies and that controlled foreign company and that other foreign company in aggregate held that interest for more than 18 months:

Provided that the provisions of subparagraph (i) shall not apply where that other foreign company is a foreign financial instrument holding company immediately before that disposal.

10) For the purposes of subsection (9)(b)(ii) the Minister may—

a) by notice in the Gazette determine that one or more foreign countries be treated as one if such foreign countries comprise a single economic market and such treatment will not lead to an unacceptable erosion of the tax base; or

b) in consultation with the Commissioner grant exemption to any person from the application of subsection (9)(b)(ii), to the extent that its application will unreasonably prejudice national economic policies or South African international trade and such exemption will not lead to an unacceptable erosion of the tax base.

11) The provisions of subsection (9)(b) to (h), inclusive shall not apply in respect of any resident, where that resident fails to comply with the provisions of section 72A.

9E. Taxation of foreign dividends

1) Deleted by the Revenue Laws Amendment Act, 74 of 2002

2) The amount of any income which shall be exempt from tax in terms of the provisions of section 10(1)(kA), shall be so much of any amount received or accrued during the relevant year of assessment by or to any company which is a resident from a source outside the Republic, which is not deemed to be from a source in the Republic, which has been or will be subject to tax in any designated country at a qualifying statutory rate as defined in section 9E.

3) Deleted by the Revenue Laws Amendment Act, 74 of 2002

9G. Taxable income in respect of foreign equity instruments

1) For the purposes of this section 'foreign currency' means any currency which is not legal tender in the Republic.

2) Notwithstanding the provisions of section 25D, the amount to be included in the gross income of a person in respect of the disposal by that person of any foreign equity instrument which constitutes trading stock, shall be determined by translating the amount received or accrued in any currency other than currency of the Republic in respect of that disposal into the currency of the Republic at the average exchange rate for the year of assessment during which that foreign equity instrument is disposed of.

3) Any –

a) expenditure incurred by a person in any currency other than currency of the Republic in respect of any foreign equity instrument which is allowable as a deduction in terms of the provisions of this Act; or

b) amount in any currency other than currency of the Republic which is taken into account in the determination of the taxable income of any person in respect of any foreign equity instrument,

shall, for purposes of determining the taxable income of that person for the year of assessment in which that foreign equity instrument is disposed of, be translated into the currency of the Republic—

i) in the case of a foreign equity instrument acquired before 1 October 2001, at the ruling exchange rate on 1 October 2001; or

ii) in any other case, at the average exchange rate for the year of assessment during which that expenditure was actually incurred by that person.

10. Exemptions

1) There shall be exempt from the tax--

a) the revenues of the Government, any provincial administration or of any other state;

b) the revenues of local authorities;

c)

i) Deleted by section 9 of Act 21 of 1994;

ii) any pension payable to any person or his surviving spouse by reason of such person having occupied the office of State President or Vice State President: Provided that the provisions of this subparagraph shall not apply to any amount payable to any person or his surviving spouse by reason of such person having occupied the office of President as elected in terms of section 77 of the Constitution;

iii) the salary and emoluments payable to any person who holds office in the Republic as an official of any government, other than the Government of the Republic, provided such person is stationed in the Republic for that purpose and is not ordinarily resident in the Republic;

iv) any salary and emoluments payable to any domestic or private servant of any person referred to in subparagraph (iii) in respect of domestic or private services rendered or to be rendered by such servant to such person if such servant is not a South African citizen and is not ordinarily resident in the Republic;

v) any salary and emoluments payable to any subject of a foreign state who is temporarily employed in the Republic, provided the exemption of such salary and emoluments is authorized by an agreement entered into by the governments of such foreign state and the Republic;

cA) the receipts and accruals of--

i) any institution, board or body (other than a company registered or deemed to be registered under the Companies Act, 1973 (Act No. 61 of 1973), or under any law repealed by that Act and any co-operative formed and incorporated or deemed to be formed and incorporated under the Cooperatives Act, 1981 (Act No. 91 of 1981), and any close corporation and any trust) established by or under any law and which, in the furtherance of its sole or principal object--

aa) conducts scientific, technical or industrial research;

bb) provides necessary or useful commodities, amenities or services to the State (including any provincial administration) or members of the general public; or

cc) carries on activities (including the rendering of financial assistance by way of loans or otherwise) designed to promote commerce, industry or agriculture or any branch thereof;

ii) any association, corporation or company contemplated in paragraph (a) of the definition of 'corppany' in section 1, all the shares of which are held by any such institution, board or body, if the operations of such association, corporation or company are ancillary or complementary to the object of such institution, board or body:

Provided that such institution, board, body or company--

a) has been approved by the Commissioner subject to such conditions as he may deem necessary to ensure that the activities of such institution, board, body or company are wholly or mainly directed to the furtherance of its sole or principal object;

b) is by law or under its constitution--

i) not permitted to distribute any of its profits or gains to any person, other than, in the case of such company, to its shareholders;

ii) required to utilize its funds solely for investment or the object for which it has been established; and

iii) required on dissolution--

aa) where the institution, board, body or company is established under any law, to transfer its assets to some other institution, board or body which has been granted exemption from tax in terms of this paragraph and which has objects similar to those of such institution, board, body or company; or

bb) where the institution, board, or body is established by law, to transfer its assets to--

A) some other institution, board or body which has been granted exemption from tax in terms of this paragraph and which has objects similar to those of such institution, board, body or company; or

B) to the State:

Provided further that--

a) where the Commissioner is satisfied that any such institution, board, body or company has during any year of assessment failed to comply with the provisions of this paragraph, he may withdraw his approval of the institution, board, body or company with effect from the commencement of that year of assessment;

b) where the institution, board, body or company fails to transfer, or take reasonabl steps to transfer, its assets as contemplated in paragraph (b)(ii) of the first proviso, the accumulated net revenue which has not been distributed shall be deemed for the purposes of this Act to be an amount of taxable income which accrued to such institution, board, body or company during the year of assessment contemplated in paragraph (a); and

c) any decision of the Commissioner in the exercise of his discretion under this paragraph shall be subject to objection and appeal;

cB) Deleted by section 21 of Act No. 30 of 2000];

cC) Deleted by section 21 of Act No. 30 of 2000];

cD) Deleted by section 21 of Act No. 30 of 2000];

cE) the receipts and accruals of any political party registered under the provisions of section 36 of the Electoral Act, 1979 (Act No. 45 of 1979);

cF) Deleted by section 21 of Act No. 30 of 2000];

cG) the receipts and accruals of any person who is not a resident, which are derived by such person from carrying on business as the owner or charterer of any ship or aircraft, if a similar exemption or equivalent relief is granted by the country of which such person is a resident, to any resident in respect of any tax imposed in that country on income which may be derived by such person from carrying on in such country any business as owner or charterer of any ship or aircraft;

cH) the receipts and accruals of any company, society or other association of persons or any trust, whether or not registered under any law (other than a co-operative formed and incorporated or deemed to be formed and incorporated under the Co-operatives Act, 1981 (Act No. 91 of 1981)), if--

i) the sole object of such company, society, association or trust is to receive, hold and apply moneys contributed to such company, society, association or trust in accordance with section 11(hA) in order to discharge any of the following or like obligations imposed upon any person in terms of any law which regulates mining operations, namely--

aa) the rehabilitation of disturbances of the surface of land and the prevention and combating of pollution of the air, land, sea or other water where such disturbances and pollution are due to mining, prospecting, quarrying or similar operations;

bb) the protection of the surface of land and water sources and the making safe of undermined ground and of dangerous excavations, tailings, waste dumps and structures, of whatsoever nature, made in the course of mining, prospecting, quarrying or similar operations; and

cc) the demolition or removal of any building, structure or other thing erected or constructed in connection with mining, prospecting, quarrying or similar operations, the removal of any debris or other objects and the restoration, as far as is practicable, of the surface to its natural state;

ii) such company, society or association is under its constitution, or such trust is under the instrument establishing such trust, not permitted to distribute any of its profits or gains to any person and is required to utilize its funds solely for the object for which it has been established: Provided that such company, society, association or trust shall be permitted to invest its funds in institutions approved by the Commissioner, until such time as such funds are required;

iii) in terms of the constitution of such company, society or association or the instrument establishing such trust it will upon its winding-up or liquidation be obliged to give or transfer its assets remaining after the satisfaction of its liabilities to some other company, society, association or trust with a similar object to that of the said company, society, association or trust; and

iv) the Commissioner has approved such company, society, association or trust on such conditions as he may deem necessary to ensure that the activities of such company, society, association or trust are wholly directed to the furtherance of its sole object;

cI) Deleted by section 21 of Act No. 30 of 2000];

cJ) Deleted by section 21 of Act No. 30 of 2000];

cK) Deleted by section 21 of Act No. 30 of 2000];

cL) Deleted by Income Tax Act No 36 of 1996];

cM) the receipts and accruals of any company formed and incorporated under section 21 of the Companies Act, 1973 (Act No. 61 of 1973), or deemed by the said section to be so formed and incorporated, which has been approved by the Commissioner, if--

i) the sole or principal object of the company is to promote and facilitate the distribution of agricultural and related commodities;

ii) such sole or principal object is actively pursued;

iii) the company is or was not knowingly a party to, or does not knowingly permit, or has not knowingly permitted, itself to be used as part of any transaction, operation or scheme of which the sole or main purpose is or was the reduction, postponement or avoidance of liability for any tax, duty or levy which, but for such transaction, operation or scheme, would have been or would have become payable by any person under this Act or any other Act administered by the Commissioner;

iv) the company does not carry on any business other than business which is directly connected with the said sole or principal object;

v) the business directly connected with the sole or principal object was previously carried on by a municipal council and the control of the company is exercised by such municipal council;

vi) in terms of the memorandum or articles of association of the company, it is upon its deregistration, winding-up or liquidation obliged to give or transfer its assets remaining after the satisfaction of its liabilities to--

aa) some other company which is exempt from tax under this paragraph; or

bb) a local authority to utilize such assets for the same objects as the aforesaid company:

Provided that--

a) where the Commissioner is satisfied that any such company has during any year of assessment failed to comply with the provisions of this paragraph, he may withdraw his approval of the company with effect from the commencement of that year of assessment;

b) where the Commissioner has withdrawn his approval of such company, it shall, within two months from the date of such withdrawal, transfer, or take reasonable steps to transfer, its remaining assets to any company which is exempt from tax under this paragraph or to a local authority to utilize such assets for the same objects as the aforesaid company;

c) where a company fails to transfer, or take reasonable steps to transfer, its remaining assets as contemplated in paragraph (b) of this proviso, the accumulated net revenue which has not been distributed shall be deemed for the purposes of this Act to be an amount of taxable income which accrued to such company during the year of assessment referred to in paragraph (a) of this proviso; and

d) any decision of the Commissioner in the exercise of his discretion under this paragraph shall be subject to objection and appeal;

cN) the receipts and accruals of any public benefit organisation which has been approved by the Commissioner in terms of section 30(3);

d) the receipts and accruals of any--

i) pension fund, provident fund, retirement annuity fund; or

ii) benefit fund, or

iii) mutual loan association, fidelity or indemnity fund, trade union, chamber of commerce or industries (or an association of such chambers), local publicity association or non-proprietary stock exchange approved by the Commissioner subject to such conditions as the Minister may prescribe by regulation; or

iv) company, society or other association of persons established to--

aa) provide social and recreational amenities or facilities for the members of such company, society or other association; or

bb) promote the common interests of persons (being members of such company, society or association of persons) carrying on any particular kind of business, profession or occupation,

approved by the Commissioner subject to such conditions as the Minister may prescribe by regulation;

e) any levy received by or accrued to--

i) any body corporate established in terms of the Sectional Titles Act, 1986 (Act No. 95 of 1986), from its members;

ii) a share block company established in terms of the Share Blocks Control Act, 1980 (Act No. 59 of 1980), from its shareholders; or

iii) any other association of persons (other than a company registered or deemed to be registered under the Companies Act, 1973 (Act No. 61 of 1973), and any co-operative formed and incorporated or deemed to be formed and incorporated under the Co-operatives Act, 1981 (Act No. 91 of 1981), and any close coporation and any trust, but including a company incorporated under section 21 of the Companies Act, 1973), from its members, where the Commissioner is satisfied that, subject to such conditions as he may deem necessary, such association of persons--

aa) has been formed solely for the purposes of managing the collective interests common to all its members, which includes expenditure applicable to the common immovable property of such members and the collection of levies for which such members are liable; and

bb) is not permitted to distribute any of its funds to any person other than a similar association of persons:

Provided that such body, company or association is or was not knowingly a party to, or does not knowingly permit or has not knowingly permitted, itself to be used as part of any transaction, operation or scheme of which the sole or main purpose is or was the reduction, postponement or avoidance of liability for any tax, duty or levy which, but for such transaction, operation or scheme, would have been or would become payable by any person under this Act or any other law administered by the Commissioner;

f) [paragraph (f) deleted by s.21 of Act No. 30 of 2000];

g) any amount received as a war pension, or as an award or a benefit under any law relating to the payment of compensation in respect of diseases contracted by persons employed in mining operations;

gA) any disability pension paid under section 2 of the Social Assistance Act, 1992 (Act No. 59 of 1992);

gB) any compensation paid in terms of the Workmen's Compensation Act, 1941 (Act No. 30 of 1941), or the Compensation for Occupational Injuries and Diseases Act, 1993 (Act No130 of 1993);

gC) any—

(i) amount received by or accrued to any resident under the social security system of any other country; or

(ii) pension received by or accrued to any resident from a source outside the Republic, which is not deemed to be from a source in the Republic in terms of section 9(1)(g), in consideration of past employment outside the Republic;

h) interest received by or accrued to--

i) any person (other than a company) who is not a resident and who does not carry on business in the Republic; or

ii) a company which is not a resident and does not carry on business in the Republic,

from stock or securities (including Treasury Bills) issued by the Government including the South African Transport Services, or any local authority within the Republic or the Electricity Supply Commission or the South African Broadcasting Corporation: Provided that, if in the case of any such stock or securities issued in respect of a loan raised in a country outside the Republic, the Treasury has, with the approval of the Minister of Finance, given an undertaking that the interest derived therefrom by any person who is not a resident shall be exempt from taxes in the Republic, the interest received by or accrued to such a person from such of the said stock or securities as were acquired by such person outside the Republic and paid for by such person in the currency of any country other than the Republic shall be exempt from normal tax even if that person carries on business in the Republic: Provided further that the exemption under this paragraph shall not apply in respect of interest which on or after 1 November 1987 is received by or accrues to--

a) a person (other than a company) who is ordinarily resident in a neighbouring country, if such stock or security was acquired by him on or after that date; or

b) a company which is incorporated, registered, managed or controlled in any neighbouring country unless the Commissioner is satisfied that such stock or security was acquired by it before that date and that on both that date and the date of receipt or accrual of such interest one or more natural persons, not ordinarily resident in the Republic, held for their own benefit all the issued shares of such company:

Provided further that the exemption under this paragraph shall not apply to any natural person unless such person was physically absent from the Republic for a period or periods of at least 183 days in aggregate during the year of assessment in which such interest was received or accrued;

hA) interest received by or accrued to a person who is not a resident: Provided that--

i) the exemption under this section shall not apply to any natural person who was at any time a resident if such person has during the year of assessment carried on business in the Republic;

ii) for the purposes of this paragraph any person who is a resident of any country which has for the purposes of applying any regulation made under section 9 of the Currency and Exchanges Act, 1933 (Act No. 9 of 1933), been included in the common monetary area, shall be deemed to be a resident of the Republic;

iii) for the purposes of this paragraph, so much of any dividend as has been distributed by any portfolio of any collective investment scheme constituting a company in terms of paragraph (e)(i) of the definition of 'company' in section 1 out of interest derived by such portfolio which is exempt from tax in the hands of such portfolio under the provisions of paragraph (iA), shall be deemed to be interest;

iv) the exemption under this paragraph shall not apply to any natural person unless such person was physically absent from the Republic for a period or periods of at least 183 days in aggregate during the year of assessment in which such interest was received or accrued; and

v) the exemption under this paragraph shall no apply to any interest received by or accrued to a company which is managed and controlled outside the Republic, if such interest is effectively connected with the business carried on by that company in the Republic.

i)

i) Deleted by section 8 of Act 36 of 1966;

ii) Deleted by section 8 of Act 36 of 1966;

iii) so much of the interest on Tax Redemption Certificates held by any one person as does not exceed the sum of fifty rand;

iv) Deleted by section 10 of Act 101 of 1990;

v) interest on any loan portion of the normal or super tax imposed under the Income Tax Act, 1953, or any subsequent Act of Parliament;

vi) Deleted by section 8 of Act 36 of 1966;

vii) Deleted by section 7 of Act 65 of 1973;

viii) Deleted by section 7 of Act 65 of 1973;

ix) Deleted by section 7 of Act 65 of 1973;

x) Deleted by section 7 of Act 65 of 1973;

xi) Deleted by section 7 of Act 104 of 1979;

xii) Deleted by section 8 of Act 36 of 1966;

xiii) Deleted by section 8 of Act 36 of 1966;

xiv) Deleted by section 8 of Act 36 of 1966;

xv) in the case of any taxpayer who is a natural person-

aa) so much of the aggregate of any foreign dividends contemplated in section 9E and interest received by or accrued to him or her from a source outside the Republic, which are not otherwise exempt from tax, as does not during the year of assessment exceed R1 000: Provided that the amount of the exemption in terms of this paragraph shall-

A) first apply in respect of any such foreign dividends; and

B) in so far as such amount exceeds the amount of such foreign dividends, apply in respect of any such interest;

and

bb) so much of the aggregate of any interest received by or accrued to him or her from a source in the Republic and any dividends (other than foreign dividends contemplated in section 9E), which are not otherwise exempt from tax, as does not during the year of assessment exceed-

A) in the case of any person who was or, had he or she lived would have been, at least 65 years of age on the last day of the year of assessment, the amount of R10 000; or

B) in any other case, the amount of R6 000, reduced by the amount of any exemption allowable in terms of paragraph (aa);

xvi) Deleted by section 21 of Act 30 of 2000;

iA) in the case of any portfolio of a collective investment scheme referred to in paragraph (e)(i) of the definition of 'company' in section 1, so much of the income received by or accrued to such portfolio as has been distributed, or as the Commissioner is satisfied will be distributed, by way of a dividend or a portion of a dividend, to persons who have become entitled to such dividend by virtue of their being holders of participatory interest in such portfolio.

j) the receipts and accruals of any bank, if the Commissioner is satisfied that such bank is not resident in the Republic and is entrusted by the Government of a territory outside the Republic with the custody of the principal foreign exchange reserves of that territory, and the Minister of Finance decides to apply the provisions of this paragraph to that bank in respect of the year of assessment under charge;

k)

i) dividends received by or accrued to or in favour of any person: Provided that this exemption shall not apply--

aa) to dividends (other than those distributed out of profits of a capital nature and those received by or accrued to or in favour of any person who is neither a resident, nor carrying on business in the Republic) distributed by a company the shares of which are 'property shares' as defined in section 47 of the Collective Investment Schemes Control Act, 2002, on shares included in a portfolio comprised in any collective investment scheme in property managed or carried on by any company registered as a manager under section 42 of that Act for purposes of Part V of that Act; or

bb) to so much of any dividend as has been distributed by any portfolio of any collective investment scheme constituting a company in terms of paragraph (e)(i) of the definition of 'company' in section 1 –

A) out of income derived by such portfolio which is exempt from tax in the hands of such portfolio under the provision of paragraph (iA), and

B) out of amounts received by or accrued to such portfolio by way of dividends referred to in section 11(s); or'

cc) to any dividend received by or accrued to or in favour of any person where such dividend constitutes or forms part of any consideration paid or payable to such person in respect of the disposal of shares (other than affected shares in respect of which the taxpayer has, in terms of the provisions of section 9B, elected the amount received or accrued on disposal to be deemed to be of a capital nature), which were held as trading stock by such person in a company and such shares were acquired by such company in terms of section 85 of the Companies Act, 1973 (Act No. 61 of 1973); or

dd) to the amount of any foreign dividend contemplated in section 9E received by or accrued to any resident, which is not exempt from tax under section 9E(7);

iA) deleted by the Revenue Laws Amendment Act, 74 of 2002

kA) so much of any amount received by or accrued to any company which is a resident from a source outside the Republic as determined in accordance with the provisions of section 9F(2);

l) any amount received by or accrued to any person which amount has been subject to withholding tax in terms of the provisions of section 35;

m) any amount received by or accrued to an author of a work in respect of the assignment of or grant of an interest in a copyright in such work, if such amount is chargeable with income tax in a country other than the Republic: Provided that this exemption shall not apply to any person who is not the first owner of a copyright under the Copyright Act, 1978 (Act No. 98 of 1978), or to a company;

mA) Deleted by section 10 of Act 28 of 1997;

mB) any benefit or allowance payable in terms of the Unemployment Insurance Act, 2001 (Act No. 63 of 2002);

n) Deleted by section 12 of Act 129 of 1991;

nA) where an employee is as a condition of his employment required while on duty to wear a special uniform which is clearly distinguishable from ordinary clothing, the value of any such uniform given to the employee by his employer, or so much of any allowance made by the employer to the employee in lieu of any such uniform as is reasonable;

nB) any benefit or advantage accruing to any employee (as defined in paragraph 1 of the Seventh Schedule) by reason of the fact that his employer (as defined in the said paragraph), has, in consequence of the transfer of the employee from one place of employment to another place of employment or the appointment of the employee as an employee of the employer or the termination of the employee's employment, borne the expense--

i) of transporting such employee, members of his household and the personal goods and possessions of him self and the members of his household from his previous place of residence to his new place of residence; or

ii) of such costs as the Commissioner may allow which have been incurred by the employee in respect of the sale of his previous residence and in settling in permanent residential accommodation at his new place of residence; or

iii) of hiring residential accommodation in an hotel or elsewhere for the employee or members of his household during the period ending 183 days after his transfer took effect or after he took up his appointment, as the case may be, if such residential accommodation was occupied temporarily pending the obtaining of permanent residential accommodation;

nC) Deleted by section 12 of Act 129 of 1991;

nD) Deleted by section 12 of Act 129 of 1991;

nE) any amount (including any taxable benefit determined under the provisions of the Seventh Schedule) received by or accrued to an employee, as so defined, under a share incentive scheme operated for the benefit of employees of the taxpayer's employer, as so defined, which was derived--

i) upon the cancellation of a transaction under which the taxpayer purchased shares under such scheme; or

ii) upon the repurchase from the taxpayer, at a price not exceeding the selling price to him, of shares purchased by him under such scheme,

if in consequence of such cancellation or repurchase the taxpayer has not received or become entitled to receive any compensation or consideration other than the repayment of any portion of the purchase price actually paid by him;

nF) Deleted by section 12 of Act 129 of 1991;

nG) the value of any benefit or advantage contemplated in paragraph 2 of the Seventh Schedule derived by an employee who, after having retired from full-time service with the employer by whom such benefit or advantage was granted, has been re-employed by such employer on a part-time basis, if--

i) the cash remuneration received by or accrued to the employee in respect of such part-time employment was payable at a rate not exceeding R5 000 per annum;

ii) the employee retired from such full-time service on or after attaining the age of 60 years or as a result of ill-health or other infirmity; and

iii) such benefit or advantage was granted before the employee so retired:

Provided that the provisions of this paragraph shall not apply to any benefit or advantage granted to an employee who is re-employed on or after 1 March 1992;

nH) 50 per cent of so much of any taxable benefit derived by the taxpayer during any year of assessment ending not later than 28 February 1995 in consequence of the granting of any loan in the circumstances contemplated in paragraph 2 (f) of the Seventh Schedule as--

i) was determined in relation to any portion of such loan which was before 15 March 1990 utilized by the taxpayer for the purpose of acquiring shares under a share incentive scheme operated by his employer and which relates to so many of such shares as the taxpayer was or is, under the conditions of such scheme as they applied immediately before the said date, prohibited from disposing of; and

ii) relates to a period in the year of assessment during which the taxpayer was so prohibited from disposing of the relevant shares;

o) any remuneration as defined in paragraph 1 of the Fourth Schedule -

i) derived by any person as an officer or crew member of a ship engaged -

aa) in the international transportation for reward of passengers or goods; or

bb) in the prospecting (including surveys and other explanatory work) for, or the mining of, any minerals (including natural oils) from the seabed outside the continental shelf of the Republic as contemplated in section 8 of the Maritime Zones Act, 1994 (Act No. 15 of 1994), where such officer or crew member is employed on board such ship solely for the purposes of the 'passage' of such ship, as defined in the Marine Traffic Act, 1981 (Act No. 2 of 1981),

if such person was outside the Republic for a period or periods exceeding 183 full days in aggregate during the year of assessment; or

ii) received by or accrued to any person during any year of assessment in respect of services rendered outside the Republic by that person for or on behalf of any employer, if that person was outside the Republic –

aa) for a period or periods exceeding 183 full days in aggregate during any 12 months period commencing or ending during that year of assessment; and

bb) for a continuous period exceeding 60 full days during that period of 12 months, and those services were rendered during that period or periods: Provided that –

A) for purposes of this subparagraph, a person who is in transit through the Republic between two places outside the Republic and who does not formally enter the Republic through a port of entry as defined in the Immigration Act, 2002 (Act No. 13 of 2002), shall be deemed to be outside the Republic; and

B) the provisions of this subparagraph shall not apply in respect of any remuneration derived in respect of the holding of any office or from services rendered for or on behalf of any employer, as contemplated in section 9(1)(e);

p) any amount received by or accrued to any person who is not a resident, for services rendered or work or labour done by him outside the Republic for or on behalf of any employer in the national or provincial sphere of Government, or any local authority in the Republic, any national or provincial public entity if not less than 80 per cent of the expenditure of such entity is defrayed directly or indirectly from funds voted by Parliament, if such amount is chargeable with income tax in the country in which he is ordinarily resident and the income tax so chargeable is borne by himself and is not paid on his behalf by the Government, the local authority concerned or such public entity;

q) any *bona fide* scholarship or bursary granted to enable or assist any person to study at a recognized educational or research institution: Provided that if any such scholarship or bursary has been so granted by an employer or an associated institution (as respectively defined in paragraph 1 of the Seventh Schedule) to an employee (as defined in the said paragraph) or to a relative of such employee in circumstances indicating that the scholarship or bursary concerned would not have been granted had that employee not been an employee of that employer, the exemption under this paragraph shall not apply--

i) if any remuneration to which the employee was entitled or might in the future have become entitled was in any manner whatsoever reduced or forfeited as a result of the grant of such scholarship or bursary;

ii) in the case of a scholarship or bursary granted to enable or assist any such relative of an employee so to study, if the remuneration derived by the employee during the year of assessment exceeded R60 000; and

iii) to so much of any scholarship or bursary contemplated in paragraph (ii) as in the case of any such relative exceeds R2 000 during the year of assessment;

qA) [para (qA) deleted by s.12(1)(j) of Act No 129 of 1991];

r) any gratuity (other than a leave gratuity) received by or accrued to any person from public funds upon his retirement from any office or employment under the Government, including the Railway Administration and any provincial administration, or from the funds of the Land and Agricultural Bank of South Africa upon his retirement as a member of the board of the said Bank, which the Treasury declares to be free of tax;

s) the receipts and accruals derived by any company from the realization of assets consisting of gold bullion or shares in companies, if such assets were acquired by such company with funds which were transferred to the Republic from any country outside the Republic by arrangement with the Treasury or with funds derived from the realization of similar assets acquired with the proceeds derived from any such assets or from dividends received in respect of such shares, and the Treasury has with the approval of the Minister of Finance given an undertaking that any such receipts and accruals shall be exempt from the tax, provided particulars of the terms and conditions of any arrangement with and any undertaking given by the Treasury and the period during which such undertaking is to endure are published in the *Gazette*;

t) the receipts and accruals--

i) of the Council for Scientific and Industrial Research;

ii) of the South African Inventions Development Corporation;

iii) deleted by section 29(c) of Act No. 30 of 1998

iv) deleted by section 10(g) of Act No. 28 of 1997

v) of the Armaments Development and Production Corporation of South Africa Limited, established under section 2 of the Armaments Development and Production Act, 1968 (Act No. 57 of 1968);

vi) of any company during any period during which all the issued shares of such company are held by the Corporation referred to in subparagraph (v), if the operations of such company are conducted in pursuance of, or are ancillary or complementary to, the objects of the said Corporation:

vii) deleted by section 10(g) of Act No. 28 of 1997

viii) deleted by Revenue Laws Amendment Act No 46 of 1996

ix) deleted by Revenue Laws Amendment Act No 46 of 1996

x) of the Development Bank of Southern Africa established on 30 June 1983;

xi) deleted by s.18 of Act No. 53 of 1999

xii) deleted by s.21 of Act No. 30 of 2000

xiii) deleted by s.9(1)(f) of Act No. 21 of 1994

xiv) deleted by Income Tax Act No 38 of 1996

xv) deleted by the Revenue Laws Amenendment Act, 74 of 2002

tA) the receipts and accruals of any company which qualifies for exemption under section 2 of the Company Tax Amendment Decree, 1994 (Decree No. 2 of 1994 of Ciskei), which are derived from a source within the territory of the former Republic of Ciskei;

u) any amount received by or accrued to any person from such person's spouse or former spouse by way of alimony or allowance or maintenance of such person or any children under an order of judicial separation or divorce granted in consequence of proceedings instituted after the twenty-first day of March, 1962, or under any agreement of separation entered into after that date;

v) deleted by section 10(1)(s) of Act No. 141 of 1992

w) deleted by section 29(e) of Act No. 30 of 1998

x) so much of any amount (being a lump sum) referred to in paragraph (d) of the definition of "gross income" in section 1 or in section 7A (4A) or (5) as does not exceed R30 000 less the sum of any other amounts which have been excluded from the taxpayer's income by virtue of the exemption conferred by this paragraph, whether in the current or any previous year of assessment: Provided that the exemption under this paragraph shall not apply in respect of any amount received by or accrued to any person upon or because of the termination or because of the impending termination of the services required to be rendered by him as the holder of any office or employment or in respect of the relinquishment, termination, loss, repudiation, cancellation or variation of his office or employment or in respect of his appointment (or right or claim to be appointed) to any office or employment, unless--

i) such person has attained the age of fifty-five years; or

ii) the termination or impending termination of such person's services or the relinquishment, termination, loss, repudiation, cancellation or variation of his office or employment or of his appointment (or right or claim to be appointed to any office or employment is due to superannuation, ill-health or other infirmity; or

iii) deleted by s.10(1)(f) of Act No. 21 of 1995

iv) the termination or impending termination of such person's services is due to his employer having ceased to carry on or intending to cease carrying on the trade in respect of which such person was employed or to such person having become redundant in consequence of his employer having effected a general reduction in personnel or a reduction in personnel of a particular class and, where such person's employer is a company, such person was not at any time a director of such company and did not at any time hold more than five per cent of the issued share capital or members' interest in such company;

Provided further that, notwithstanding the provisions of section 37D, any such amount which was received by or accrued to a married woman and which was in whole or in part excluded from her husband's taxable income under the provisions of this paragraph, shall for the purposes of determining the exemption under this paragraph in respect of any such amount subsequently received by or accrued to either spouse be deemed to be an amount which was received or accrued to the husband.

y) deleted by section10 of Act 101 of 1990

z) any amount received by or accrued to or in favour of any person from the State by way of a subsidy on interest payable by him on any amount owing by him on any loan or advance utilised by him for the purposes of pastoral, agricultural or other farming operations carried on by him;

zA) any amount by way of rebate or other assistance received by or accrued to or in favour of any person under any scheme for the promotion or financing of exports which is for the purposes of this paragraph approved by the Minister of Trade and Industry with the concurrence of the Minister of Finance.
Provided that where the person entitled to claim such amount from the State has, under an agreement directly connected with the export trade carried on by him, agreed to pay the whole or any portion of such amount to any other person, the exemption under this paragraph shall also apply to the whole or such portion of such amount received by or accrued to such other person under the said agreement;

zB) any amount received by or accrued to any employer from a fund which has under an industrial council agreement been established as contemplated in section 48 (1) (d) of the Labour Relations Act, 1956 (Act No. 28 of 1956) or section 39 (4) of the Manpower Training Act, 1981 (Act No. 56 of 1981), for the training of employees for skilled work, if such employer has undertaken such training in respect of his employees;

zC) any amount received by or accrued to or in favour of any person from the State by way of a subsidy under any scheme designed to encourage the establishment, expansion or carrying on of industrial or commercial undertakings in an economic development area, if such subsidy was granted in respect of--

i) wages paid by such person in carrying on any such undertaking; or

ii) the expenses incurred by such person in training employees employed by him in such undertaking;

zD) any amount received by or accrued to or in favour of any person by way of a reimbursement by the State of expenditure incurred by him in relocating in an economic development area any industrial or commercial undertaking, or part of such an undertaking, carried on by him elsewhere than in such area, except to the extent that the said amount relates to any expenditure claimed by and allowed to such person as a deduction from his income under the provisions of this Act or has been taken into account in the determination under this Act of the value of any machinery or plant for the purposes of determining any allowance in respect of such machinery or plant;

zE) any amount received by or accrued to the Small Business Development Corporation, Limited, by way of any subsidy or assistance payable by the State;

zF) deleted by the Revenue Laws Amenentment Act, 74 of 2002

zG) any amount which on or after 15 May 1989 was received by or accrued to a film owner (as defined in section 24F) by way of a subsidy payable by the State under any scheme designed to promote the production of films (as defined in the said section);

zH) any amount received by or accrued to or in favour of any person from the State in terms of--

i) the Regional Industrial Development Programme which came into operation on 1 May 1991;

ii) the Simplified Regional Industrial Development Programme, which came into operation on 1 October 1993 by way of a grant;

iii) the Small/Medium Manufacturing Development Programme, which came into operation on 1 October 1996 by way of a grant;

iv) the Tax Holiday Scheme contemplated in section 37H, which came into operation on 1 October 1996 by way of a grant.

v) the Small, Medium Enterprise Development Programme, which came into operation on 1 September 2000; and

vi) the Critical Infrastructure Programme, which came into operation on 1 September 2000.

2) Notwithstanding the exemptions provided for in paragraphs (h) and (k) of subsection (1)--

a) all amounts falling within the scope of the said paragraphs shall be set out by the taxpayer in the return rendered by him; and

b) the said exemptions shall not apply in respect of any portion of an annuity.

3) The exemptions provided by any paragraph of subsection (1) shall not extend to any payments out of the revenues, receipts, accruals or profits mentioned in such paragraph.

11. GENERAL DEDUCTIONS ALLOWED IN DETERMINATION OF TAXABLE INCOME

1) For the purpose of determining the taxable income derived by any person from carrying on any trade , there shall be allowed as deductions from the income of such person so derived--

a) expenditure and losses actually incurred in the production of the income, provided such expenditure and losses are not of a capital nature;

b) deleted by section 15 of Act 59 of 2000

bA) any interest (including related finance charges) which is not otherwise allowable as a deduction under this Act, which has been actually incurred by the taxpayer on any loan, advance or credit utilized by him for the acquisition, installation, erection or construction of any machinery, plant, building, or any improvements to a building, or any pipeline, transmission line or cable or railway line as contemplated in section 12D, or any aircrafy hangar, apron, runway or taxiway as contemplated in section 12F, to be used by him for the purposes of his trade, and which has been so incurred in respect of a period prior to such machinery, plant, building, improvements, pipeline, transmission line or cable, railway line, aircrafy hangar, apron, runway or taxiway being brought into use for the purposes of the taxpayer's trade, such deduction to be allowed in the year of assessment during which such machinery, plant, building, improvements, pipeline, transmission line or cable, railway line, aircrafy hangar, apron, runway or taxiway is or are brought into use for the said purposes;

bB) any finance charge incurred by the taxpayer in respect of the purchase or contract price owing under an agreement for the acquisition, installation, erection or construction of any machinery, plant, aircraft, implement, utensil, article or livestock used by him for the purposes of his trade, including (but not limited to) mining, shipping or farming, which deduction shall be in lieu of any deduction or allowance in respect of such finance charge which may be allowable under any other provision of this Act: Provided that any such finance charge (other than a finance charge which falls to be dealt with in terms of the provisions of section 24J) which is calculated or payable in respect of a period of more than 12 months extending beyond the end of the year of assessment shall for the purposes of this paragraph be deemed to have been incurred from day to day during the said period;

c) any legal expenses (being fees for the services of legal practitioners, expenses incurred in procuring evidence or expert advice, court fees, witness fees and expenses, taxing fees, the fees and expenses of sheriffs or messengers of court and other expenses of litigation which are of an essentially similar nature to any of the said fees or expenses) actually incurred by the taxpayer during the year of assessment in respect of any claim, dispute or action at law arising in the course of or by reason of the ordinary operations undertaken by him in the carrying on of his trade: Provided that the amount to be allowed under this paragraph in respect of any such expenses shall be limited to so much thereof as--

i) is not of a capital nature; and

ii) is not incurred in respect of any claim made against the taxpayer for the payment of damages or compensation if by reason of the nature of the claim or the circumstances any payment which is or might be made in satisfaction or settlement of the claim does not or would not rank for deduction from his income under paragraph (a) or (b); and

iii) is not incurred in respect of any claim made by the taxpayer for the payment to him of any amount which does not or would not constitute income of the taxpayer; and

iv) is not incurred in respect of any dispute or action at law relating to any such claim as is referred to in paragraph (ii) or (iii) of this proviso;

cA) an allowance in respect of any amount actually incurred by such person in the course of the carrying on of his trade, as contemplated in respect of any restraint of trade imposed on any other person who--

i) is a natural person;

ii) is or was a labour broker as defined in the Fourth Schedule (other than a labour broker in respect of which a certificate of exemption has been issued in terms of such Schedule);

iii) is or was a personal service company as defined in the Fourth Schedule; or

iv) is or was a personal service trust as defined in the Fourth Schedule,

to the extent that such amount constitutes or will constitute income of the person to whom it is paid: Provided that the amount allowed to be deducted under this paragraph shall not exceed for any one year the lesser of--

aa) so much of such amount so incurred as is equal to such amount divided by the number of years, or part thereof, during which the restraint of trade shall apply; or

bb) one-third of such amount so incurred;

d) expenditure actually incurred during the year of assessment on repairs of property occupied for the purpose of trade or in respect of which income is receivable, including any expenditure so incurred on the treatment against attack by beetles of any timber forming part of such property and sums expended for the repair of machinery, implements, utensils and other articles employed by the taxpayer for the purposes of his trade;

e) save as provided in paragraph 12(2) of the First Schedule, such sum as the Commissioner may think just and reasonable as representing the amount by which the value of any machinery, plant, implements, utensils and articles (other than machinery, plant, implements, utensils and articles in respect of which a deduction may be granted under section 12B or 12C used by the taxpayer for the purpose of his trade has been diminished by reason of wear and tear or depreciation during the year of assessment: Provided that--

i) where a deduction has been allowed under paragraph (d), the Commissioner shall take into consideration the sum allowed under that paragraph in determining the sum to be allowed under this paragraph;

ii) in no case shall any allowance be made for the depreciation of buildings or other structures or works of a permanent nature;

iiA) where any machinery, implement, utensil or article qualifying for an allowance under this paragraph is mounted on or affixed to any concrete or other foundation or supporting structure and the Commissioner is satisfied--

aa) that the foundation or supporting structure is designed for such machinery, implement, utensil or article and constructed in such manner that it is or should be regarded as being integrated with the machinery, implement, utensil or article;

bb) that the useful life of the foundation or supporting structure is or will be limited to the useful life of the machinery, implement, utensil or article mounted thereon or affixed thereto,

the said foundation or supporting structure shall for the purposes of this paragraph not be deemed to be a structure or work of a permanent nature but shall for the purposes of this Act be deemed to be a part of the machinery, implement, utensil or article mounted thereon or affixed thereto;

iii) no allowance shall be made under this paragraph in respect of any ship to which the provisions of section 14(1)(a) or (b) apply or in respect of any aircraft to which the provisions of section 14bis(1)(a), (b) or (c) apply;

iiiA) no allowance shall be made under this paragraph in respect of any machinery, implement, utensil or article of which the cost has been allowed as a deduction from the taxpayer's income under the provisions of section 24D;

iv) the value of new or unused machinery, implements, utensils or articles which--

aa) were used by the taxpayer directly in a process of manufacture or, if brought into use on or after 15 March 1961, in any other process which in the opinion of the Commissioner is of a similar nature or, where the taxpayer is an agricultural co-operative (as defined in section 27(9)), for storing or packing pastoral, agricultural or other farm products or for subjecting such products to a primary process as defined in the said section 27(9); and

bb) were acquired to replace machinery, implements, utensils or articles which were damaged or destroyed, shall be reduced by any amount which has been recovered or recouped as contemplated in paragraph (a) of subsection (4) of section 8 or the corresponding provisions of any previous Income Tax Act in respect of the damaged or destroyed machinery, implements, utensils or articles and has been excluded from the taxpayer's income in terms of paragraph (e) of the said subsection or the corresponding provisions of any previous Income Tax Act, and not included in the taxpayer's income in terms of the proviso to the said paragraph or the corresponding provisions of any previous Income Tax Act in the current or any previous year of assessment;

v) the value of any machinery, implements, utensils or articles used by the taxpayer for the purposes of his trade shall be increased by the amount of any expenditure (other than expenditure referred to in paragraph (a)) which is proved to the satisfaction of the Commissioner to have been incurred by the taxpayer in moving such machinery, implements, utensils or articles from one location to another;

vi) the value of any machinery, implements, utensils or articles used by the taxpayer for the purposes of his trade shall be reduced by the amount of any deduction which may be made under subsection (1) of section 12 or under that subsection as applied by subsection (3) of the said section, or under the corresponding provisions of any previous Income Tax Act or under section 12A(2) or under section 27(2)(d);

vii) where the value of any such machinery, implements, utensils and articles acquired by the taxpayer on or after 15 March 1984 is for the purposes of this paragraph to be determined having regard to the cost of such machinery, implements, utensils and articles, such cost shall be deemed to be the cost which, in the opinion of the Commissioner, a person would, if he had acquired such machinery, implements, utensils and articles under a cash transaction concluded at arm's length on the date on which the transaction for the acquisition of such machinery, implements, utensils and articles was in fact concluded, have incurred in respect of the direct cost of the acquisition of such machinery, implements, utensils and articles, including the direct cost of the installation or erection thereof;

viii) where in respect of any machinery, implement, utensil or article required by the taxpayer on or after 21 June 1993, a deduction or allowance was previously granted to a connected person in relation to the taxpayer under this paragraph or section 12B (1) or 12C (1), or under section 27 (2) (d) prior to the deletion thereof by section 28 (b) of the income Tax Act, 1991 (Act No. 129 of 1991), the allowance under this paragraph shall be calculated on the lesser of the cost of such machinery, implement, utensil or article to such connected person or the market value thereof as determined on the date upon which it was acquired by the taxpayer;

ix) where any such machinery, plant, implement, utensil or article was used by the taxpayer during any previous financial year or years for the purposes of any trade carried on by such taxpayer, the receipts and accruals of which were not included in the income of such taxpayer during such year or years, the Commissioner shall take into account the period of use of such asset during such previous year or years in determining the amount by which the value of such machinery, plant, implement, utensil or article has been diminished;

f) an allowance in respect of any premium or consideration in the nature of a premium paid by a taxpayer for--

i) the right of use or occupation of land or buildings used or occupied for the production of income or from which income is derived; or

ii) the right of use of any plant or machinery used for the production of income or from which income is derived; or

ii)bis the right of use of any motion picture film or any sound recording or advertising matter connected with such film, if such film, sound recording or advertising matter is used for the production of income or income is derived therefrom; or

iii) the right of use of any patent as defined in the Patents Act, 1978 (Act No. 57 of 1978), or any design as defined in the Designs Act, 1993 (Act No. 195 of 1993), or any trade mark as defined in the Trade Marks Act, 1993 (Act No. 194 of 1993), or any copyright as defined in the Copyright Act, 1978 (Act No. 98 of 1978), or of any other property which is of a similar nature, if such patent, design, trade mark, copyright or other property is used for the production of income or income is derived therefrom; or

iv) the imparting of or the undertaking to impart any knowledge directly or indirectly connected with the use of such film, sound recording, advertising matter patent, design, trade mark, copyright or other property as aforesaid:

Provided that--

aa) the allowance under sub-paragraph (i), (ii), (ii)bis or (iii) shall not exceed for any one year such portion of the amount of the premium or consideration so paid as is equal to the said amount divided by the number of years for which the taxpayer is entitled to the use or occupation, or one twenty-fifth of the said amount, whichever is the greater,

bb) if the taxpayer is entitled to such use or occupation for an indefinite period, or if, in the case of any such right of use or occupation granted under an agreement concluded on or after 1 July 1983, the taxpayer or the person by whom such right of use or occupation was granted holds a right or option to extend or renew the original period of such use or occupation, he shall be deemed, for the purposes of this paragraph, to be entitled to such use or occupation for such period as in the opinion of the Commissioner represents the probable duration of such use or occupation; and

cc) the allowance under sub-paragraph (iv) shall not exceed for any one year such portion (not being less than one twenty-fifth) of the amount of the premium or consideration so paid as the Commissioner may allow having regard to the period during which the taxpayer will enjoy the right to use such film, sound recording, advertising matter, patent, design, trade mark, copyright or other property as aforesaid and any other circumstances which in the opinion of the Commissioner are relevant;

dd) the provisions of this paragraph shall not apply in relation to any such premium or consideration paid by the taxpayer which do not for the purposes of this Act constitute income of the person to whom it is paid, unless such premium or consideration is paid under a written agreement formally and finally signed before 10 April 1984 by every party to the agreement;

g) an allowance in respect of any expenditure actually incurred by the taxpayer, in pursuance of an obligation to effect improvements on land or to buildings. incurred under an agreement whereby the right of use or occupation of the land or buildings is granted by any other person, where the land or buildings are used or occupied for the production of income or income is derived therefrom: Provided that--

i) the aggregate of the allowances under this paragraph shall not exceed the amount stipulated in the agreement as the value of the improvements or as the amount to be expended on the improvements or, if no amount is so stipulated, an amount representing in the opinion of the Commissioner the fair and reasonable value of the improvements;

ii) any such allowance shall not exceed for any one year such portion of the aggregate of the allowances under this paragraph as is equal to the said aggregate divided by the number of years (calculated from the date on which the improvements are completed, but not more than 25 years) for which the taxpayer is entitled to the use or occupation;

iii) if the taxpayer is entitled to such use or occupation for an indefinite period, he shall for the purposes of this paragraph be deemed to be entitled to such use or occupation for such period as in the opinion of the Commissioner represents the probable duration of such use or occupation;

iv) the aggregate of the allowances under this paragraph in respect of any building or improvements referred to in section 13(1) or (4) or 27(2)(b) shall not exceed the cost (after the deduction of any amount which has been set off against the cost of such building or improvements under section 13(3) or section 27(4)) to the taxpayer of such building or improvements less the aggregate of the allowances in respect of such building or improvements made to the taxpayer under the said section 13(1) or (4) or 27(2)(b) or the corresponding provisions of any previous Income Tax Act;

v) where expenditure has been incurred by the taxpayer in respect of the cost of any improvements to land or buildings (other than improvements consisting of any building or improvements referred to in paragraph (iv) of this proviso or in section 13bis and other than any residential unit referred to in section 13ter) and such expenditure or a portion thereof has qualified or will qualify for deduction from the taxpayer's income by way of a deduction of expenditure or an allowance in respect of expenditure under any other provision of this Act, the aggregate of the allowances under this paragraph in respect of such improvements shall not exceed the amount or value referred to in paragraph (i) of this proviso less an amount equal to the aggregate of the amounts which have so qualified or will so qualify for deduction from the taxpayer's income under the said other provision, whether in the current or any preceding or subsequent year of assessment;

vi) the provisions of this paragraph shall not apply in relation to any such expenditure incurred under an agreement concluded on or after 1 July 1983, if the value of such improvements or the amount to be expended on such improvements, as contemplated in paragraph (h) of the definition of "gross income" in section 1, does not for the purposes of this Act constitute income of the person to whom the right to have such improvements effected has accrued;

gA) an allowance in respect of any expenditure (other than expenditure which has qualified in whole or part for deduction or allowance under any of the other provisions of this section or the corresponding provisions of any previous Income Tax Act) actually incurred by the taxpayer--

i) in devising or developing any invention as defined in the Patents Act, 1978 (Act No. 57 of 1978), or in creating or producing any design as defined in the Designs Act, 1993 (Act No. 195 of 1993), or any trade mark as defined in the Trade Marks Act, 1993 (Act No. 194 of 1993), or any copyright as defined in the Copyright Act, 1978 (Act No. 98 of 1978), or any other property which is of a similar nature; or

ii) in obtaining any patent or the restoration of any patent under the Patents Act, 1978, or the registration of any design under the Designs Act, 1993, or the registration of any trade mark under the Trade Marks Act, 1993, or under similar laws of any other country; or

iii) in acquiring by assignment from any other person any such patent, design, trade mark or copyright or in acquiring any other property of a similar nature or any knowledge connected with the use of such patent, design, trade mark, copyright or other property or the right to have such knowledge imparted,

if such invention, patent, design, trade mark, copyright, other property or knowledge, as the case may be, is used by the taxpayer in the production of his income or income is derived by him therefrom: Provided that--

aa) where such expenditure exceeds R5 000, and was incurred--

A) before 29 October 1999, the allowance shall not exceed for any one year such portion of the amount of the expenditure as is equal to such amount divided by the number of years which, in the opinion of the Commissioner, represents the probable duration of use of the invention, patent, design, trade mark, copyright, other property or knowledge, or four per cent of the said amount, whichever is the greater;

B) on or after 29 October 1999, the allowance shall not for any one year exceed an amount equal to--

AA) five per cent of the amount of the expenditure in the case of any invention, patent, trade mark, copyright or other property of a similar nature or any knowledge connected with the use of such invention, patent, trade mark, copyright or other property or the right to have such knowledge imparted; or

BB) 10 per cent of the amount of the expenditure in the case of any design or other property of a similar nature or any knowledge connected with the use of such design or other property or the right to have such knowledge imparted;

bb) where such expenditure was incurred before the commencement of the year of assessment in question the allowance shall be calculated on the amount of such expenditure, less an amount equivalent to the sum of the allowances to which the taxpayer was entitled under this paragraph and the allowances to which, in the opinion of the Commissioner, the taxpayer would have been entitled under this paragraph if this paragraph had been applicable, in respect of such expenditure in respect of previous years of assessment, including any year of assessment under any previous Income Tax Act;

cc) no allowance shall be made in respect of any such invention, patent, design, trade mark, copyright or other property or knowledge so acquired or obtained by the taxpayer on or after 24 June 1988, but prior to 1 July 1993 from any other person who is a resident of the Republic or who is ordinarily resident in a neighbouring country (or, in the case of a company, is incorporated or has its place of effective management in a neighbouring country), if--

A) the taxpayer or such other person is a company and such other person or the taxpayer, as the case may be, is interested in more than 50 per cent of any class of shares issued by such company, whether directly as a shareholder in that company or indirectly as a shareholder in any other company; or

B) both the taxpayer and such other person are companies and any third person is interested in more than 50 per cent of any class of shares issued by one of those companies and in more than 50 per cent of any class of shares issued by the other company, whether directly as shareholder in the company by which the shares in question were issued or indirectly as a shareholder in any other company;

dd) where any such invention, patent, design, trade mark, copyright or other property or knowledge was so acquired or obtained by the taxpayer on or after 1 July 1993 from any other person who is a resident of the Republic or who is ordinarily resident in a neighbouring country (or, in the case of a company, is incorporated or has its place of effective management in a neighbouring country), and who is a connected person in relation to the taxpayer, the allowance under this paragraph shall be calculated on the lesser of the cost of such invention, patent, design, trade mark, copyright or other property or knowledge to such connected person or the market value thereof as determined on the date upon which such invention, patent, design, trade mark, copyright or other property or knowledge was acquired or obtained by the taxpayer;

ee) no allowance shall be made in respect of any expenditure incurred by such taxpayer on or after 29 October 1999, in respect of the acquisition from any other person of any trade mark or other property of a similar nature or any knowledge connected with the use of such trade mark or the right to have such knowledge imparted;

gB) expenditure (other than expenditure which has qualified in whole or part for deduction or allowance under any of the other provisions of this section) actually incurred by the taxpayer during the year of assessment in obtaining the extension of the term of any patent under the Patents Act, 1978 (Act No. 57 of 1978), or the extension of the registration period of any design under the Designs Act, 1993 (Act No. 195 of 1993), or the renewal of the registration of any trade mark under the Trade Marks Act, 1993 (Act No. 194 of 1993), or under similar laws of any other country, if such patent, design or trade mark is used by the taxpayer in the production of his income or income is derived by him therefrom;

gC) deleted by section 15 of Act 59 of 2000.

h) such allowance in respect of amounts included in the taxpayer's gross income under paragraph (g) or paragraph (h) of the definition of "gross income" in section 1 as the Commissioner may deem reasonable having regard to any special circumstances of the case and, in the case of an amount so included under the said paragraph (h), to the original period for which the right of use or occupation was granted or, in the case of any amount so included under the said paragraph (h) in consequence of an agreement concluded on or after 1 July 1983, to the number of years taken into account in the determination of the relevant allowance granted to any other person under the provisions of paragraph (g) of this section: Provided that where there has on or after the twenty-ninth day of March, 1972, accrued to the taxpayer the right to have improvements effected on land or to buildings by any other person and an amount is required to be included in the taxpayer's gross income under the said paragraph (h) with respect to such improvements, no allowance shall be made to the taxpayer under this paragraph in respect of such amount, if--

i) the taxpayer or such other person is a company and such other person or the taxpayer, as the case may be, is interested in more than fifty per cent of any class of shares issued by such company, whether directly as a shareholder in that company or indirectly as a shareholder in any other company; or

ii) both the taxpayer and such other person are companies and any third person is interested in more than fifty per cent of any class of shares issued by one of those companies and in more than fifty per cent of any class of shares issued by the other company, whether directly as a shareholder in the company by which the shares in question were issued or indirectly as a shareholder in any other company;

hA) so much of any amount paid (other than an amount in respect of which any deduction or allowance has been or will be granted under any other provision of this Act) by a taxpayer engaged in mining, prospecting, quarrying or similar operations to a company, society, association of persons or trust referred to in section 10(1)(cH) to be used by such company, society, association or trust for the purposes contemplated in such section: Provided that such an amount shall be determined and such payment shall be made in accordance with--

i) the constitution of such company, society or assiciation of persons; or

ii) the instrument establishing such trust,

as has been approved by the Commissioner in terms of section 10(1)(cH); and

i) the amount of any debts due to the taxpayer which have during the year of assessment become bad, provided such amount is included in the current year of assessment or was included in previous years of assessment in the taxpayer's income;

j) such an allowance as may be made each year by the Commissioner in respect of such debts due to the taxpayer as he considers to be doubtful: Provided that such allowance shall be included in the income of the taxpayer in the following year of assessment;

k)

i) any sum contributed during the year of assessment to any pension fund by way of current contribution by any person who holds any office or employment, where such contribution is made by reason of the holding of such office or employment, or by any person who is a partner referred to in paragraph (ii)(ee) of the proviso to paragraph (c) of the definition of pension fund in section 1: Provided that the total deduction to be allowed in respect of contributions by such person to any one or more pension fund or funds shall not in the year of assessment exceed the greater of R1 750 or 7,5 per cent of the remuneration (being the income or part thereof referred to in the definition of "retirement-funding employment" in section 1) derived by such person during such year in respect of his retirement-funding employment;

ii) any sum paid during the year of assessment to any pension fund by any person who, as a member of such fund, has in terms of the rules governing such fund undertaken to pay such sum in respect of any past period which is to be reckoned as pensionable service of that member: Provided that--

aa) the deduction to be allowed in respect of any sums so paid shall not in the year of assessment exceed the sum of R1 800;

bb) any amount, being a portion of a sum so paid, which has been disallowed solely by reason of the fact that it exceeds the amount of the deduction allowable in respect of the year of assessment shall be carried forward and be deemed for the purposes of this paragraph to be a sum so paid in the next succeeding year of assessment;

cc) the provisions of this subparagraph shall apply for the purpose of determining the taxpayer's total taxable income for any year of assessment ended or ending on or after 28 February 1981 whether such taxable income is derived from the carrying on of any trade or otherwise;

dd) no deduction shall be made under this paragraph in respect of so much of any amount carried forward in terms of paragraph (bb) of this proviso as has been accounted for under paragraph (d) of the definition of "formula B" in paragraph 1 of the Second Schedule or the first proviso to paragraph 6 of that Schedule;

l) any sum contributed by an employer during the year of assessment for the benefit of his employees to any pension fund, provident fund or benefit fund (other than a fund contemplated in paragraph (a) of the definition of 'benefit fund'): Provided that--

i) in respect of any lump sum contribution, the Commissioner may determine that the said sum shall be deducted in a series of annual instalments, so that only a portion thereof is deducted in the year of assessment in which it is contributed, and the residue in such subsequent years of assessment and in such proportions as the Commissioner may determine, until the contribution is extinguished;

ii) if the contributions (including any lump sum payments) made by the employer in respect of any employee during any year of assessment to such funds exceed an amount equal to ten per cent of the approved remuneration of such employee for such year of assessment, and the Commissioner is satisfied that the aggregate of such contributions and the total remuneration accrued during such year of assessment to such employee in respect of his employment by the employer is excessive or unjustifiable in relation to the value of the services rendered by such employee to the employer, and having regard to other benefits, if any, derived by him from his employment by the employer, only so much of such contribution as appears to the Commissioner to be reasonable, but not less than an amount equal to ten per cent of the approved remuneration of such employee for such year of assessment, shall be allowed to be deducted under this paragraph;

iii) for the purposes of paragraph (ii) of this proviso "approved remuneration", in relation to any employee for any year of assessment, means so much of the total remuneration accrued to such employee during such year of assessment in respect of his employment by the employer concerned as the Commissioner considers to be fair and reasonable in relation to the value of the services rendered by such employee during such year of assessment to the employer and having regard to other benefits, if any, derived by him from his employment by the employer;

iv) where any contributions are made to any such fund by the members of a partnership in their capacity as employers, the references in paragraph (ii) of this proviso to an employer shall be construed as applying to the partnership as though its members were one person;

v) the references in this paragraph to employees or any employee shall, where the employer is a partnership and contributions are made by the employer to a pension fund, be construed as including references to any member of such partnership who was previously an employee in the undertaking carried on by the partnership and who has been permitted to retain his membership of such pension fund as contemplated in paragraph (ii) (ee) of the proviso to paragraph (c) of the definition of "pension fund" in section 1, and, for the purposes of paragraphs (ii) and (iii) of this proviso "approved remuneration", in relation to such member, shall be construed as including the amount of his pensionable emoluments referred to in the said paragraph (ii) (ee);

vi) any decision of the Commissioner under this paragraph, not being a decision under paragraph (i) of this proviso, shall be subject to objection and appeal;

m) any amount paid by way of annuity during the year of assessment by any taxpayer--

i) to a former employee who has retired from the taxpayer's employ on grounds of old age, ill health or infirmity; or

ii) to a person who was for a period of at least five years a partner in an undertaking carried on by the taxpayer and who retired from the partnership in respect of that undertaking on grounds of old age, ill health or infirmity, provided that the amount so paid to such person is reasonable, having regard to the services rendered by such person as a partner: in such undertaking prior to his retirement and the profits made in such undertaking, and that the said amount does not represent consideration payable to such person in respect of his interest in the partnership; or

iii) to any person who is dependent for his maintenance upon a former employee or a former partner in an undertaking carried on by the tarpayer or (where such former employee or former partner is deceased) was so dependent immediately prior to his death:

Provided that the deduction under subparagraph (iii) shall not exceed in respect of the persons so dependent on any one retired or deceased employee or former partner, the sum of R2 500;

n)

aa) so much of the total current contributions to any retirement annuity fund or funds made during the year of assessment by any person as a member of such fund or funds as does not in the case of the taxpayer exceed the greatest of--

A) 15 per cent of an amount equal to the amount remaining after deducting from, or setting off against, the income derived by the taxpayer during the year of assessment (excluding income derived from any retirement funding employment (being the income or part thereof referred to in the definition of "retirement funding employment" in section 1)) the deductions or assessed losses admissible against such income under this Act (excluding this paragraph, sections 17A, 18, 18A and 19(3) of this Act and paragraph 12(1)(c) to (i), inclusive, of the First Schedule); or

B) the amount, if any, by which the amount of R3 500 exceeds the amount of any deduction to which the taxpayer is entitled under paragraph (k)(i) in respect of the said year; or

C) the amount of R1 750;

bb) so much of the total of any contributions to any retirement annuity fund or funds made during the year of assessment by any person as a member of such fund or funds as does not exceed R1 800 in the case of the taxpayer, where such contributions are made under conditions prescribed in the rules of the fund whereby a member who has discontinued his contributions prematurely is entitled to be reinstated as a full member thereof and the current contributions to the fund have been paid in full:

Provided that--

i) no deduction shall be made under subparagraph (aa) in respect of any amount paid into a retirement annuity fund for the benefit of a member of such fund where such amount is a lump sum benefit derived by the member from a pension fund, a provident fund or a retirement annuity fund and that amount has under the provisions of paragraph 6 (a), (b) or (c) of the Second Schedule qualified for deduction from any amount to be included in the member's gross income;

ii) the deductions in terms of subparagraph (aa) shall not exceed an amount equal to the amount remaining after deducting from or setting off against the income derived by the taxpayer during the year of assessment the deductions and assessed losses admissible against such income under this Act (excluding the said subparagraph, sections 17A and 19(3) of this Act and paragraph 12(1)(c) to (i), inclusive, of the First Schedule);

iii) any current contributions (excluding any amount referred to in paragraph (i) of this proviso) to any retirement annuity fund or funds which are made by such person as a member of such fund or funds during a year of assessment and do not qualify for deduction from his income for that year under subparagraph (aa) shall be carried forward and, except to the extent that such contributions have been accounted for under paragraph (d) of the definition of "formula B" in paragraph 1 of the Second Schedule or the first proviso to paragraph 6 of that Schedule, be deemed for the purposes of the said subparagraph to be current contributions made to the fund or funds in question during the next succeeding year of assessment;

iv) no deduction shall be made under subparagraph (bb) in respect of an contribution relating to any year of assessment which, if such contribution had been made during that year, would not have qualified for deduction under this paragraph, as applicable in relation to the said year;

v) any amount being a portion of a contribution made as contemplated in subparagraph (bb) and which has been disallowed solely by reason of the fact that it exceeds the amount of the deduction allowable in respect of the year of assessment, shall be carried forward and be deemed for the purposes of the said paragraph to be a contribution so made in the next succeeding year of assessment;

vi) the provisions of this paragraph shall apply for the purpose of determining the taxpayer's total taxable income whether derived from the carrying on of any trade or otherwise;

vii) Deleted by section 12 of Act 21 of 1995;

viii) where any such contribution was allowed as a deduction to a person, no deduction in respect of such contribution shall be allowed to such person's spouse;

ix) any such contribution which has been made by a married woman to any such fund of which she became a member before 1 March 1992 shall, at the option of such married woman, be deemed for the purposes of this paragraph as applicable in any year of assessment ending not later than 28 February 1997 to be a contribution made by such married woman's husband as a member of such fund;

o) save as provided in paragraph 12(2) of the First Schedule, an allowance in respect of--

i) any building (or portion thereof) referred to in section 13(1) or (4) or section 13bis(1) or section 27(2)(b) or of any improvements (or portion thereof) to such building; or

ii) any shipbuilding structure referred to in section 13(8) or of any improvement to such shipbuilding structure; or

iii) any residential unit referred to in section 13ter; or

iv) any permanent work, road pavement or ancillary service referred to in section 24G; or

v) any machinery, plant, implements, utensils or articles used by the taxpayer for the purposes of his trade; or

vi) any transmission line or cable or railway line referred to in section 12D; or

vii) any aircraft hangar or any apron, runway or taxiway referred to in section 12F,

which have been scrapped by such taxpayer during the year of assessment, such allowance to be the excess of the original cost to such taxpayer of such building (or portion thereof), improvements (or portion thereof) to such building, shipbuilding structure, improvements to such shipbuilding structure, residential unit, permanent work, road pavement, ancillary service, machinery, plant, implements, utensils, articles, transmission line or cable, railway line, aircraft hangar, apron, runway or taxiway over the total amount arrived at by adding

aa) all the allowances made in respect thereof under the provisions of paragraph (e) of this section, or section 12(1), or section 12(1) as applied by section 12(3), or section 12A(2), or section 12B, or section 12C, or section 12D, or section 12F, or section 13(1), or section 13(1) as applied by section 13(8), or section 13bis(1), (2) or (3), or section 13ter(2) or (3), or section 14(1)(a) or (b), or the corresponding provisions of any previous Income Tax Act, or section 14bis(1)(a), (b) or (c), or section 24F, or section 24G, or section 27(2)(b), or

bb) in the case of any building (or portion thereof), improvements (or portion thereof) to such building, shipbuilding structure, improvements to such shipbuilding structure, residential unit, permanent work, road pavement, ancillary service, machinery, plant, implements, utensils, articles, transmission line or cable, railway line, aircraft hangar, apron, runway or taxiwaywhich was during any previous financial year or years used by the I taxpayer in the course of any trade carried on by such taxpayer, the receipts and accruals of which were not included in the income of such taxpayer during such year or years, all the allowances which could have been made in terms of the provisions referred to in item (aa) as if such receipts and accruals had been included in such taxpayer's income,

to any amount or the value of any advantage accruing to the taxpayer in respect of the sale or other disposal of such building, shipbuilding structure, improvements, residential unit, permanent work, road pavement, ancillary service, machinery, plant, implements, utensils, articles, transmission line or cable, railway line, aircraft hangar, apron, runway or taxiway: Provided that--

i) no allowance shall be made in the case of any such building (or portion thereof), improvements (or portion thereof) to such building, shipbuilding structure, improvements to such shipbuilding structure, residential unit, transmission line or cable, railway line, aircraft hangar, apron, runway or taxiway which has or have been scrapped within a period of ten years from the date of erection or purchase, or in the case of any such residential unit in respect of which any amount has fallen for inclusion in the taxpayer's income under the provisions of section 13ter(7)(a), whether in the current or in any previous year of assessment;

ii) for the purposes of this paragraph the cost of any building (or portion thereof), improvements (or portion thereof) to any building, shipbuilding structure, improvements to any shipbuilding structure, residential unit, transmission line or cable, railway line, aircraft hangar, apron, runway or taxiway shall be deemed to be that portion of the actual cost on which the allowance in question was made;

iii) for the purposes of this paragraph the cost of any machinery, implements, utensils or articles shall be deemed to be the actual cost plus the amount by which the value of such machinery, implements, utensils or articles has been increased in terms of paragraph (v) of the proviso to paragraph (e) or the corresponding provisions of any previous Income Tax Act, and less the amount by which such value has been reduced in terms of paragraph (iv) of the said proviso or the corresponding provisions of any previous Income Tax Act;

iiiA) for the purposes of paragraph (iii) of this proviso, the actual cost of any machinery, implements, utensils or articles acquired by the taxpayer on or after 15 March 1984 shall be deemed to be the cost of such machinery, implements, utensils or articles as determined under the provisions of paragraph (vii) of the proviso to paragraph (e);

iv) for the purposes of this paragraph the cost of any aircraft in respect of which any allowance has been made to the taxpayer under the provisions of section 14bis shall be deemed to be the actual cost less any amount (not being an amount which has been included in the income of the taxpayer for any year of assessment in terms of section 8 (4) (i)) by which the cost or estimated cost price of such aircraft has in the calculation of such allowance been reduced in terms of section 14bis (2) (a);

v) for the purposes of this paragraph the cost of any ship in respect of which any allowance has been made to the taxpayer under the provisions of section 14 shall be deemed to be the actual cost less any amount (not being an amount which has been included in the income of the taxpayer for any year of assessment in terms of section 8(4)(d)) by which the cost or estimated cost price of such ship has in the calculation of such allowance been reduced in terms of the definition of "adjustable cost" or "adjustable cost price" in section 14(2);

vi) no allowance shall be made under this paragraph in respect of any machinery, implement, utensil or article of which the cost has been allowed as a deduction from the taxpayer's income under the provisions of section 24D;

vii) no allowance shall be made under this paragraph in respect of any building, improvements to such building, shipbuilding structure, improvements to such shipbuilding structure, residential unit, permanent work, road pavement, ancillary service, machinery, plant, implements, utensils, articles, transmission line or cable or railway line which is disposed of by that person to any other person who is a connected person in relation to that person: Provided that any amount which is disallowed as a deduction under this subparagraph may be deducted by that person from any amount received by or accrued to that person from that other person, which must be included in the gross income of that person, in that year of assessment or any subsequent year of assessment, if that other person is still a connected person in relation to that person.

p) expenditure (other than expenditure in respect of which any deduction or allowance has been or will be granted under any other provision of this Act) incurred during the year of assessment by any taxpayer--

i) for the purpose of scientific research undertaken by him for the development of his business, if such expenditure is not of a capital nature; or

ii) by way of contributions to any association, institute, college or university, to be used in scientific research relating to the taxpayer's own business, if the Council for Scientific and Industrial Research certifies to the Commissioner that it approves the proposals of such association, institute, college or university in regard to such research and that it is satisfied that such contributions will be used in such research;

q) save as provided in paragraph 12 (2) of the First Schedule, if expenditure of a capital nature (other than expenditure in respect of which any deduction or allowance has been or will be granted under any other provision of this Act) has been incurred by a taxpayer for the purpose of scientific research undertaken by him for the development of his business, and the Council for Scientific and Industrial Research certifies to the Commissioner that during the year of assessment in question such research was carried on and was financed by such expenditure, an amount in respect of the year of assessment in which such research commenced and of any succeeding year of assessment calculated at the rate of 25 per cent of such expenditure: Provided that--

i) the total deduction under this paragraph shall not exceed the amount of such expenditure; and

ii) if in any year of assessment the taxpayer discontinues such research or if the Council for Scientific and Industrial Research is unable, in respect of any year of assessment, to certify as provided in the foregoing provisions of this paragraph, there shall be included in the taxpayer's income for that year of assessment the total of the deductions under this paragraph or the corresponding provisions of any previous Income Tax Act, whether in the current or any previous year of assessment, less one-tenth of the amount of such expenditure in respect of each completed period of one year, not exceeding ten, contained in the period during which such research was carried on;

r) Deleted by section10 of Act 52 of 1970;

s) in the case of a company the shares of which are 'property shares' as defined in section 47 of the Collective Investment Schemes Control Act, 2002, the dividends (other than those distributed out of profits of a capital nature) distributed by such company during the year of assessment on shares included in a portfolio comprised in any collective investment scheme in property managed or carried on by any company registered as a manager under section 42 of that Act for the purposes of Part V of that Act;

t) in the case of any taxpayer (excluding any taxpayer who derives income from the sale of immovable property to persons who are not employed by him) who during any year of assessment incurs expenditure in connection with the erection of any dwelling or who, for the purpose of financing in whole or in part the erection by any person during the said period of any dwelling, advances or donates to any person any amount during any such year of assessment, and who satisfies the Commissioner that that dwelling will be occupied exclusively by persons or the households of persons who are his employees and are employed by him for the purposes of his trade (other than mining or farming), an allowance in respect of the said year of assessment equal to 50 per cent of the expenditure so incurred or of the amount so advanced or donated: Provided that--

i) where any company is mainly engaged in the provision of housing facilities for the employees of its sole or principal shareholder or for the employees of any other company the shares in which are held wholly by the sole or principal shareholder in such firstmentioned company, the employees of such shareholder or such other company, as the case may be, shall for the purposes of this paragraph be deemed to be the employees also of such firstmentioned company;

ii) the aggregate of all the allowances made under this paragraph or the corresponding provisions of any previous Income Tax Act in respect of the erection of any one dwelling shall not exceed the sum of R6 000;

iii) if in any year of assessment any dwelling in relation to the erection of which an allowance has been made to any taxpayer under this paragraph or the corresponding provisions of any previous Income Tax Act, whether in the current or any previous year of assessment, is occupied by any person or by the household of any person who is not an employee of that taxpayer, there shall be included in the income of the said taxpayer for the current year of assessment the amount of such allowance less an amount equal to one-tenth of the said allowance in respect of each completed period of one year, but not exceeding ten years, during which such dwelling was occupied by an employee or the household of an employee of that taxpayer,

and for the purposes of this paragraph "employee" in relation to any taxpayer does not include any person who is a relative of that taxpayer or who, if the taxpayer is a company, is a shareholder (or a relative of a shareholder) in that company or in any company which is associated with that company by virtue of shareholding, not being a shareholder who holds all his shares in that company solely because he is employed by that company and who will, in terms of the articles of association of that company, not be entitled to continue to hold those shares after he ceases to be so employed;

u) so much of the entertainment expenditure (including club subscriptions) incurred by any taxpayer who is a natural person during the year of assessment as the Commissioner is satisfied was so incurred directly in connection with the taxpayer's trade and which is not such expenditure as is referred to in paragraph (a): Provided that--

i) the deduction under this paragraph shall be limited to an amount equal to the lesser of--

aa) R2 500; or

bb) R300 plus 5 per cent of so much of the taxable income (as determined before any deduction is made under this paragraph) derived by the taxpayer from carrying on during the year of assessment any trade in connection with which such expenditure was incurred, as exceeds R6 000;

ii) no deduction shall be made under this paragraph in respect of any such expenditure as is incurred in connection with any employment or office in respect of which the taxpayer derives remuneration as defined in paragraph 1 of the Fourth Schedule, unless that person is an agent or representative whose remuneration is normally derived mainly in the form of commissions based on his or her sales or the turnover attributable to that person;

aa) the Commissioner is satisfied that such employment or office is of such a nature that the taxpayer's duties regularly and necessarily involve incurring such expenditure; and

bb) the taxpayer receives in respect of such expenditure a reimbursive allowance which is included in his gross income under the provisions of paragraph (iii) of the proviso to paragraph (c) of the definition of "gross income" in section 1;

iii) [deleted by the Taxation Laws Amendment Act, 2002]

iv) [deleted by the Taxation Laws Amendment Act, 2002]

v) Deleted by section 9 of Act 65 of 1973

w) an allowance in respect of any premium which was actually paid by the taxpayer under any policy of insurance taken out upon the life of an employee of the taxpayer or, in the case of a company, upon the life of a director or an employee of that company, the amount of such allowance to be as follows, namely--

i) where the life of the employee or director is insured for a period of not more than one year or where the only premiums payable under the said policy are premiums of equal amount payable at regular intervals of not more than one year until benefits (other than interim or temporary benefits) become payable or commence to become payable under that policy, an amount equal to the amount of the premium which became payable under such policy during the year of assessment; or

ii) in any other case, an amount equal to such portion of the premium paid under the said policy as, in the opinion of the Commissioner (having regard *inter alia* to the terms of the policy and, in the appropriate circumstances, to the expectation of life of the employee or director) should be regarded as relating to the year of assessment; or

iii) if, during the year of assessment, any sum (being a lump sum included in the taxpayer's gross income under paragraph (m) of the definition of "gross income" in section 1) has been received by or has accrued to the taxpayer under or upon the surrender or disposal of the said poiicy, an amount (not exceeding such lump sum) equal to so much of the premiums paid by the taxpayer under the said policy as has not qualified for deduction (whether by way of an allowance under this paragraph or otherwise) from the taxpayer's income in the said year of assessment and preceding years of assessment under this Act and any previous Income Tax Act:

Provided that--

aa) no allowance shall be made under this paragraph in respect of any premium under any policy which was at the time of the payment of such premium the property of any person other than the taxpayer;

bb) no allowance in respect of any premium under any policy of insurance shall be made under this paragraph (except, in the appropriate circumstances, an allowance under subparagraph (iii)) in respect of any year of assessment--

A) if during such year any person other than the taxpayer was entitled. or would have been entitled, to any benefits that were or could have become payable under the said policy; or

B) if any loan or advance (other than a loan or advance referred to in paragraph (m) of the definition of "gross income" in section 1) was made to any person on the security or strength of such policy and any amount was during the said year owing in respect of such loan or advance or in respect of interest or other charges relating thereto. unless the Commissioner is satisfied that the loan or advance was obtained in order to obtain funds required by the taxpayer for the purposes of his trade in consequence of the employee's or director's ill-health, infirmity, incapacity, retirement or cessation of services occurring after the said policy was acquired by the taxpayer, or

C) if the said premium fell due before the commencement of the year of assessment ending the twenty-eighth day of February, 1971.

cc) the sum of the allowances made under this paragraph in respect of any insurance premium shall not exceed the amount of such premium;

dd) no allowance shall be made under this paragraph in respect of any premium paid under any insurance policy unless--

A) such policy was effected in terms of a written proposal accepted by the insurer before 1 June 1982 or the proposal for such policy was made before 25 May 1982 and accepted by the insurer not later than 21 June 1982; or

B) the only benefit payable under the policy is a benefit payable within a period fixed in such policy upon or by reason of the death or disablement of the employee or director whose life is insured under the policy or the policy is a disability policy as defined in section 1 of the Long-term Insurance Act, 1998 (Act No. 52 of 1998); or

C) the Minister of Finance has by regulation prescribed requirements in regard to terms and conditions with which insurance policies shall conform for the purposes of this subparagraph and the policy conforms with such requirements;

ee) the allowance under this paragraph in respect of premiums paid by the taxpayer during any year of assessment shall, except as provided in subparagraph (iii), be limited--

A) in the case of premiums paid under a policy referred to in subparagraph (A) of paragraph (dd) of this proviso, to so much of such premiums as were payable in terms of the conditions contained in that policy on 31 May 1982; or

B) in the case of premiums paid under one or more policies referred to in subparagraph (C) of the said paragraph (dd) upon the life of a particular employee or director, to an amount equal to 10 per cent of the remuneration (as defined in the definition of 'remuneration' in paragraph 1 of the Fourth Schedule) derived by such employee or director from the taxpayer during the said year of assessment;

ff) no deduction shall be made from the income of any taxpayer in respect of premiums paid by him under any policy of insurance of which he is the owner on the life of an employee of that taxpayer or, where the taxpayer is a company, of a director or employee of that company, except in so far as an allowance may be made under this paragraph or, in the case of a policy which is not a life policy or a disability policy as defined in section 1 of the Long-term Insurance Act, 1998, a deduction which may, in appropriate circumstances, be made under paragraph (a) or (b) of this section;

x) any amounts which in terms of any other provision in this Part, are allowed to be deducted from the income of the taxpayer.

STAMP DUTY, INCOME TAX, SECONDARY TAX ON COMPANIES, TAX ON RETIREMENT FUNDS, VALUE-ADDED TAX AND UNCERTIFICATED SECURITIES TAX IMPLICATIONS OF LENDING ARRANGEMENTS IN RESPECT OF MARKETABLE SECURITIES

1) Introduction

In drawing up standards for clearance and settlement procedures an international working committee found that the settlement status in South African equity markets differed from the settlement status adopted by most countries internationally. The committee recommended that securities lending be encouraged as a method of expediting the settlement of security transactions. Securities lending also improves liquidity, encourages investment and increases pricing efficiency.

Consequently, in 1996 certain amendments were effected to the Stamp Duties Act, No 77 of 1968 (the SD Act) and Income Tax Act, No 58 of 1962 (the IT Act), to introduce the concept of a lending arrangement. The amendments to the IT Act are based on the principles contained in the tax systems of various other countries, such as Australia, Canada, Japan, the United Kingdom and the United States. According to those tax systems the lender of the loaned securities is deemed still to be the owner thereof and no gain or loss arises in the hands of the lender or borrower as a result of the transfer of the loaned securities between the lender and borrower. Payments made in respect of such securities will, however, have certain tax implications.

The provisions of this Practice Note are applicable to residents and non-residents who are subject to the taxes imposed in terms of the various Acts addressed in this Practice Note.

2) Stamp Duty

Section 23 (1) of the SD Act defines a "lending arrangement" as--

"any arrangement or agreement in terms of which--

a) a person (hereinafter referred to as the lender), lends a marketable security to another person (hereinafter referred to as the borrower), in order to enable the borrower to effect delivery of the marketable security under a transaction entered into by the borrower to sell the marketable security; and

b) the borrower in return undertakes to transfer a marketable security of the same kind and of the same or equivalent quantity and quality to the lender within a period of twelve months from the date of such loan."

Research has shown that a number of countries which levy a duty on share transfers exempt transfers from the duty if the transfer is effected in terms of a lending arrangement. In line with international practice, an appropriate exemption was inserted in the SD Act. Exemption (nB) of Item 15 of Schedule 1 to the SD Act accordingly exempts from stamp duty--

"Any registration of transfer of any marketable security in the name of the lender of a marketable security, if such registration of transfer is effected in consequence of the return to that lender of a marketable security previously lent to the borrower in question in terms of a lending arrangement."

The exemption applies only in the following circumstances:

a) If the purpose of the borrower of the securities is to enable the borrower to deliver such securities under a transaction entered into by the borrower to sell such securities. If the borrower has any other purpose e.g. to deliver the borrowed securities in terms of another lending arrangement, the stamp duty exemption does not apply.

b) The borrower must undertake to return marketable securities of the same kind and of the same or equivalent quantity and quality to the lender within a period of 12 months from the date of the loan (prior to 29 June 1998 this period was 6 months).

In terms of the definition the following agreements will, for example, not qualify for the exemption:

i) loans for a period exceeding 12 months;

ii) loans, outstanding for a period exceeding 6 months, prior to 29 June 1998; and

iii) agreements in terms of which the 12-month period is rolled over (extended for a further period).

The words "... the borrower in return undertakes to transfer..." appearing in the definition of a lending arrangement, read together with the wording of paragraph (nB) of the exemptions to Item 15(3) are interpreted to mean that the marketable securities must, prior to expiry of the period, be reregistered in the lender's name before the exemption is applicable.

To qualify for the exemption the borrower or his agent must certify that the registration of transfer is due to the fact that a marketable security previously loaned to the borrower in terms of a lending arrangement, as defined, was returned to the lender.

3) Income Tax

3.1) Manufactured interest

Securities lending arrangements in respect of interest-bearing instruments normally provide that the borrower will compensate the lender for any coupon or other interest received by the borrower who is the registered owner of the interest-bearing instrument during the term of the lending arrangement. The "manufactured interest" is specifically provided for in the definition of "interest" in section 24J(1) of the IT Act and is, therefore, to be treated as such for the purposes of section 24J. This provision will apply, irrespective of whether the lending arrangement is entered into for a period of less than 12 months, or not.

If all the requirements of section 10(1)(hA) of the IT Act are met, the "manufactured interest" contemplated in the definition of "interest" in section 24J(1) may be exempted in the hands of the recipient who is a non-resident.

3.2) Manufactured dividends

Securities lending arrangements also normally provide that the borrower shall pay to the lender a "manufactured dividend" in lieu of any dividends declared in respect of the security borrowed from the lender. The "manufactured dividend" may include adjustments for the effects of Income Tax or Secondary Tax on Companies (STC). Any payment made by the borrower to the lender as a "manufactured dividend" is not a dividend for Income Tax purposes and must not be treated as a dividend by either the lender or the borrower. The "manufactured dividend" will constitute gross income in the hands of the lender and will not qualify for the exemption in terms of section 10(1)(k). The person who is responsible for the payment of a "manufactured dividend" will only be allowed a deduction in the determination of his taxable income of the amount paid, if the amount meets the requirements of section 11(a) of the IT Act.

3.3) Secondary Tax on Companies

The lender may not reduce the amount on which its liability for STC is calculated by the "manufactured dividend" received. The borrower will, therefore, not be liable for the payment of STC on the "manufactured dividend" paid to the lender.

3.4) Trading stock

Although the lender of marketable securities which constitute trading stock in his or her hands, is not the registered owner of the marketable security loaned to the borrower in terms of a lending arrangement, the lender is, in substance, the owner of a marketable security of the same kind, quantity and quality as the marketable security loaned to the borrower.

In terms of section 22(4A) of the IT Act the marketable security which has been loaned in terms of a lending arrangement, as defined, is therefore, for the purposes of section 22(4), deemed not to have been acquired by the borrower thereof. The marketable security which is returned to the lender by the borrower within the period of 12 months, as replacement for the marketable security loaned, is deemed not to have been acquired by the lender for the purposes of section 22(4).

Section 22(9) of the IT Act deems the marketable security, which has been loaned by the lender and has not been returned by the borrower at year-end, to remain closing stock in the hands of the lender. Such marketable security is also excluded from the closing stock of the borrower if he or she is in possession of such a marketable security at his or her year-end.

Where a marketable security loaned does not comply with the requirements of a "lending arrangement", as defined in the SD Act, the provisions of sections 22(4A) and 22(9) will not be applicable.

3.5) Listed shares

For the purposes of section 9B of the IT Act, a share loaned in terms of a lending arrangement is deemed not to be a disposal in the hands of the lender and the share loaned and any replacement share will be regarded as one and the same share in the hands of the lender. Where a lender lends shares to a specific borrower and the marketable securities are not re-registered in the lender's name prior to expiry of the 12-month period, the loan of the shares will not constitute a lending arrangement. The lender will, for purposes of section 9B, have disposed of his shares on the date the shares were transferred to the borrower in terms of the arrangement.

3.6) Repurchase and resale agreements

The definition of "instrument" in section 24J(1) of the IT Act includes repurchase and resale agreements. In essence these agreements provide for the disposal of an asset by a person to another person, at a consideration and subject to an undertaking that the other person will, at a future date, resell the asset or a similar asset to the person who first disposed of the asset. These agreements do not qualify as lending arrangements, as defined in the SD Act and must, therefore, for Income Tax and Stamp Duty purposes, be treated as a sale of and transfer of ownership in the asset between the parties to the agreement.

Any "manufactured dividend" or "manufactured interest" which is payable or receivable or which forms part of the consideration in respect of a repurchase or resale agreement will be taken into account in determining the amount of interest to be incurred or accrued in terms of section 24J of the IT Act, in respect of the relevant agreement.

4) Tax on Retirement Funds

The Tax on Retirement Funds Act, No 38 of 1996, defines "rental income" to include, inter alia, any consideration payable by a borrower to a lender, in respect of any lending arrangement as consideration for the use of the marketable security in so far as such amount is not included in the definition of interest in section 24J of the IT Act. Therefore, the fee in respect of the lending of interest-bearing marketable securities, as well as the lending of marketable securities which are equity, will constitute "rental income", as defined.

As the "manufactured interest" is included in the definition of "interest", as contemplated in section 24J of the IT Act, such amounts are also subject to the Tax on Retirement Funds.

A "manufactured dividend" in respect of a "lending arrangement" does not constitute "interest" or "rental" as defined in the Tax on Retirement Funds Act.

5) Value-Added Tax

In terms of the Value-Added Tax Act, No 89 of 1991 (VAT Act), the supply of goods or services by a vendor in the course or furtherance of any enterprise carried on by him is subject to VAT at the standard rate, unless the supply is specifically exempt or subject to VAT at the zero rate.

Section 12(a) of the VAT Act exempts from tax the supply of any financial services, as defined in section 2 of the VAT Act, except where such services are subject to the zero rate, e.g. certain supplies of services to non-residents.

As regards scrip lending, the following provisions of section 2 are applicable:

"Financial services.

1) For the purpose of this Act, the following activities shall be deemed to be financial services:

a) ......

b) ......

c) The issue, allotment, drawing, acceptance, endorsement or transfer of ownership of a debt security;

d) the issue, allotment or transfer of ownership of an equity security;

e) ......

f) the provision by any person of credit under an agreement by which money or money's worth is provided by that person to any other person who agrees to pay in the future a sum or sums exceeding in aggregate the amount of such money or money's worth;

g) - (l):

Provided that the activities contemplated in paragraphs (a), (b), (c), (d) and (f) shall not be deemed to be financial services to the extent that the consideration payable in respect thereof is any fee, commission merchant's discount or similar charge, excluding any discounting cost."

A fee or commission charged by a vendor for making scrip available to another person, is, in view of the proviso to section 2(1), not consideration for a financial service and is, accordingly, subject to VAT.

The view is, however, held that a "manufactured dividend" or "manufactured interest" constitutes consideration for the supply of a financial service, as envisaged in section 2(1)(c), (d) and (f), and does not constitute a fee, commission or similar consideration, as envisaged in the proviso. Such consideration is therefore in respect of the supply of a financial service which is exempt from VAT in terms of section 12(a) of the VAT Act.

If a single amount is payable to a lender and such amount constitutes both a fee or commission and a "manufactured dividend" or "manufactured interest", it is essential that, for purposes of section 10(22) of the VAT Act, the amounts attributable to the fee or commission and that attributable to the "manufactured dividend" or "manufactured interest" be indicated at the time the agreement is entered into. Failing a split into the separate elements, the full amount will be subject to VAT.

6) Uncertificated Securities Tax Act, No 31 of 1998 (UST Act)

The UST Act will come into operation on a date to be determined by the President by proclamation in the Gazette. The purpose of imposing this tax is to provide for the dematerialisation of securities listed on the JSE in a Central Securities Depository (CSD).

In terms thereof all share certificates which are deposited in the CSD will be cancelled and shareholding will be represented by entries in the accounts maintained by participants who act on behalf of the shareholders. From a tax point of view it was necessary to introduce a duty on the transfer of uncertificated securities, as the issue of securities and the transfer of beneficial and legal ownership thereof will occur without the filing of any paper.

"beneficial ownership", is defined in the UST Act as--

" in relation to a security, includes any one or more of the following:

a) the right or entitlement to receive any dividend or interest payable in respect of that security; or

b) the right to exercise or cause to be exercised in the ordinary course of events, any or all of the voting, conversion, redemption or other rights attaching to such security.".

In terms of section 6(1)(b)(iv) of the UST Act an exemption will apply to a change in beneficial ownership in securities in relation to lending arrangements:

"if the change in beneficial ownership is from a lender to a borrower, or vice versa, in terms of a lending arrangement and the lender or borrower, as the case may be, who has acquired beneficial ownership has certified to the participant that the change is in terms of such a lending arrangement".

7) Conclusion

It has come to the attention of this Office that practices have developed whereby instruments are, for example, endorsed as exempt from stamp duty, in circumstances where not all the elements of a lending arrangement as contemplated in terms of the SD Act are present. The purpose of this Practice Note is therefore to provide taxpayers with clear guidelines regarding the tax consequences of lending arrangements.

Persons who are responsible for the endorsement of these types of instruments must, therefore, ensure that all the relevant requirements have been met, in order to qualify for the relief provided for, as outlined in this Practice Note.

SARS, however, would like to emphasise that, should the relevant unacceptable practices not cease, SARS will have no alternative than to request the Minister of Finance to recommend to Parliament that the relevant relief and facilitating provisions be withdrawn.

INCOME TAX ACT TABLE OF CONTENTS

8. Certain amounts to be included in income or taxable income
8A. Gains made by directors of companies...
8E. Dividends on certain shares deemed to be interest...
9. Circumstances in which amounts deemed to have accrued...
9A. Blocked foreign funds
9B. Circumstances in which certain amounts received or accrued...
9D Net income of controlled foreign companies
9E. Taxation of foreign dividends
9F. Income from foreign sources
9G. Taxable income in respect of foreign equity instruments
10. Exemptions
10A. Exemption of capital element of purchased annuities.
11. General deductions allowed in determination of taxable income.
11bis. Marketing allowance.
11sex.Deduction of compensation for railway operating losses.
12B. Deduction in respect of certain machinery, plant, etc...
12C. Deduction in respect of certain machinery, plant, etc...
12D. Deduction in respect of certain pipelines, transmission lines and railway lines
12E. Deduction in respect of certain plant and machinery of small business corporations
12F. Deduction in respect of certain aircraft hangars, aprons. runways and taxiways
12G. Additional Industrial investment allowance in respect of industrial assets
12H. Deductions in respect of learnership agreements
13. Deductions in respect of buildings used in a process of manufacture
13bis. Deductions in respect of buildings used by hotelkeepers
13ter. Deductions in respect of residential buildings.
14. Deductions in respect of ships
14bis. Deductions in respect of aircraft.
15. Deductions from income derived from mining operations
17A. Expenditure incurred by a lessor of land...
18. Deduction in respect of medical and dental expenses.
18A. Deduction of donations to certain public benefit organisations
20. Set-off of assessed losses.
21. Deduction of alimony, allowance or maintenance.
22. Amounts... in respect of values of trading stocks.
22A. Schemes of arrangement involving trading stock.
23. Deductions not allowed in determination of taxable income.
23A. Limitation of allowances granted to lessors of certain assets
23B. Prohibition of double deductions
23C. Reduction of cost or market value of certain assets.
23D. Limitation of allowances granted in respect of certain assets.
23E. Provisions relating to leave pay.
23F. Acquisition or disposal of trading stock.
23G. Sale and leaseback arrangements.

Part I: Returns

- 65. Returns to be in form prescribed by Commissioner
- 66. Notice by Commissioner requiring returns for assessment...
- 68. Income and capital gain of married persons and minor children
- 69. Duty to furnish returns as to employees, etc...
- 70. Duty of companies to furnish returns.
- 70A. Return of information by Portfolio of Collective Investment Scheme
- 70B. Return of information in respect of financial instruments administered by portfolio ad
- 71. Return of payments in respect of bearer warrants.
- 72. Return as to shareholdings.
- 72A. Return as to participation right in controlled foreign company
- 73. Duty of persons submitting accounts in support of returns...
- 73A. Record keeping by persons deriving income other than remuneration
- 73B. Record keeping in relation to taxable capital gain or assessed capital loss
- 73C. Retention period of records where objection and appeal lodged
- 74. General provisions with regard to information, etc...
- 74A. Furnishing of information, documents... by any person
- 74B. Obtaining of information, documents... at certain premises
- 74C. Inquiry
- 74D. Search and seizure
- 75. Penalty on default
- 75A. Publication of names of Offenders
- 76. Additional tax in the event of default or omission.

Part II: Assessments

- 77. Assessments and recording thereof
- 78. Estimated assessments.
- 79. Additional assessments
- 79A. Reduced Assessments
- 79B. Withdrawel of assessments
- 80. Inspection of record of assessments.

Part III: Objections and Appeals

- 81. Objection against assessment
- 82. Burden of proof as to exemptions, deductions...
- 83. Appeals to tax court against assessment
- 83A. Appeals to tax board
- 84. Summoning of witnesses and penalty for non-attendance.
- 85. Contempt of tax court
- 86A. Appeals against decisions of a tax court
- 87. Members of courts not disqualified from adjudicating.
- 88. Payment of tax pending appeal.

Part IV: Payment and Recovery of Tax

- 89. Appointment of day for payment of tax...

South African Revenue Service

TAX RATES

Rates of normal tax payable by persons (other than companies) in respect of the years of assessment ending 28 February 2003, and by companies in respect of years of assessment ending during the period of 12 months ending 31 March 2003.

(Section 8 of Act 30 of 2002)

1) The rates of normal tax referred to in section 8 of the Revenue Laws Amendment Act, 2002 in respect of persons (other than companies) are as follows:

a) In respect of the taxable income of any person (other than a company or a person in respect of which subparagraph (b) applies), an amount of tax calculated in accordance with the table below:

Taxable Income	Rates of Tax
Where the taxable income--	
does not exceed R40 000	18 per cent of each R1 of the taxable income;
exceeds R40 000 but does not exceed R80 000	R7 200 plus 25 per cent of the amount by which the taxable income exceeds R40 000;

exceeds R80 000 but does not exceed R110 000	R17 200 plus 30 per cent of the amount by which the taxable income exceeds R80 000;
exceeds R110 000 but does not exceed R1700 000	R26 200 plus 35 per cent of the amount by which the taxable income exceeds R110 000;
exceeds R170 000 but does not exceed R240 000	R47 200 plus 38 per cent of the amount by which the taxable income exceeds R170 000;
exceeds R240 000	R73 800 plus 40 per cent of the amount by which the taxable income exceeds R240 000.

b) in respect of the taxable income of any trust (other than a special trust), an amount of 40 cents on each rand of taxable income.

2) The rates of normal tax referred to in section 8 of the Revenue Laws Amendment Act, 2002 in respect of companies are, subject to the provisions of paragraph 4, as follows:

a) On each rand of the taxable income of any company (excluding taxable income referred to in subparagraphs (b), (c), (d), (e), (f), (g) and (h)), 30 cents, or, in the case of a company which mines for gold on any gold mine and which is in terms of an option exercised by it exempt from the payment of secondary tax on companies, 38 cents;

b) in respect of the taxable income of any company which qualifies as a small business corporation as defined in section 12E of the Income Tax Act, 1962, on each rand of the taxable income as does not exceed R150 000, 15 cents, and on each rand of the taxable income of such company as exceeds R150 000, 30 cents;

c) on each rand of the taxable income of any employment company, as defined in section 12E of the Income Tax Act, 1962, 35 cents;

d) on each rand of the taxable income derived by any company from mining for gold on any gold mine (with the exclusion of so much of the taxable income as the Commissioner for the South African Revenue Service determines to be attributable to the inclusion in the gross income of any amount referred to in paragraph (j) of the definition of "gross income" in section 1 of the Income Tax Act, 1962, but after the set-off of any assessed loss in terms of section 20(1) of the Income Tax Act, 1962), a percentage determined in accordance with the formula:

$$y = 37 - \frac{185}{x}$$

or, in the case of a company which is in terms of an option exercised by it exempt from the payment of secondary tax on companies, in accordance with the formula:

$$y = 46 - \frac{230}{x}$$

in which formulae y represents such percentage and x the ratio expressed as a percentage which the taxable income so derived (with the said exclusion, but before set-off of any assessed loss or deduction which is not attributable to the mining for gold from the said mine) bears to the income so derived (with the said exclusion);

e) on each rand of the taxable income of any company, the sole or principal business of which in the Republic is, or has been, mining for gold and the determination of the taxable income of which for the period assessed does not result in an assessed loss, which the Commissioner determines to be attributable to the inclusion in its gross income of any amount referred to in paragraph (j) of the definition of "gross income" in section 1 of the Income Tax Act, 1962, a rate equal to the average rate of normal tax or 30 cents, whichever is higher: Provided that for the purposes of this subparagraph, the average rate of normal tax shall be determined by dividing the total normal tax (excluding the tax determined in accordance with this subparagraph for the period assessed) paid by the company in respect of its aggregate taxable income from mining for gold on any gold mine for the period from which that company commenced it's gold mining operations on that gold mine to the end of the period assessed, by the number of rands contained in the said aggregate taxable income;

f) on each rand of the taxable income derived by any company from carrying on long-term insurance business in respect of its individual policyholder fund, company policyholder fund and corporate fund, 30 cents;

g) on each rand of the taxable income (excluding taxable income referred to in subparagraphs (b), (c), (d), (e), (f) and (h)) derived by a company which has its place of effective management outside the Republic and which carries on a trade through a branch or agency within the Republic, 35 cents;

h) on each rand of the taxable income derived by a qualifying company as contemplated in section 37H of the Income Tax Act, 1962, subject to the provisions of the said section, zero cents:

Provided that the tax determined in accordance with any of subparagraphs (a) to (h), inclusive, shall be payable in addition to the tax determined in accordance with any other of the said subparagraphs.

3) The rates set forth in paragraphs 1 and 2 shall be the rates required to be fixed by Parliament in accordance with the provisions of section 5(2) of the Income Tax Act, 1962.

4) For the purposes of paragraph 2, income derived from mining for gold shall include any income derived from silver, osmiridium, uranium, pyrites or other minerals which may be won in the course of mining for gold, and any other income which results directly from mining for gold.

5) In this Schedule, unless the context otherwise indicates, any word or expression to which a meaning has been assigned in the Income Tax Act, 1962, bears the meaning so assigned.

STRATEGIC ECONOMIC AND BUSINESS INFORMATION

CURRENT ECONOMIC TRENDS

South Africa has a GDP of USD 126 billion with significant growth potential, enjoys easy access to other markets in Africa has sophisticated financial institutions and capital markets, a good communication infrastructure, lower labor costs than western industrialized countries and inexpensive electrical power and raw materials. Since 1994 when the first democratic elected government came into power, the country became politically stable with a more open and outwardly oriented economy. South Africa has, however, yet to develop to its full potential because of years of isolation, former inward-looking trade and investment policies and low savings and investment rates. It continues to lack skilled labor and around one quarter of the labor force is unemployed. The skills' shortage results from the inherited shortcomings of the old "apartheid" educational system as well as the escalating departure of skilled labor from South Africa to more lucrative employment opportunities abroad.

The South African government is steadily addressing the many serious challenges it is faced with, some with more success than others however. These include: the still huge income inequality between the different race groups; ever-increasing crime; job losses; poor quality schools, need for skills training as well as social services for all; HIV/AIDS; poverty; corruption and disappointing economic growth rates especially during the preceding two years.

GDP OUTLOOK

The South African economy is adjusting well to the challenges posed by a changing global economy. The foundations are being laid for improved long-term economic growth and a series of growth-oriented microeconomic reforms introduced will complement and sharpen the broader structural changes that have taken place through the economy.

Following two years of sluggish growth brought on by the emerging markets crisis, the South African economic outlook improved considerably during 2000. The percentage increase in real GDP growth improved to 3.1 percent in 2000 after 1.9 percent and 0.7 percent growth in 1999 and 1998 respectively. From 1994 to 2000, the annual average was 2.7 percent. For 2001, however, most analysts have revised their economic growth forecasts downwards to 2.8 percent because of the deceleration of world economic growth.

Sound management at the macro-economic level continued to characterize the public finances during 2000/01 and the budget deficit as a percentage of the GDP was reduced further to 2 percent. Overall there are grounds for optimism about the future prospects of the South African economy.

These include:

- The economy has been in a recovery phase of the business cycle since about the third quarter of 1999, yet it has not developed any of the usual imbalances typical of economic expansions in the past.
- Inflation has been moderate and appreciably lower than during previous recoveries (5.3 percent for 2000), as has been the growth in unit labor costs.
- The growth of asset prices is not excessive.
- The balance sheets of banks and other financial intermediaries are sound.
- The exposure of the corporate sector to external debts does not pose any serious threat.
- The financial position of the household sector is far healthier than in previous expansions and bankruptcies of individuals have fallen sharply.

• Private fixed-capital formation is rising but there is apparently no danger of creating excess capacity.
• The deficit on the current account of the balance of payments was turned into a surplus, led by an expansion in export earnings.
• The exchange rate of the Rand has fallen to a level where domestic producers can compete aggressively in export markets.

The prime-lending rate, which peaked at 25 percent in 1998, has since declined to acceptable levels. The latest reduction in June 2001 brings the rate down to 13.75 percent. As a result, private consumption, particularly of durable goods, as well as recapitalization by industry is expected to rise.

The volatility experienced in the Rand exchange rate in recent years continues. This pressure stems mainly from outflows via the financial account of the balance of payments. Although institutional foreign investment outflows have been constrained somewhat by the March 2001 foreign exchange regulations, there exists significant scope for the path of individuals to expand offshore holdings. However, the significant inflows expected from the government's privatization program until 2005 should support the currency.

3. REGIONAL ROLE.

South Africa's geographic position offers access to markets, not only throughout Africa, but also farther a field in the southern hemisphere. As a member state of the Southern African Development Community (SADC), it plays an important role in developing regional trade and cooperation and benefits from the SADC Free Trade Agreement that came into operation in September 2000.

South Africa has by far the largest economy in the region. However, South Africa's reputation as an emerging market also suffers from its proximity to the instability and conflicts that have appeared its certain northern neighbors and in and around the central African sub-region. The 2000/2001 land invasions in Zimbabwe and the resultant instability had a harmful impact on South Africa's currency and ability to attract foreign investment.

Regional stability and investment growth are priorities for the government. Together with Algeria and Nigeria, South Africa is involved in the Millennium African Recovery Program (MAP), a comprehensive plan for Africa's development. MAP document aims to create pre-conditions for sustainable development, enhance economic governance, human resource development, infrastructure provision, diversification of goods and services production, open international trade markets, increase capital flows and realign institutional arrangements.

4. PRINCIPAL GROWTH SECTORS

AGRICULTURE

Although South African agricultural production has almost doubled over the past 30 years, erratic weather has caused significant production variations from year to year. The country is self-sufficient in primary foods with the exception of wheat, oilseeds, and rice. The contribution of agriculture, fishery and forestry to value added at basic prices (total value of output less the value of intermediate consumption) increased from R20.1 billion in 1999 to about R25.4 billion in 2000, while the percentage contribution increased from 2.8 to 3.2 percent. The increase in production was mainly due to improved rainfall. However, producer prices increased by 5.1 percent compared to a 0.2 percent increase in 1999. Producer prices of field crops decreased by 6.8 percent while prices for horticultural products and animal products increased by 9.1 percent and 11.4 percent respectively.

The real contribution of agriculture to the national economy is often obscured by its nominally low direct contribution to GDP (less than 4 percent). However, if the full impact of the "agro-industrial" complex with backward and forward employment linkages and multiplier effects on the rest of the economy are included, agriculture contributes at least 15 percent to the GDP. In 2000, the gross value of agricultural production is estimated at R45 billion, an increase of 2.8 percent. Major contributing products include poultry meat production 13.9 percent, corn 12.5 percent, and cattle slaughtered 8.7 percent. Gross farm income from all products increased by 2.9 percent, while consumption expenditure on food increased by 9.6 percent to R108.7 billion.

South Africa has a market-oriented agricultural economy and is a net exporter of agricultural products. The positive agricultural balance of trade amounted R6.2 billion. Agricultural exports varied between 8 and 10 percent of total exports, while agricultural imports varied between 6 and 7 percent of total imports. The value of farm exports rose from R14.8 billion in 1999 to R15.8 billion in 2000, partly because of the devaluation of the Rand, while the value of agricultural imports increased from R9 billion in 1999 to R9.6 billion in 2000. Major products exported included sugar (R1,862 million), wine (R1,690 million), citrus fruit (R1,582 million), and grapes (R1,255 million). Rice (R939 million), wheat (R634 million), and vegetable protein meal (R485 million), were the most important imports.

The United States is a major supplier of agricultural products to South Africa, contributing 9.6 percent of its imports in 2000. In 2000, total value of U.S. agricultural exports to South Africa amounted to USD 133 million, down from USD 297 million in 1996. The decrease in U.S. exports was principally due to the decline in the value of the Rand relative to the US Dollar. The United States is a growing market for South Africa's agricultural products. In 2000, 5.8 percent of the country's agricultural exports went to the U.S. For the first time the value of agricultural exports to the U.S. was equal to the imports from the U.S. When fishery and forestry products are added, South Africa enjoyed a USD 33 million positive trade balance with the U.S.

CELLULAR TELEPHONY

Cell C was finally awarded the third cellular license in February 2001 by the Minister of Communications, Ms. Ivy Matsepe-Casaburi. The new operator is to invest some R3-billion on cellular network infrastructure. The estimated expenditure for Cell C was calculated by looking at what it takes to set up a basic network and making assumptions about how extensive its network will be. At the same time, the two cellular incumbents, MTN and Vodacom will scale back spending for the next few years, as their network infrastructure is relatively complete.

According to local telecommunications analysts, the investment by Cell C will create new opportunities, but by 2003, spending on cellular infrastructure will begin to fall. The next big boost in the cellular market will be when operators have to introduce third-generation networks to meet demand for fast and bandwidth-hungry applications such as internet access and video streaming to cell phone handsets. Telecoms consultancy group, BMI-T estimates their total investment to be anywhere between R15-billion to R30-billion.

Cell C in May 2001 began its rollout after lengthy delays caused by rival bidder Nextcom challenging the licensing process. The new operator has awarded its initial network infrastructure contracts to Siemens Telecommunications and Accenture, in deals believed to add up to approximately R2-billion.

Overall, investments in telecommunications infrastructure will grow by about 10% a year, from R15.2 billion in 2000 to R24.9 billion by 2005. Of that, R10bn-R15bn will come from investments by an as yet unlicensed second fixed-line operator. The bulk of the R15bn per annum that is presently spent on telecommunications infrastructure comes from the cellular industry. Nine out of 10 handsets sold in South Africa are cell phones as opposed to fixed-line phones.

Sales will also grow for firms supplying software such as billing systems, customer relationship management and network monitoring systems. Video conferencing will also become more ubiquitous, growing at a rate of 35% per annum, albeit it from a low base.

ELECTRONIC COMMERCE

Since the four basic requirements for electronic commerce - electricity, a telephone connection, a computer, and electronic credit – are still out of reach for the vast majority of South Africans, South Africa represents enormous medium term potential and opportunity for e-commerce. In the "first-world" component of South Africa, businesses are rapidly embracing e-commerce to compete globally, but are hampered by lack of cost-effective telecommunications infrastructure (due to parastatal Telkom's monopoly, which is hoped to end in the4th quarter 2001) and a severe shortage of skilled IT professionals. The skills shortage is being addressed to a certain extent by companies creating training centers in various universities and technikons in order to ensure their own growth, but at present demand is still far ahead of supply.

COMPUTER SOFTWARE AND SERVICES.

The local computer software and services market has shown strong growth over the past few years, and to date those IT companies focused in promising sectors has rewarded investors. From high margin businesses such as networking and systems integration to lower margin businesses such as hardware distribution, there are many opportunities in the local software and services market for companies with the right management approach. Key trends in this market include:

- Electronic Commerce
- Internet-oriented software and services
- Convergence of technologies
- Increased focus on outsourcing

The convergence of technology and specifically the conversions of voice-to-text and vice-versa on advanced platforms are crucial for future growth. More and more demand will be placed on integrating voice into an IT solution. Demand for networking products as well as highly specialized software will enable communications and value-added services on all communications platforms. Value-added software is a key to long-term growth.

Software retail growth in South Africa, which has been consistently higher than the world average over the past several years, is expected to continue showing substantial growth for the foreseeable future. South Africa is however of course not immune to the IT gloom affecting the world economy at present.

(ECO-) TOURISM

Tourism in South Africa is a fast-growing industry, annually contributing between USD 3 to 4 billion to the economy. The drop in the value of the South African currency over recent years has made tourism for visitors from places such as the UK, Europe and the US very economical. The number of travelers arriving to South Africa has grown steadily from 5.2 million in 1996 to an estimate of 6 million in 2000. From January to June 2000, a total of 3 million foreign tourists arrived in South Africa. During this 6 months South Africa attracted 173,821 visitors from the UK, 96,721 from Germany and 85,478 from the US.

Tourism has a great potential to create jobs in South Africa. The total number of employment opportunities sustained by tourism amounted to 574,236 during 2000. Between 1994 and 2000, the growth rate in tourism employment was an average of 7 percent per year.

The tourism accommodation industry in South Africa provides a wide spectrum of lodgings – from the formal hotel sector to the informal holiday flats and cottages, game lodges and reserves, guest-houses, youth hostels, and bed-and-breakfast inns. Of the estimated 30,000 rooms available in South Africa's hotels, about 46 percent are categorized as "not graded" while about 20 percent are graded "four-star" or better. The lack of five star accommodation, particularly on Durban beaches (situated in the KwaZulu-Natal province), has been an obstacle for tour operators looking for business in up-market areas. A number of major development opportunities exist, with projects already under development and further sites already identified as prospective locations for the development of tourism infrastructure. For U.S. exports, key sectors identified as having the greatest commercial potential include information systems, marketing, design, architecture, finance and planning. The lack of local expertise in areas ranging from management skills to education and training creates an excellent opportunity for U.S. firms. Opportunities for U.S. investment may also exist in making tourist facilities accessible to the disabled.

The SA Government has introduced a policy of commercialization and privatization of certain of its National Parks to allow the private sector into that market. Furthermore the scope of government incentives schemes, announced during 2001, was extended to also include the tourism industry. The state-owned Industrial Development Corporation (IDC) has also prioritized tourism and increasingly provides the industry with financial assistance for medium to large commercial projects.

The fastest growing segment of tourism in South Africa is ecological tourism (eco-tourism), which encompasses fauna to flora, action holidays and, increasingly, local community empowerment and development. Linked to sound environmental management, growth in eco-tourism allows South Africa to make the most of its unique environmental heritage that contributes to sustainable socio-economic development and quality of life. South Africa's first three declared World Heritage Sites highlight the relationship and interdependence of tourism growth with the protection and conservation of the environment. These sites – Robben Island, the Greater St Lucia Wetland Park and Sterkfontein Caves -- reflect South Africa's rich cultural and natural heritage and are major tourism attractions. Their new status has benefited local communities who participate in the resulting economic expansion.

SECURITY AND SAFETY EQUIPMENT.

With the increasing loss of cars due to theft and hijacking, a great need exists for vehicle security systems. Bank robberies persist, albeit with reduced frequency. Another major source of concern has been heists on cash-in-transit vehicles by highly organized and heavily armed groups. As a consequence of the amount of criminal activity, there continues to be a strong demand in South Africa for security and self-defense related products and services. For example, large retailers are beginning to take pilferage very seriously and are installing substantial surveillance systems in their shop fronts. CCTV is ideal for this purpose, being accepted as evidence in court.

The commercial and industrial security industry in South Africa is valued at approximately USD 1.8 billion. Of this aggregate value, the most promising sub-sectors include:

- Vehicle security (car alarms, anti-carjacking devices and satellite tracking systems) - USD 417 million
- Perimeter security and access control (e.g., fencing, wire, and security gates) - USD 154 million

- Detection devices and building protection (e.g., close circuit TV and security glass) - USD 149 million
- Internal physical security and turnkey systems (e.g., security doors and computer based microprocessor systems) - USD 96 million

Chemical Industry

The South African chemical industry is driven by the relatively large South African home market that accounts in many instances for the bulk of sub-Saharan African consumption. Some 2,300 chemical operations in South Africa focus predominantly on basic upstream chemical manufacturing and downstream formulation and polymer conversion. Current South African market prospects are positive and stand to provide impetus for further imports. The chemical and related industry is import-oriented, with export levels approximately half of import levels. In chemicals alone the trade deficit is R9 billion, 57% of which pertains to downstream fine chemicals. The total import of chemical products in 2000 estimated at R25 billion, consists of chemicals (87%), plastic products (8%) and rubber products (9%). A significant level of chemical goods are imported for use in sectors outside the chemical industry, including sectors such as leather processing textiles, glass manufacturing, mining, pulp and paper.

Chemical imports where no local supply capacity exists include:
Bauxite
Nylons
Terephthalic Acid
Isocyanates tdi, mdi
Polyurethanes
Polyacrylamides
Acrylic acid testers
Styrene
Polystyrene
ABS resins
Ethylene Glycol
Butadiene
Propylene Oxide
Propylene Glycol

A significant portion of the balance of basic chemical imports is for aromatic organic chemicals such as terephthalic acid. Other prospects in the chemical industry include bio-technology where current industry activities are restricted to lysine, enzymes and vaccines production.

The major sources of imported chemicals are the USA, UK, Germany, Australia, Switzerland, Netherlands, Belgium, France, Italy and Japan. South Africa is also well positioned to also enable the exports of chemicals to major regional destinations that include Zimbabwe, Zambia, Kenya, Mozambique and Angola.

Mining and Minerals

Minerals have played a major role in the creation of wealth and the industrialization and economic development of the country. The mines generated employment for an untrained labor force, earned export revenues, and attracted foreign investment, skills and technology. The mining industry was and remains market-oriented, almost exclusively in the hands of the private sector, and a major contributor to the economy.

Mining's direct contribution appears to have declined as the SA economy has grown and diversified. However, much of the growth in manufacturing and chemicals has been mineral-based as local processing increased. Prior to 1991, gold dominated the industry's total sales and export earnings. Since then, the contributions from other mining, the ferrous and steel industry and (in 2000) the Platinum Group Metals (PGMs) have exceeded gold's contribution with coal and coal-petrochemicals and plastics rapidly reducing the gap.

Mining's direct contribution to the GDP has declined fairly steadily from the high of 22 percent in 1980 (with a gold price of USD800 per ounce) to 6.5 percent in 2000. However, estimates show that the additional contributions from processed mineral products plus the associated multiplier effects would add another 20-25 percent to this, giving a mineral-related GDP contribution of more than 26 percent.

Mining directly contributes some 9 percent to the Gross Domestic Fixed Investment (GDFI) and this will increase significantly if all the identified projects are implemented - R70 billion over the next five years, excluding energy and oil and gas projects plus R20-30 billion for pipelines. In 2000, 78 percent of primary mineral sales revenues came from exports, which accounted for 47 percent of total exports. This increases to 59 percent when taking account of both primary and beneficiated mineral exports, but not including manufactured products such as catalytic converters (15 percent of world supply), automobiles and stainless steel bulk containers of which SA is the world's largest producer.

Direct employment in the industry currently accounts for 3-4 percent of the total workforce, and has declined by more than 50 percent over the past decade and by 15 percent since 1998, most of this in the gold mines. This, together with an increase in the proportion of skilled workers and mechanization has improved productivity, significantly increased real average wages per worker, and reduced costs and consequently the ability to mine lower grade ores.

South Africa's mineral wealth is found in diverse geological formations, some of which are unique in size and quality by world standards. These include deposits containing metals and industrial minerals such as gold, platinum group metals (PGMs), coal, diamonds, manganese, chromium, vanadium, titanium, phosphates, iron, zirconium, zinc, aluminum-silicates, uranium, vermiculite, asbestos and fluorspar, to name but a few. Overall, SA produces over 60 different mineral commodities of which 78 percent are exported. The size of many of the deposits can be gauged by the fact that after more than a 100 years of mining, SA still has very large reserves and resources of most of these minerals.

World-class and competitive industries, infrastructure, technologies and skills have been developed and built on the availability and development needs of these huge resources. These include: transportation and water infrastructure; coal-based electrical network that accounts for more than half the continent's power; synthetic fuels and petrochemical products also produced from coal; ferroalloys of manganese, chrome, vanadium and silicon; carbon-, alloy-, ultra-thin and stainless steels; fertilizers; titanium powders and pigments; refined precious and base metals of gold, PGMs, copper, zinc, nickel and others; aluminum smelters using imported alumina; and others. And around these has grown a major export industry.

The restructuring and globalization of the minerals industry continued during 2000/01 with De Beers being bought out for USD 19-20 billion, forming a strategic alliance with LVMH, the French luxury goods company, for the marketing of diamond jewelry. This buy-out done in part to solving Anglo's evaluation and rating problems on the London Securities Exchange.

In view of the importance of minerals to the economy, the SAG has recently promulgated a new draft Minerals Bill that will give the State exclusive custodianship of all mineral rights. The stated objective of this bill is to open up dormant resources to international mining and to create opportunities for the small mining sector and black empowerment groups previously excluded from the industry. Final details on the bill are still being negotiated.

SA is a relatively mature mining country and new green-field deposits may not be as easily found as in other parts of Africa. However, South Africa's infrastructure, large known reserves of a variety of minerals and sophisticated minerals-based industries provide numerous opportunities for investment in, and development of value-added and manufactured mineral products, particularly for the export market. SA also provides a convenient and secure stepping-stone to the mineral opportunities in the countries of the SADC region.

SPATIAL DEVELOPMENT INITIATIVES (SDIS).

SDIs are strategically located development regions aimed at unlocking the economic potential in selected areas. A single SDI may offer, among others, opportunities in construction, tourism, agriculture, and manufacturing. Because the initiatives are multifaceted they are implemented through consortia. The SDI program consists of ten local SDIs and four Industrial Development Zones (IDZs) at varying stages of development. The initiatives should provide U.S. companies with infrastructure, technological and investment opportunities. The aims of spatial development initiatives include:

- Facilitate sustainable and equitable growth and development
- Generate sustainable employment
- Maximize private sector investment
- Exploit South Africa's under-used locational and economic advantages

General information on SDIs and links to the individual project initiatives can be found on the Internet please see www.dti.gov.za

MAJOR TRENDS

With the peaceful democratic elections and smooth transition to majority rule in 1994, South Africa embarked on a structural transformation of its economy aimed at redressing racial inequalities and fostering long-term, outward-oriented growth. The country has a fair-sized domestic market of USD 133.4 billion (1998) with significant growth potential and is increasingly becoming free-market oriented. It enjoys easy access to other markets in Africa and has well-developed financial institutions and capital markets, a good communication infrastructure, lower labor costs compared to western industrialized countries and inexpensive electrical power and raw materials. It has, however, yet to develop to its full potential because of years of isolation, former inward-looking trade and investment policies, low savings rate and a largely unskilled labor force with attendant low productivity.

President Thabo Mbeki has repeatedly stressed his determination to meet the challenges facing the South African economy, particularly fighting crime and corruption; creating jobs; providing education, training, housing, and health care – including confronting the scourge of HIV/AIDS; stimulating growth in the economy; and alleviating poverty. South Africa continues to lack skilled labor, not only in professional fields relating to the sciences, medicine, technology and mathematics, but also in practical technical fields. This skills' shortage results from the inherited shortcomings of the educational system as well as the departure of skilled labor from South Africa to more lucrative employment opportunities abroad.

The South African government is addressing these problems through a number of policies, including the "Growth, Employment and Redistribution" (GEAR) macroeconomic policy, based on sound economic principles, which have earned international praise. The policy calls for foreign as well as domestic investment, privatization of government-owned enterprises and the restructuring of industry along globally competitive lines.

South Africa's proactive quest for foreign investment is a key part of its GEAR macroeconomic policy. In his July 1999 "State of the Nation" speech, newly inaugurated President Thabo Mbeki announced his plan for creating a prestigious International Investment Council which would include leading players in the global economy to ensure South Africa's attractiveness as a destination for foreign investment. Business has reacted positively to Minister of Trade and Industry Alec Erwin's April 1999 announcement of a new phase of the Department of Trade and Industry's (DTI) investment promotion campaign, which includes a late September 1999 roadshow to New York City and Los Angeles. Minister Erwin identified auto components, chemicals, electronics, information technology, pharmaceuticals, telecommunications and tourism as priority areas for attracting U.S. investment into South Africa.

Progress on privatization has been slower than expected, delayed by the government's strong desire to achieve consensus among business, government and labor in order to sustain the momentum of reform. South Africa has taken a number of steps to make its economy more open and attractive to global business including: reducing import tariffs and subsidies to local firms; eliminating the discriminatory non-resident shareholders tax; removing certain limits on hard currency repatriation; reducing the secondary tax on corporate dividends; lowering the corporate tax rate on earnings to 30 percent; and reducing tariff rates (although South Africa's tariff system remains complex and subject to rapid change).

As part of the opening of its economy, South Africa is working to develop and strengthen its trading relations with the world. In one such step on March 24, 1999 the South African Cabinet, the European Council of Ministers and the European Commission approved and endorsed the South Africa/European Union Trade, Development, and Cooperation Agreement. The EU and South Africa are expected to ratify the Agreement in time for implementation on January 1, 2000.

One of the provisions of the SA-EU Agreement is for a Free Trade Area (FTA). Under the FTA provision the EU is committed to the full liberalization of 95 percent of South African imports over a 10-year transitional period, while South Africa is to liberalize 86 percent of EU imports over a 12-year transitional period. Further, duty-free South African goods entering the EU are to increase by twenty percentage points over the next ten years. Many goods, especially agricultural goods, are currently subject to EU quotas that will be increased under the FTA.

GDP OUTLOOK AND REGIONAL ROLE

South Africa's economic growth has been sluggish at 2.5 percent in 1997 and 0.5 percent in 1998. The decline was largely due to the Asian crisis, the delayed effects of South Africa's economic isolation during the Apartheid era and very high real positive interest rates. The fall in 1999 of the gold price to its lowest level in 20 years and low commodity prices in general brought on by the global economic slow-down have also had a clearly negative effect on the country. In July of 1999, the SA Rand was at 6.0 to the US Dollar.

Recent positive economic indicators include the substantial drop in key interest rates and the stabilization of the Rand, the South African currency. Inflation, which was in double digits for nearly twenty years, has been reduced to around 7% and the fiscal deficit to about 3 percent of gross domestic product (GDP). New South African government figures also indicate that the economy is more heavily weighted toward the service sector than previously thought, with primary and secondary sectors comprising only 34.5 percent total GDP, while the tertiary (services) sector comprises 65.5 percent.

A recent Reuters poll shows economists believe that South Africa's economy will be characterized by improving growth, stable inflation, a steady exchange rate and lower interest rates. They believe that South Africa has now emerged from the 1998 emerging financial market crisis, and will start to benefit from a return of foreign capital to lift growth this year and next year. The poll of 30 South African and European economists forecasts growth in 1999 at 0.9 percent and at 3.0 percent in 2000. Steep cuts in interest rates are predicted to free up consumer spending, which has been tied with rates that peaked at 25.5 percent in 1998, dropping to 16.5 percent by August 1999.

2.1 Regional Role. While South Africa's reputation as an emerging market suffers from its proximity to the tangle of conflicts that have engulfed its northern neighbors in and around the central African sub-region, its geographic position offers access to markets not only throughout Africa but also farther afield in the southern hemisphere.

The Southern African Development Community (SADC) was founded in 1980 is the most important regional organization in the continent. South Africa has been a member of SADC since 1994 and chairs the organization until September 1999. The SADC is a sub-regional organization created from the South African Development Coordinating Conference (SADCC) in 1980. The organization seeks to foster economic growth and development through increased economic integration among its 14 member states with approximately 180-million inhabitants: Angola, Botswana, Lesotho, Malawi, Mozambique, Namibia, South Africa, Swaziland, Zambia and Zimbabwe Mauritius and Tanzania, the Democratic Republic of Congo (former Zaire), and the Seychelles. These countries range from some of the poorest in the world, like Mozambique to the power-house of Africa - South Africa. Angola and Mozambique should be among Africa's wealthiest countries, but they have been devastated by war.

The SADC Trade Protocol is the cornerstone of SADC's sub-regional trade integration effort. On August 24, 1996 eleven SADC member states signed the SADC Trade Protocol, and to date Botswana, Mauritius, Namibia, Tanzania and Zimbabwe have ratified it. South African officials made a detailed proposal to their SADC counterparts indicating they are prepared to take steps toward ratification. At present there are intense discussions on the tariff reduction schedule and the rules of origin. Insufficient analytical capacity, perceptions of uneven benefits, non-tariff trade barriers and the absence of agreement on customs procedures and standards have slowed the implementation process. Nonetheless, there remains optimism that the SADC Free Trade Area (FTA) will come into effect in early 2004.

South Africa has been a member of the South African Customs Union (SACU) since its inception in 1910. The SACU agreement was renegotiated in 1969 following the independence of Botswana, Swaziland, and Lesotho. Namibia joined SACU in 1990.

SACU aims to promote free trade and cooperation on customs matters among its five member states. There are presently no internal tariff barriers between SACU member states, but because of different tax regimes, there are some tax adjustments that occur at the borders. All SACU members, except Botswana, share a common currency as members of the Common Monetary Area.

PRINCIPAL GROWTH SECTORS

3.1 Agriculture. For South Africa's farmers, 1998 was slightly less prosperous than 1997, although the historical trend in output was not down significantly (agriculture's economic performance in both 1996 and 1997 was above average). The contribution of agriculture to GDP increased from R23.8 billion in 1997 to R24.0 billion in 1998, although the percentage contribution decreased from about 4.5 percent to 4.1 percent in 1998. The main reason for the decrease in agricultural production during 1998 was dry and hot conditions with below average rainfall during the first half of the year. During the year, the estimated volume of agricultural production fell 4.8 percent below 1997 with the volume of field crop production (grains and oilseeds) declining by 13 percent as a result of the drought.

The real contribution of the agricultural sector to the national economy is often obscured by its nominally low direct contribution to GDP (less than 5 percent) and employment (about 13 percent). However, if the full impact of income and employment linkages and multipliers are included, agriculture contributes about 12 percent to GDP, and 30 percent to employment. About two-thirds of agricultural output is used as intermediate inputs in the manufacturing sector. This fact is borne out by the large impact of drought on GDP; more severe droughts have caused a decline in total GDP of as much as 0.5 to 2 percent, a high figure for a sector playing a relatively small role in the economy.

South Africa has a market-oriented agricultural economy, with significant volumes of both agricultural imports and exports. The decline in the value of the South African Rand relative to the dollar over the last two years has had a beneficial effect on the country's agricultural export earnings. Exports rose to R13.4 billion in 1998 compared to about R12.3 billion in 1997. Principal exports in 1998 included fresh and processed fruits and vegetables worth about R4.4 billion and sugar worth about R1.7 billion. Agricultural exports contributed more than 30 percent of the gross value of agricultural production in 1998 while imports were equal to about 21 percent of the value of output..

The United States plays a major role in the South African agricultural market, supplying 11.5 percent of imports and taking 4.5 percent of the country's exports. Total U.S. agricultural exports to South Africa climbed to $296 million in 1996, but fell back to $195 million in 1998, mainly due to the decline in the value of the Rand. As of July 1999, the SA Rand was at 6.0 to the US Dollar.

3.2 Air Pollution and Waste Management. South Africa's reintegration into the global economy necessitates improved pollution and waste management systems. Also, beginning with the country's first democratic elections, South Africa's role and influence in the Southern African Development Community (SADC) suggests that it should take the lead in promoting clear air and waste management technology within southern Africa. Key issues include water, air and land pollution, and poor disposal of waste. The potential air pollution resulting from industrial parks and residential areas has to date not been adequately considered during the planning stages of many initiatives. Moreover, control equipment is poorly maintained and often non-operational.

With knowledge of the potential hazards of pollution, a growing need exists for measurement and analysis instruments - specifically for instruments that are able to measure a number of parameters simultaneously and handle a number of observations over time. There is also a need in the market place for American "know-how"; the expertise which goes along with such products.

(For further information, refer to Air Pollution and Waste Management, under Leading Sectors for US Exports and Investment: Best Prospects for Non-Agricultural Goods and Services, page 35)

3.3 Cellular Telephony. The explosive growth of South Africa's cellular industry continued to outpace industry forecasts during the year under review. The industry has two principal operators, Vodacom and MTN, with licensing for a third mobile cellular operator scheduled for early next year. The Vodacom Group, in which Telkom has a 50 percent equity stake, saw its customer base climbing to two million by the end of 1998, of which 1.5 million were active subscribers, representing an increase of some 50 percent. Turnover rose by 56 percent to R6.8 billion from the previous year's R4.4 billion, while operating profit stood at R1.5 billion. Based on call traffic volumes, the regional distribution of users are 29 percent in Gauteng (the Johannesburg and Vereeniging area excluding Pretoria), 24 percent in Pretoria, Northern Province and Mpumalanga, 19 percent in the Western Cape, 4 percent in the Free State and Northern Cape, 7 percent in Eastern Cape and 17 percent in KwaZulu-Natal.

The Vodacom Board approved a capital expenditure program of R 2.5 billion for the year, an investment that was entirely self-funded. Included in the program were 100 micro-base stations, six voicemail platforms and two additional Intelligent Network platforms. Network expansion is ongoing and expenditure is expected to exceed R 2.3 billion in the coming financial year.

Another milestone for Vodacom was its entry into the Internet market with the launch of Vodacom Internet Company, its new Internet Service Provider (ISP), and Yebo!Net, which offers prepaid access to the Internet at local Telkom rates.

MTN (Mobile Telephone Networks), a privately-held company with shareholders in South Africa (a 25 % shareholder being Transtel, a parastatal South African organization and subsidiary of Transnet) and the United Kingdom, was recently awarded a second network operator's license in Uganda and a first operator's license in Rwanda. It is currently bidding for licenses in several other sub-Saharan countries. MTN's strategy in these countries is one of alliance-building to promote local job creation, entrepreneurship, skill-training, empowerment and enhanced socio-economic integration.

As the only telecommunications company in the southern hemisphere and one of only three in the world to have been awarded ISO 9001 quality accreditation, MTN has been approached by Visa Mastercard, Verifone and First National Bank to be the network carrier for the pilot project for retailer on-line verification. This will allow on-line retail point-of-sale transactions to be done without a phone line, thus opening up additional opportunities for rural areas.

MTN's coverage presently extends to over 34 percent of South Africa's geographical area. MTN had installed of over 6,500 of MTN's community payphones by December 1997 – well in excess of the numbers agreed to in terms of license obligations.

Potential investors and operators have thus far supported the South African government's efforts to create a favorable investment environment. In particular the low cost of market entry has been seen as a golden opportunity. Cellular networks can currently operate at a maximum speed of 9.6 kilobits per second (kbps). MTN recently carried out tests in conjunction with Ericsson (cellphone manufacturer) where speeds of up to 56kbps were achieved. Once speed of two to three gigabits (gbps) is reached, there is no reason why South Africa should be dependent on fixed lines for carrying voice or data. MTN predicts that speeds ranging from 28 to 56 kbps will become a commercial reality within the next 18 months, and that within three to five years this will be increased to speeds of 2 to 3 gbps. Increased speed across the networks will encourage the use of cellular telephony for data communications, which currently account for less than 2 percent of cellular usage. Moreover, once network speeds increase, opportunities will exist for carrying video to the cellular handset with video capability over the Internet using Internet protocol, the telephone network, or satellite infrastructure.

3.4 Computer Software and Services. The local computer software and services market has shown strong growth over the past few years, and to date investors have been rewarded by those IT companies focused in promising sectors. From high margin businesses such as networking and systems integration to lower margin businesses such as hardware distribution, there are many opportunities in the local software and services market for companies with the right management approach. Key trends in this market include:

- Electronic Commerce
- Internet-oriented software and services
- Convergence of technologies
- Increased focus on outsourcing

The convergence of technology and specifically the conversions of voice-to-text and vice-versa on advanced platforms are crucial for future growth. More and more demand will be placed on integrating voice into an IT solution. Demand for networking products as well as highly specialized software will enable communications and value-added services on all communications platforms. Value-added software is a key to long-term growth.

Software growth in South Africa, which has been consistently higher than the world average over the past several years, is expected to show substantial growth for the next two to three years.

(For further information, refer to Computer Software and Services, under Leading Sectors for US Exports and Investment: Best Prospects for Non-Agricultural Goods and Services, page 35)

3.5 (Eco) Tourism. With its return to the "global village," South Africa is fast becoming a popular tourist destination. In a recent report, the World Tourism Organization (WTO) ranked South Africa as the 25th most frequented tourist destination in 1998, a significant move upward from the 1990 ranking at 50th. The most recent figures on tourism illustrate that the number of travelers arriving to South Africa has grown steadily grown from 5.2 million in 1996, to 5.4 million in 1997, and 5.7 million in 1998. September was the most popular month for foreign arrivals in 1998. The number of Americans arriving to South Africa increased 16 percent between 1997 and 1998, and at 166,071 arrivals, American visitors represent the third largest overseas market after the U.K. (321,281) and Germany (195,878).

The number of American visitors is expected to continue rising through the year 2000 as a result of two agreements recently signed between the U.S. and South Africa. The first of these, a bilateral tourism initiative to promote co-operation in the tourism sector, was signed in mid-1995. In addition, the U.S. and South Africa signed a Civil Aviation Agreement that increased the number of weekly direct flights between the U.S. and South Africa from 7 to 11, effective 1 April 1996. This number will increase annually to 21 per week by 1 April 2000.

The tourism accommodation industry in South Africa provides a wide spectrum of lodgings – from the formal hotel sector to the informal holiday flats and cottages, game lodges and reserves, guest-houses, youth hostels, and bed-and-breakfast inns. Of the estimated 30,000 rooms available in South Africa's hotels, about 46 percent are categorized as "not graded"; 5 percent as "one and two-star"; 31 percent as "three-star"; 13 percent as "four-star"; and 5 percent as "five-star." The lack of five star accommodation, particularly on Durban beaches (situated in the KwaZulu-Natal province) has been an obstacle for tour operators looking for business in up-market areas. To improve the area's tourism potential, KwaZulu-Natal authorities have established a Tourism Authority, which is also empowered to engage in joint ventures with private enterprise. A number of major development opportunities exist, with projects already under development and further sites already identified as prospective locations for the development of tourism infrastructure.

The fastest growing segment of tourism in South Africa is ecological tourism (ecotourism), which encompasses fauna to flora, action holidays and, increasingly, local community empowerment and development. For U.S. exports, key sectors identified as having the greatest commercial potential include information systems, marketing, design, architecture, finance and planning - particularly with respect to the long-term development of the Kwa-Zulu Natal and the Western Cape as a tourist destination. The lack of local expertise in these areas creates an excellent opportunity for U.S. firms in fields ranging from management skills to education and training. Additional opportunities for U.S. investment may also exist in making tourist facilities accessible to the disabled.

3.6 Electronic Commerce. Over the next few years, electronic commerce or e-commerce (which encompasses all business conducted by means of computer networks), is likely to radically transform the way most South Africans do business. It reflects a paradigm shift driven principally by a wide range of converging technological developments and the emergence of the "knowledge economy." There are already a growing number of South African companies actively conducting electronic business via the Internet. The value of business conducted electronically has consistently increased on a month-by-month basis, with the overall transactional value growth of 140 percent over the past twelve months.

For developing countries like South Africa, e-commerce presents important new opportunities to achieve a more level playing field vis-à-vis larger, more developed economies; it reduces existing drawbacks relating to cost, communication, and information, and has the potential to create huge new markets for U.S. products and services. One of the leading areas for continued growth is Internet security. Merchants and consumers who regularly engage in online trade are expressing growing concerns over security infrastructures on the Internet, and are demanding more secure session technology to guarantee the confidentiality of data exchanged during online transactions. Other promising areas include new technologies and business development concepts in e-commerce.

(For further information, refer to Electronic Commerce, under Leading Sectors for US Exports and Investment: Best Prospects for Non-Agricultural Goods and Services, page 35)

3.7 Mining. The mining industry has played a significant role in the economic development of South Africa. In terms of the world's mineral reserves' base, South Africa ranks number one for gold, platinum, manganese, chromium, vanadium, alumino-sillicates and titanium, second for vermiculite and zirconium, third for fluorspar, fourth for antimony, and fifth for zinc, coal, lead and uranium. While the reserve base for diamonds is not known, South Africa ranks second or third in terms of the value of current global diamond exports. In total the country produces some sixty mineral commodities of which gold, platinum group metals (PGM) coal and ferro-alloy account for 86 % of mineral exports and some 50 % of total merchandized exports. During the past decade South Africa's mining sector has undergone a major transformation. The gold mines in particular have seen costs increase significantly while both the tonnage and grades of ore produced have declined.

The result has been the restructuring of a number of mining companies, for example Anglogold, Goldfields and Billiton. Thus far, the declining SA Rand-Dollar exchange rate, together with increased sales of PMGs, iron ore, copper, nickel and zinc as well as diamonds and coal have partially offset the declining export earnings of the gold sector. Improving economic conditions in many parts of the world however, including Japan's industrial production, should eventually flow through to mining. Thomas MacNamara, representing New York investment firm CIBC Oppenheimer, suggests that fundamental demand for gold continues to grow, while the world's central banks are not likely to sell as much of their gold reserves as previously believed.

In recent years, the coal sector has also seen significant expansion in terms of export earnings. However, intense competition in key markets and global oversupply of sea borne steam coal have been two factors contributing to downward pressure on spot and forward coal prices. At the same time the emerging markets financial crisis has led to reduced industrial output and hence a decreased demand for energy, resulting in a decline in the demand for coal.

Importantly, a number of resource-based mega-projects (e.g., Columbus Stainless Steel and Billiton's Hillside Aluminum Smelter) have allowed South Africa to move beyond exporting primary commodities to become a world-class exporter of processed industrial minerals. New investments in a small number of resource-based projects have accounted for almost half of recorded formal sector economic growth since 1994. Such investments are largely a consequence of increased investor confidence in the country's long-term political stability, and enabled South Africa to cross an important threshold in 1995 when for the first time exports of processed primary products exceeded gold exports. Looking forward, a host of natural resource and metals projects offer the potential for sustained industrial growth in the coming years.

Recognizing this potential, South Africa's industrialization program focuses heavily on resource-based manufacturing and processing to stimulate growth – especially in the minerals processing, petrochemicals, jewelry, and metal fabrication industries. This will, however, require massive investment and continued access to foreign markets. Competition for market share has increased at the same time that commodity prices have fallen and demand in East Asian countries has generally decreased. The key to the industry's survival lies in improved productivity which can be achieved, in part, through greater education, training, and motivation of the workforce.

Although the mining industry's contribution to the South African economy has declined since the early 1970's, it remains a substantial contributor both in terms of foreign exchange earnings and GDP. In 1998, the mining industry contributed 6.03 percent to GDP, or approximately 13 percent if indirect multiplier effects associated with the industry's effect on the economy are included. While the relative importance of gold mining has declined over the last decade in line with fluctuations in the gold price, gold mining still contributes a little more than 2 percent to GDP. Observers calculate that the mining industry contributes more than 50 % to South Africa's merchandized exports; this excludes the domestically generated beneficiation of these resources. With this value-added component, the contribution to exports could be as high as 70%.

For the year under review, mining also continued to contribute significantly to gross domestic fixed investment (GDFI) and gross capital formation, contributing 8.6 percent to GDFI. The industry also contributed significantly to the national fiscus, both directly and indirectly. For the fiscal year 1998/99, estimated total direct taxation paid by the industry was some R1.7 billion, representing 1 percent of total tax revenue. Mining also contributes indirectly through taxation paid by employees and by industries that supply the mining industry or use mining industry products and through indirect taxes paid by mines on input costs (such as the fuel levy).

3.8 Security and Safety Equipment. With the increasing loss of cars due to theft and hijacking, a great need exists for vehicle security products. Bank robberies persist, albeit with less frequency. Another major source of concern has been the heists on cash-in-transit vehicles by highly organized and heavily armed groups. As a consequence of the amount of criminal activity, there continues to be a strong demand in South Africa for security and self-defense related products and services. For example, large retailers are beginning to take pilferage very seriously and are installing substantial surveillance systems in their shop fronts. CCTV is ideal for this purpose, particularly because it produces concrete evidence in court.

The commercial and industrial security industry in South Africa is valued at approximately USD 1.8 billion Dollars. Of this aggregate value, the most promising sub-sectors include:
- Vehicle security (car alarms, anti-carjacking devices and satellite tracking systems) - USD 417 million
- Perimeter security and access control (e.g., fencing, wire, and security gates) - USD 154 million
- Detection devices and building protection (e.g., close circuit t.v. and security glass) - USD 149 million
- Internal physical security and turnkey systems (e.g., security doors and computer based microprocessor systems) - USD 96 million

(For further information, refer to Security and Safety Equipment, under Leading Sectors for US Exports and Investment: Best Prospects for Non-Agricultural Goods and Services, page 35)

3.9 Spatial Development Initiatives (SDIs). SDIs are strategically located development regions aimed at unlocking the economic potential in selected areas. A single SDI may offer, among others, opportunities in construction, tourism, agriculture, and manufacturing. Because the initiatives are multifaceted they are implemented through consortia. The SDI program consists of ten local SDIs and four Industrial Development Zones (IDZs) at varying stages of development. To date, the current portfolio of SDIs has identified 518 investment opportunities valued at approximately R115.4 billion (USD 19.2 billion) with the capacity to generate more than 118,000 new jobs. The initiatives are the practical implementation of the government's economic strategy as set out in its GEAR policy framework, and should provide U.S. companies with infrastructure, technological and investment opportunities. Former South African President Nelson Mandela likened the SDI program to an industrial revolution, stating the ultimate vision was to open the entire South African market through public-private partnerships. The aims of spatial development initiatives include:
- Facilitate sustainable and equitable growth and development
- Generate sustainable employment
- Maximize private sector investment
- Exploit South Africa's under-utilized locational and economic advantages

General information on SDIs and links to the individual project initiatives can be found on the Internet at www.sdi.org.za or at www.transport.gov.za/projects/sdi.html. Brief descriptions of the major SDIs are below.

3.9.1 The Lubombo Initiative. The Lubombo Initiative is a concerted program by the governments of Swaziland, Mozambique, and South Africa to ensure that new investment occurs rapidly in the area. An essential infrastructure project is the upgrade of secondary roads and construction of a tar road through the SDI to link the major South African coastal road, the N2, to Maputo, the capital of Mozambique. Tourism anchor projects being proposed are the Ponta to Puro-Kosi Bay and Futi/Tembe/Usuthu transnational tourism nodes, the Greater St. Lucia Wetland Park, a tourism cluster at Lake Sibayi, an integrated Mlawula-Hlane wildlife project, the Lavumisa-Pongola Trans-Frontier Complex and the Lubombo tourism train route. In all 694 projects have been identified to the estimated value of R148 billion in the tourism, education, craft, commercial and agriculture sectors, including substantial opportunities for communities and small businesses.

3.9.2 West Coast Initiative. The West Coast Investment Initiative is focused on the opportunities created by the mini mill of Saldanha Steel as well as under utilized opportunities in agriculture, tourism, manufacturing and fishing in the region. This initiative opens a window of opportunity to potential investors in an area with a significant resource base, and adequate and improving infrastructure. In addition, an investor friendly package of incentives and institutional arrangements is in place to enhance innovative and sound investments. One hundred and twenty investment projects were launched at the investment conference held in Saldanha Bay on the West Coast from 25 to 27 February 1998.

Additional information can be found on the Internet at www.westcoast.org.za. Also see Appendix H.

The Fish River Initiative. The Fish River initiative has evolved to promote employment in the Port Elizabeth and East London parts of the Eastern Cape. The primary focus of the Fish River SDI is on "crowding in" new investment from the private sector. Sectors under consideration include the automobile industry, supplier development, agro processing and forestry. The Fish River Initiative offers exciting opportunities for investors and has been designed to provide local entrepreneurs, international and national investors and fledgling businesses with a broad range of investment options.

The Maputo Corridor. The Maputo Corridor, a development axis between Johannesburg and the city and port of Maputo, Mozambique, has seen considerable success since its launch in 1998 and is the most widely known development initiative. There has been a continual process of identifying investment opportunities in the following sectors: infrastructure, agriculture, mining, energy, chemicals, tourism and manufacturing. There are currently 180 projects under consideration with a total value estimated at approximately R42 billion (USD 7 billion).

Wild Coast Initiative. The Wild Coast is a stretch of approximately 280 kilometers (174 miles) situated between the Mtamvuna River in the north and the Great Kei River in the south. The lull of perfect beaches attracts the majority of visitors to the resorts along the coastline, and the Wild Coast Initiative builds on this attraction through agri-tourism projects. Forestry and agriculture projects are also in development.

Rustenburg (Platinum) Initiative. The Platinum SDI forms part of the Coast2Coast SDI that links Maputo Port in Mozambique to Walvis Bay in Namibia. Most of the Platinum SDI falls inside South Africa's North West Province, with direct links to import tourism, industrial and agriculture processing activities in the North West Province, and to the Mabopane-Centurion Development Corridor around Pretoria. The region has a wealth of raw materials, which can be used in processing and manufacturing industries. It also has tremendous potential to develop a tourist industry considering its existing tourism infrastructure and attractions, including big five nature reserves. An appraisal of the economic potential of this area has identified approximately 200 potential projects and project opportunities in tourism, manufacturing, agriculture and mining.

The Platinum SDI management team will provide additional information upon request.

Rustenburg (Platinum) SDI Project Manager
Mr. Rekwele Mmatli
Tel: (27 11) 313-3331
Fax: (27 11) 313-3000

Phalaborwa SDI. The Phalaborwa Initiative, broadly covering the Northern Province and Mpumalanga, is in the process of identifying and preparing attractive projects and investment opportunities in agriculture, forestry, tourism, mining, and mineral processing. The region is a significant supplier and processor of wood fiber in South Africa and internationally; it also includes a wide range of tourist attractions centered primarily in and adjacent to the famous Kruger National Park. The Phalaborwa SDI is linked to Maputo Development Corridor, and therefore has access to Maputo and international markets.

The Phalaborwa SDI management team will provide additional information upon request.

Phalaborwa SDI Project Manager
Mr. Jurgens van Zyl
Tel: (27 11) 313-3518
Fax: (27 11) 313-3086

Richards Bay Initiative. The Richards Bay Investment Center officially opened its doors in October 1998 to assist companies that want to establish a presence in the region. Industrial projects identified by the Industrial Development Corporation include opportunities in aluminum, heavy minerals, chemicals, wood, and sugar clusters. Tourism is also expected to become a key industry for the region. Richards Bay acts as a gateway to the Lubombo region, and the harbor is within a 45 minute drive of "big five" game viewing opportunities.

KwaZulu-Natal SDI. One of nine provinces of South Africa, KwaZulu-Natal stretches over 57,000 square miles on South Africa's eastern seaboard. KwaZulu-Natal is a competitive region for the attraction of foreign investment and nine target areas have been identified for this purpose. These areas include: textiles, clothing, plastic products, chemicals, fabricated metal products, automotive components, wood and wood products, footwear, machinery and appliances. During the three-year period ending March 1998, 47 foreign companies established operations in the region, primarily in four sectors: textiles, clothing and leather (38.3%), chemicals and plastics (21.3%), fabricated metal products and machinery (19.2%) and paper and paper products (17.0%).

Additional information can be found on the Internet at www.kmi.co.za.

GOVERNMENT ROLE IN THE ECONOMY

South Africa under the former Nationalist Party government pursued a strategy of import substitution and industrial development which protected local industries by means of high tariff barriers and heavy state involvement in electrical, transportation, communications and service industries. In 1994, the ANC inherited an economy in which roughly half of all capital assets were owned by the government, a quarter of which were parastatal corporations.

A key element of GEAR is the "restructuring of state assets." In 1995, under a "National Framework Agreement" (NFA), tripartite stakeholders from government, business, and labor agreed to a substantial program of restructuring and privatization of state assets. President Mbeki has repeatedly reaffirmed the South African government's commitment to the privatization program. Partial or complete privatization of several parastatals has been completed, including: The Airports Company, (an umbrella company for the country's major airports); six radio stations of the South African Broadcasting Corporation (SABC); Sun Air (a small former homeland airline); and Telkom (the national telecommunications company). South Africa's most recent privatization was the June 25, 1999 sale of 20 percent of South African Airways (SAA) to Swissair for USD 230 million. The sale puts the total value of the airline at USD 1.2 billion, making the deal South Africa's second-largest privatization effort. The South African government has indicated that as much as 40 percent of SAA could be in private hands by the end of 1999.

In his June 1999 "State of the Nation" speech, President Mbeki stated "some of the most important developments with regard to the restructuring of state assets will relate to Transnet" (the transportation parastatal). According to President Mbeki, "the priority given to this corporation arises from the fact that the transport and logistic system it contains underpins the success of other major investment projects." Priority will also be given to the liquid fuels and petrochemical industry through a joint effort of the Ministries of Minerals and Energy, Trade and Industry, and Public Enterprises. This effort will include the finalization of discussions with the Government of Mozambique on a gas pipeline that is to run from Mozambican gas fields to South Africa. Mbeki also noted that there would be further developments with the issuing of new licenses in the telecommunications sector.

Although present government policy is to refrain from competing with private entities in the private sector, the following firms enjoy a degree of protection through direct or indirect allowances from the government which give them a financial advantage vis-à-vis private entrants: ADE (diesel engines); SASOL (synthetic fuels and petrochemicals); IDC (industrial development corporation); CSIR (scientific and industrial research and marketing innovations); and the Central Energy Fund family of companies, including Mossgas, the Strategic Fuel Fund, and Soekor, the state oil exploration company. In addition, Telkom (the state telecommunications company) enjoys a monopoly until the year 2002 on providing international and fixed line telecommunications services. If Telkom's strategic equity partners meet certain performance targets, the South African government will consider an extension of this monopoly until 2003. Transnet enjoys a monopoly on most transport and port services and Eskom (the state electricity monopoly) operates as a non-taxed company, which pays dividends to the state as its sole shareholder.

BALANCE OF PAYMENTS SITUATION

Decreased demand in the South African economy contributed to a reversal of the deficit on the current account of the balance of payments into a surplus of R2.0 billion in the first quarter of 1999. At a seasonal adjusted annualized rate, the surplus in the first quarter is equal to 0.8% of GDP. The improvement came largely from a substantial decline in the value of merchandise goods imported and an equally substantial increase in the value of merchandise exports. The decline in the exchange value of the Rand also assisted in creating the surplus (see Appendix C 2). The value of South Africa's net gold exports however declined due to a lower volume of exports as well as lower realized prices.

The slowdown of financial flows to emerging market economies was echoed in a contraction of financial flows to South Africa during 1998. Foreign direct investment in South African assets declined sharply – from R17.6 billion in 1997 to R3.1 billion in 1998. The outflow of capital arising from acquisitions of foreign direct investment assets by South African entities maintained a steady flow from R10.8 billion in 1997 and R9.6 billion in 1998. The inflow of capital resulting from portfolio investment by non-residents has varied since early 1998 with an inflow of R26.5 billion in the first quarter of 1998, followed by an outflow of R1.1 billion in the third quarter, and then inflows of R2.5 billion and R10.9 billion in the fourth quarter of 1998 and first quarter of 1999. The variety of these demonstrates flow reflect the liquidity of the South African markets.

The fourth and first quarter inflows reflect continued confidence by short-term foreign investors in the South African economy. This was echoed by the recent U.S. Duff and Phelps credit rating for South Africa, which maintained the country's long-term foreign currency and Rand debt ratings at BBB- and A- respectively. The rating was largely based on Duff and Phelps' positive view of the South African government's macroeconomic framework including its fiscal consolidation, flexible monetary policy and external liberalization.
U.S. trade with South Africa totaled USD 4.67 billion in total (two-way) goods trade during 1998.

U.S. exports to South Africa increased by 49% over the years from 1992 to 1998. Imports from South Africa have risen 77% over the last six years.

INFRASTRUCTURE

International Trade Infrastructure. The exploitation of natural resources over the past century has created a transportation infrastructure in South Africa that dominates the subcontinent. South Africa provides more tonnage through its ports than the combined facilities of Angola, Gabon, Kenya, Mozambique, Tanzania, and the Democratic Republic of Congo; and more air transport than all other countries of Southern, Central and East Africa combined. South Africa's international trade infrastructure is relatively well-developed, while in the context of the developing world it ranks as excellent. However, a 1996 analysis conducted by the Department of Transport identified the following problem in terms of international transport:

- With the exception of world-class bulk transport systems in two key corridors, freight transport in general does not meet the needs of customers in terms of both cost and service.

The last few years have seen significant steps to enhance the effectiveness of South Africa's physical and service infrastructure. Trade support services such as cargo inspection, standards information and certification, and credit insurance have been improved, and the country's major ports (Durban, Cape Town, Richards Bay, and Port Elizabeth) are well-equipped to move cargo of all types.

Infrastructure in Rural Areas. The quality of infrastructure in the rural areas and the former homelands (the geographic ethnic-statehoods created and imposed by the previous National Party government) varies, and most townships (urban and peri-urban residential areas of mostly economic and sub-economic housing inhabited by the Black populace) remain in need of road development and improvement. The South African government continues to look for projects in the framework of its Spatial Development Initiatives Program (SDIs), in urban and rural centers, and in partnership with other countries in the region in order to improve infrastructure. The government is also working to shift the weight of funding in public transport in favor of public transportation infrastructure, and is providing support to provincial Roads Departments to assist them in restructuring and rationalizing infrastructure delivery institutions. This support is intended to ensure that the level of expenditure on overhead is reduced in favor of expenditure targeted at the provision of new road infrastructure (particularly in rural areas), as well as to the rehabilitation and ongoing maintenance of existing provincial roads.

Transnet. The government department, South African Transport Services, was restructured into a public company (with share capital controlled by the Minister for Public Enterprises) in 1989, and became Transnet in 1990. Transnet's position as a profit-seeking, commercialized company, migrating towards a holding company over the next five to seven years, allows the company to pursue initiatives such as joint ventures and private/public sector partnerships as well as maintain competitiveness in a global business environment. Transnet's transport holdings include: Spoornet (rail), Portnet (ports), Metrorail (rail), Autonet (roads), Fastforward (trucking), Petronet (pipelines), and South African Airways (SAA), each of which operates as a separate company. The next few years may continue to see a restructuring in Transnet as the company aims to secure private capital and reduce state debt. Transnet reported a R426 million loss for the year to March compared with the R278 million profit previously and has been identified by President Mbeki and Public Enterprises Minister Jeff Radebe as a "key priorty." Already the partial privatization of Spoornet has opened the opportunity for private rail companies to gain concession for operating lines. Also, several private sector companies provide trucking services, and recently a number of private airlines have begun to provide services which compete with those offered by the government owned SAA. The successful restructuring of Transnet is expected to generate business opportunities in the following areas:

- Stand-alone Core Business
- New Business Opportunities
- Strategic Business Development (national/international)
- Black Empowerment
- Logistics

SUPPLEMENTS

SELECTED GOVERNMENT CONTACTS

FINANCE

Internet: http://www.gov.za/ministry/finance.htm

Mail Private Bag X115 PRETORIA 0001	**Street** 240 Vermeulen Street 26th Floor cor Andries and Vermeulen Streets PRETORIA	**Tel:** (012) 323 8911 **Fax:** (012) 323 3262
Mail PO Box 29 CAPE TOWN 8000	**Street** 120 Plein Street Room 309 CAPE TOWN	**Tel:** (021) 464 6100 **Fax:** (021) 461 2934

Media Liaison Officer
Ms Pippa Green
Cellphone: 082 854 3716

Administrative Secretary
Ms Patti Smith
Tel: (012) 315 5372 or (021) 464 6102
Cellphone: 083 375 8486
E-mail: SmithP@finance.pwv.gov.za

PROVINCIAL AND LOCAL GOVERNMENT*

Minister
Mr FS Mufamadi (ANC)
Internet: http://www.gov.za/ministry/province.htm

Mail Private Bag X802 PRETORIA 0001	Street 87 Hamilton Street S Floor Arcadia PRETORIA	Tel: (012) 334 0705 Fax: (012) 326 4478
Mail Private Bag X9123 CAPE TOWN 8000	**Street** 120 Plein Street Room 1113 CAPE TOWN	**Tel:** (021) 462 1441 **Fax:** (021) 461 0851

Media Liaison Officer
Mr Andre Martin
Tel: (012) 334 0681
Cellphone: 082 465 6166
E-mail: andre@dso.pwv.gov.za

Private Secretary
Ms Nomsa Maphisa
Cellphone: 082 497 3808

PUBLIC ENTERPRISES *

Minister
Mr JT Radebe (ANC)
Internet: http://www.gov.za/ministry/enterprises.htm

Mail Private Bag X15 HATFIELD 0028	Street Infotech Building Suite 401 1090 Arcadia Street Hatfield PRETORIA	Tel: (012) 342 7111 Fax: (012) 342 7224
Mail Private Bag X9079 CAPE TOWN 8000	**Street** 120 Plein Street 16th Floor Room 1618 CAPE TOWN	**Tel:** (021) 461 6376/7/8/9 **Fax:** (021) 465 2381 / 461 1741

Director : Public Relations
Mr Zaid Nordien
Fax: (012) 342 7226
Cellphone: 082 453 6224
E-mail: znordien@anc.org.za

Private Secretary
Mr Lucky Montana

Fax: (012) 342 7226
Cellphone: 082 771 4698

PUBLIC SERVICE AND ADMINISTRATION *

Minister
Ms GJ Fraser-Moleketi (ANC)
Internet: http://www.gov.za/ministry/pubserv.htm

Mail Private Bag X884 PRETORIA 0001	**Street** Transvaal House 22nd Floor cor Vermeulen and van der Walt Streets PRETORIA	**Tel:** (012) 314 7911 **Fax:** (012) 328 6529
Mail Private Bag X9148 CAPE TOWN 8000	**Street** 120 Plein Street 13th Floor Room 1318 CAPE TOWN	**Tel:** (021) 465 5491/2/3 **Fax:** (021) 465 5484

Head: Ministerial Services
Dr Gonda Perez
Tel: (012) 314 7438
Fax: (012) 328 6565
Cellphone: 082 807 6811

Private Secretary
Ms Florance Maleka
Tel: (012) 314 7201 or (021) 461 6679
Fax: (012) 461 4445
Cellphone: 082 808 5620
E-mail: FloranceM@dpsa.pwv.gov.za

TRADE AND INDUSTRY *

Minister
Mr A Erwin (ANC)
Internet: http://www.gov.za/ministry/trade.htm

Mail Private Bag X274 PRETORIA 0001	**Street** House of Trade and Industry 11th Floor Prinsloo Street PRETORIA	**Tel:** (012) 322 7677/8/9 **Fax:** (012) 322 7851
Mail Private Bag X9047 CAPE TOWN	**Street** 120 Plein Street 6th Floor, Room 618	**Tel:** (021) 461 7191/2/3 **Fax:** (021) 465 1291

8000	CAPE TOWN	

Media Liaison Officer
Mr Edwin Smith
Tel: (012) 310 1376
Cellphone: 082 783 6025

Secretary
Mr Cobs Pillay
Tel: (012) 310 1371/2
Cellphone: 082 558 7074
E-mail: cobs@dti.pwv.gov.za

TRANSPORT *

Minister
MR AM Omar (ANC)
Internet: http://www.gov.za/ministry/transport.htm

Mail Private Bag X193 PRETORIA 0001	**Street** Forum Building Room 4111 cor Struben and Bosman Streets PRETORIA	**Tel:** (012) 309 3131 **Fax:** (012) 328 3194
Mail Private Bag X9129 CAPE TOWN 8000	**Street** 120 Plein Street 13th Floor Room 1339 CAPE TOWN	**Tel:** (021) 465 7260-4 **Fax:** (021) 461 6845

Media Liaison Officer
Mr Mike Mabasa (Acting)
Cellphone: 083 680 7048
E-mail: mike@ndot.pwv.gov.za

Private Secretary
Ms Sunita Dalla
Cellphone: 082 806 0728
E-mail: sunita@ndot.pwv.gov.za

TAX GUIDE FOR

SMALL BUSINESSES

2006/07

SARS
At Your Service

www.sars.gov.za

CONTENTS

1. OVERVIEW

This guide contains information about the tax laws and some other statutory obligations that apply to small businesses. It describes some of the forms of business organisations in South Africa – sole proprietorship, partnership, close corporation and a private company – and explains in general terms the tax responsibilities of each.

This edition also contains general information, such as the type of business organisation, registration, aspects of record keeping, relief measures for small business corporations, manufacturing enterprises, how net profit/loss and taxable income/assessed loss are determined. This helps to illustrate the specific tax considerations for the different types of business organisations. Furthermore, it contains information on some of the other taxes you may have to pay in addition to income tax.

The information in this publication applies to different kinds of businesses and is of a general nature. Specific types of businesses are not discussed such as insurance companies, banks and investment companies. However, the requirements of the tax laws regarding registration, filing of tax forms, etc. also apply to them.

1.1 Glossary

Act	:	Income Tax Act, No 58 of 1962
CGT	:	Capital Gains Tax
Commissioner	:	Commissioner for the South African Revenue Service
ITAC	:	International Trade Administration Commission
PAYE	:	Pay-As-You-Earn (Employees' Tax)
RBT	:	Residence Basis of Taxation
RSA	:	Republic of South Africa
SARS	:	South African Revenue Service
SBCs	:	Small Business Corporations
SDL	:	Skills Development Levy
SMMEs	:	Small, Medium and Micro Enterprises
STC	:	Secondary Tax on Companies
TCC	:	Tax Clearance Certificate
UIC	:	Unemployment Insurance Contributions
UST	:	Uncertificated Securities Tax
VAT Act	:	Value-Added Tax Act, No. 89 of 1991
VAT	:	Value-Added Tax

Important Note: Tax Amnesty for Small Businesses

The Minister of Finance announced in the 2006 Budget that Government will introduce a tax amnesty for small businesses.

For more information see page 25 in this Guide under the heading: Tax Amnesty for Small Businesses.

2. GENERAL CHARACTERISTICS OF DIFFERENT TYPES OF BUSINESSES

2.1 Introduction

Once you have decided to start a business, you must also decide (which will be your own choice entirely) what type of business entity to use. There are legal, tax and other considerations that can influence this decision. The legal and other considerations are beyond the scope of this guide while the tax consequences of conducting business through each type of entity will be an important element in making your decision.

The purpose of this guide is not to advise you on the type of business vehicle through which to conduct your business, but to provide entrepreneurs with information to assist them to make their own informed decisions when starting a business.

- Sole Proprietorship

A sole proprietorship is a business that is owned / operated by one person. This is the simplest form of business organisation. The business has no existence (therefore not a legal person such as a company) separate from the owner who is called the proprietor. The owner must include the income from such business in his/her own income tax return and is responsible for the payment of taxes thereon. Only the proprietor has the authority to make decisions for the business. The proprietor assumes the risks of the business to the extent of all of his or her assets whether used in the business or not.

Some advantages of a sole proprietorship are:

- It is simple to establish and operate.
- The owner is free to make decisions.
- It has a minimum of legal requirements.
- The owner receives all the profits.
- It is easy to discontinue the business.

Some disadvantages of a sole proprietorship are:

- Unlimited liability of the owner. The individual owner is legally liable for all the debts of the business. Not only the investment or business property, but any personal and fixed property may be attached by creditors.
- Limited ability to raise capital. The business capital is limited to whatever the owner can personally secure. This limits the expansion of a business when new capital is required. A common cause of failure of this form of business organisation is lack of funds. This restricts the ability of a sole proprietor to operate the business effectively and survive at an initial low profit level, or to get through an economic "rough spot".
- Limited skills. One individual alone has limited skills, although the owner may be able to hire employees with sought after skills.

- Partnership

A partnership (or unincorporated joint venture) is the relationship existing between two or more persons who join together to carry on a trade, business or profession. A partnership is also not a separate legal person/taxpayer. Each partner is taxed on his/her share of the partnership profits. Each person may contribute money, property, labour or skills, and each expects to share in the profits and losses of the business. It is similar to a sole proprietorship except that a group of owners replaces the individual owner. The number of persons who may form a partnership agreement is limited to twenty. As is the case for a sole proprietorship the partnership has advantages and disadvantages.

Some advantages of a partnership are:

- It is easy to establish and operate.
- It has greater financial strength.
- It combines the different skills of the partners.
- Each partner has a personal interest in the business.

Some disadvantages of a partnership are:

- Unlimited liability of the partners. Each partner may be held liable for all the debts of the business. Therefore, one partner not exercising sound judgment could cause the loss of the assets of the partnership as well as the personal assets of all the partners.
- The authority for decision-making is shared and differences of opinion could slow the process down.
- It is not a legal entity.
- Lesser degree of business continuity as the partnership technically dissolves every time a partner joins or leaves the partnership.
- Number of partners restricted to 20, except in the case of certain professional partnerships such as accountants, attorneys, etc.

- **Close Corporation**

A close corporation is similar to a private company. It is a legal entity with its own legal personality and perpetual succession and must register as a taxpayer in its own right. The owners of the close corporation are the members. Members do not hold shares but have a membership interest in the close corporation. This interest is expressed as a percentage. A close corporation has no share capital and therefore no shareholders. Membership, generally speaking, is restricted to natural persons or (from 11 January 2006) a trustee of an inter vivos trust or testamentary trust as contemplated in section 29(1A) or 29(2)(b) of the Close Corporation Act No. 69 of 1984. A close corporation may not have an interest in another close corporation. The minimum number of members is one and the maximum number of members is ten. For tax purposes, a close corporation is dealt with as if it were a company.

Some advantages of a close corporation are:

- It is relatively easy to establish and operate.
- The life of the business is perpetual (i.e. continues uninterrupted as members change).
- The members have limited liability, i.e. they are generally not liable for the debt of the close corporation. However, it should be noted that certain tax liabilities do exist. One such instance is where an employer / vendor is a close corporation, every member and person who performs functions similar to a director of a company, who controls or is regularly involved in the management of the company's overall financial affairs will be personally liable for the employees' tax, value-added tax, additional tax, penalty or interest for which the company is liable, i.e. where these taxes have not been paid to SARS within the prescribed period.
- The transfer of ownership is easy.
- Fewer legal requirements than a private company.

Some disadvantages of a close corporation are:

- Number of members restricted to a maximum of ten.
- More legal requirements than a sole proprietorship or partnership.

- Private Company

A company is treated by law as a separate legal entity and must also register as a taxpayer in its own right. It has a life separate from its owners with rights and duties of its own. The owners of a private company are the shareholders. The managers of a private company may or may not be shareholders. A company may not have an interest in a close corporation. The maximum number of shareholders is restricted to fifty.

Some advantages of a private company are:

- The life of the business is perpetual (i.e. it continues uninterrupted as shareholders change).
- The shareholders have limited liability, i.e. they are generally not responsible for the liabilities of the company. However, it should be noted that certain tax liabilities do exist. One such instance is where an employer / vendor is a company, every shareholder and director who controls or is regularly involved in the management of the company's overall financial affairs shall be personally liable for the employees' tax, value-added tax, additional tax, penalty or interest for which the company is liable, i.e. where the taxes have not been paid to SARS within the prescribed period.
- The Companies Act, No 61 of 1973 imposes personal liability on directors where in common law such liability may not exist, or be difficult to prove. Any person, not only a director, who is knowingly a party to the carrying on of a business in a reckless (gross carelessness or gross negligence) or fraudulent manner can be personally liable for all or any of the debts of the company.
- The transfer of ownership is easy.
- It is easier to raise capital and to expand.
- Efficiency of management is maintained.
- It is adaptable to both small and medium to large business.

Some disadvantages of a private company are:

- It is subject to many legal requirements.
- It is more difficult and expensive to establish and operate than other forms of ownership.

- Other types of business entities as described in the Act

  - Personal Service Company and Personal Service Trust

  A personal service company or personal service trust is any company or trust (other than a labour broker) where services are rendered on behalf of that company or trust to a client of that company or trust personally by any person who is a connected person[1] in relation to that company or trust, and –

  o that connected person would be regarded as an employee of that client if that service was rendered by that connected person directly to the client; or

[1] A connected person generally means –

- in the case of a natural person, a relative of a natural person, any trust of which a natural person is a beneficiary;
- in the case of a trust, a beneficiary of a trust and any relative in relation to such beneficiary;
- in the case of a company, the holding company, subsidiaries, any other company where both such companies are subsidiaries of the same holding company and any person other than a company who individually or jointly with any other connected person in relation to him/herself holds directly or indirectly at least 20 per cent of the company's equity share capital or voting rights.

For the complete definition of a connected person, see section 1 of the Act.

- o that connected person or that company or trust is subject to the control or supervision of that client as to the manner in which or the hours during which the duties are performed in rendering that service; or
- o the amounts paid or payable in respect of that service consist of or include earnings which are payable at regular intervals, daily, weekly, monthly or other intervals; or
- o more than 80% on the income of that company or trust consists of amounts directly or indirectly received from one client.

Where the company or trust employs more than three full-time employees throughout the year of assessment who are engaged in the business of the company or trust, it will not be classified as a personal service company/personal service trust.
Furthermore, the employee may not be a connected person in relation to the company or trust for the year of assessment.

Payments made to personal service companies and personal service trusts are subject to the deduction of employees' tax.

For further information, refer to the *EMP 10 – volume 47 – Guidelines for Employers*, on the SARS website.

– Labour Broker

A labour broker is any person who carries on the business, for reward, of providing clients with persons to render a service to such clients for which such persons are remunerated.

Employers are required to deduct employees' tax from all payments made to a labour broker, unless the labour broker is in possession of a valid exemption certificate from SARS.

An exemption certificate will be issued by SARS under the following circumstances if -
- o the person carries on an independent trade and is registered as a provisional taxpayer;
- o the labour broker is registered as an employer; and
- o all returns required by the Commissioner, have been submitted.

The Commissioner will not issue an exemption certificate if -
- o more than 80% of the gross income of the labour broker during the year of assessment consists of amounts received from any one client of the labour broker. However, if the labour broker has employed more than three full-time employees throughout the year of assessment who are on a full time basis engaged in the business of the labour broker, a certificate may be issued. These employees may, however, not be connected persons in relation to the labour broker; or
- o the labour broker provides to any of its clients the services of another labour broker; or
- o the labour broker is contractually obliged to provide a specified employee of the labour broker to the client.

Persons who render services to or on behalf of a labour broker without an exemption certificate are also subject to the deduction of employees' tax.

A labour broker that is a company without an exemption certificate and a personal service company cannot be a small business corporation.

For further information, refer to the *EMP 10 – volume 47 – Guidelines for Employers*, on the SARS website.

Note: Limitation of Deductions

The deduction of expenses incurred by the personal service company, personal service trust or labour broker without an exemption certificate is limited to the amounts paid to the employees of such personal service company/trust or labour broker for services rendered that will comprise taxable income in the hands of those employees.

– Independent Contractor

The concept of an independent trader or independent contractor remains one of the more contentious features of the Fourth Schedule to the Act.

An amount paid or payable for services rendered or to be rendered by a person in the course of a trade carried on by him or her independently of the person by whom the amount is paid or payable is excluded from remuneration for employees' tax purposes.

However, a person is deemed not to be carrying on a trade independently if –

- he or she is subject to control or supervision as to the manner in which his or her duties are performed or as to his or her hours of work; or
- the amounts paid or payable for his or her services are payable at regular daily, weekly, monthly or other intervals.

An amount paid to a person who is deemed not to carry on a trade independently will constitute "remuneration" and will be liable to the deduction of employees' tax.

For a detailed and thorough explanation on Independent Contractors, refer to Interpretation Note No. 17, which is available on the SARS website. Also refer to the *EMP 10 – volume 47 – Guidelines for Employers,* on the SARS website.

- Small, Medium and Micro Enterprises (SMMEs)

Information on SMMEs, details of various assistance schemes, rebates, incentives and information such as how to start a business, type of business entities and requirements of registration of a business entity may be obtained from the Department of Trade and Industry or on their website www.dti.gov.za.

3. YOUR BUSINESS AND SARS

3.1 Introduction

Now that you are starting a business, it will be helpful if you have a general understanding of the various activities of SARS, as well as your duties and obligations in terms of the tax laws.

The tax laws are administered by the Commissioner, acting through SARS offices situated in various centres throughout the country.

SARS is obligated by law to determine and collect from each taxpayer only the correct amount of tax that is due to the Government. The SARS offices are the representatives of the Commissioner and in that capacity must ensure that the tax laws are administered correctly and fairly so that no one is favoured or prejudiced above the rest.

3.2 Income Tax

- General

  Income tax is the State's main source of income and is levied on taxable income determined in terms of the Act.

- Registration

  As soon as you commence business (whether as a sole proprietor, partner or any other form), you are required to register with your local SARS office in order to obtain an income tax reference number. You must register within 60 days after you have commenced business by completing an IT 77 form, which can be obtained from your local SARS office or from the SARS website.

  If you start your business *via* a close corporation (CC) or private company you must register with the Registrar of Close Corporations or Companies to obtain a business reference number. Your CC or company will then be registered automatically as a taxpayer. If you do not hear from SARS after registering with the Registrar contact your SARS office.

  Depending on other factors such as turnover, payroll amounts, whether you are involved in imports and exports, etc. you could also be liable to register for other taxes and duties such as VAT, PAYE, Customs, Excise, SDL and UIC.

- Filing

  Income tax returns are issued annually to registered taxpayers after the end of each tax year. The tax year for individuals covers a period of 12 months and commences on 1 March of a specific year and ends on the last day of February of the following year. However, in some circumstances you may be allowed to draw up your financial statements for your business to dates other than the end of February. For more details take note of Interpretation Note 19: *Year of Assessment: Accounts Accepted to a Date Other than the Last Day of February*, which is available on the SARS website: www.sars.gov.za.

  A company/close corporation on the other hand is permitted to have a tax year ending on a date that coincides with its financial year. If the financial year-end is 30 June, its tax year or year of assessment will run from 1 July to 30 June.

Income tax returns must be submitted by a specific date each year.

If you are unable to render the return within the prescribed period, you must apply for an extension at your local SARS office. Online applications for extensions can also be made on the SARS website, under e-Commerce / Extensions.

- Change of address

The Act requires that if a person's address which is normally used by the Commissioner for any correspondence with that person changes, the person must, within 60 days after the change, notify SARS of the new address for correspondence.

- e-Filing

The primary objective of e-Filing is to facilitate the electronic submission of tax returns and payments by taxpayers. Currently e-filing makes provision for VAT 201 returns, PAYE / SDL / UIC returns (EMP 201), and provisional tax returns (IRP 6).

With effect 1 June 2006 individual taxpayers who earn a basic salary and allowances such as travel and are in receipt of IT 12S or IT 12SS returns can also submit their annual tax returns through the electronic submission facility. The following should, however, be noted:

- SARS will under certain circumstances still require the submission of original documents for purposes of verification
- SARS will do extensive validation checks on the data submitted to ensure its accuracy, including validations against the electronic IRP5's submitted by employers to SARS
- Taxpayers must retain all supporting documents for a period of five years should they be required by SARS for audit purposes
- SARS will issue these assessments electronically

e-Filing also makes provision for the e-stamp initiative and the electronic transfer duty system. The e-filing service will in time be expanded to include the following:

- Tax on retirement funds
- Secondary tax on companies
- Air passenger departure tax
- Applications for tax clearance certificates for tenders.

In order to expedite the awarding of tenders and reduce the incidence of fraudulent certificates, the tax clearance system will allow government procurement officers access to the tax status of applicants that have given consent to such access.

e-Filing also makes provision for tax directives and secure internet payment facilities.
e-Filing is now being offered free-of-charge and if more details are required, visit the e-filing website at www.sarsefiling.gov.za.

- Payments at Banks

  Payment of taxes can be made via the First National Bank, ABSA, Nedbank and Standard Bank internet facilities. Over the counter payment of taxes can also be done at First National Bank, ABSA and Nedbank. Standard Bank is currently in the process of finalising their over the counter payment facility.

  Taxes that are covered by this medium are as follows: VAT, STC, Assessed Tax, PAYE, Provisional Tax, Tax on Retirement Funds, SDL, Customs, and Air Passenger Departure Tax. If more details are required, visit the SARS website at www.commerce.sars.gov.za.

  This initiative is in line with SARS' continued efforts to improve its services to all taxpayers and traders.

- Provisional Tax

  As soon as you commence business, you will also be required to register with your local SARS office as a provisional taxpayer. Close corporations and companies are automatically registered as provisional taxpayers. The payment of provisional tax is intended to assist taxpayers in meeting their tax liabilities. This occurs by the payment of two instalments in respect of income received or accrued during the relevant tax year and an optional third payment after the end of the tax year, thus obviating, as far as possible, the need to make provision for a single substantial tax payment on assessment after the end of the tax year. The first provisional tax payment must be made six months after the commencement of the tax year and the second payment not later than the last day of the tax year. The third or topping up payment is voluntary and may be made within six months after the end of the tax year if your accounts close on a date other than the last day of February. If your tax year ends on the last day of February, the third payment must be made within seven months after the end of the tax year. Further information regarding the payment of provisional tax, can be found in the *Guide for Provisional Taxpayers*, (IRP 12), obtainable from your local SARS office and which is also available on the SARS website, under PAYE/Guidelines/Income Tax Tables.

- Employees' Tax (PAYE)

  Employees' tax is a system in terms of which an employer, as an agent of government, deducts tax from the earnings of employees and pays it over to SARS on a monthly basis. This tax serves as a tax credit that is set-off against the final tax liability of an employee, which is determined on an annual basis. A business that pays salaries, wages and other remuneration to any of its employees that is above the tax thresholds (where liability for tax arises, namely R40 000 for individuals under 65 years and R65 000 for individuals 65 years and older), must register with SARS for employees' tax purposes. This is done by completing an EMP 101 form and submitting it to SARS. The EMP 101 is available at all SARS offices and on the SARS website, www.sars.gov.za under "PAYE". Once registered, the employer will receive a monthly return (EMP 201) that must be completed and submitted together with the deducted employees' tax within seven days of the month following the month for which the tax was withheld.

  Further information can be found in the *EMP 10 – volume 47 - Guidelines for Employers*, which is sent to all registered employers and is also available on the SARS website under "PAYE".

- **Directors' Remuneration**

  The remuneration of directors of private companies (including individuals in close corporations performing similar functions) is subject to employees' tax.

  The remuneration of private company directors is often only finally determined late in the year of assessment or in the following year. The directors in these circumstances finance their living expenditure out of their loan accounts until the remuneration is determined. To overcome the problem of no monthly remuneration being payable from which tax can be withheld, a formula is used to determine deemed monthly remuneration upon which the company must pay employees' tax on behalf of the director. More information on the application of the formula and relief from hardship is available in Interpretation Note 5: *Employees' Tax – Directors of Private Companies.*

  A director is not entitled to receive an employees' tax certificate (IRP 5) in respect of the amount of employees' tax paid by the company on the deemed remuneration if the company has not recovered the employees' tax from the director.

- **How to determine net profit or loss**

  In order to prepare your income tax return, you will need to understand the basic steps for determining your business's profit or loss. This procedure is fairly simple and is much the same for each type of business organisation. Basically, profit or loss is determined as follows:

  Income – Expenses = Profit (Loss)
  You will use this formula with some slight changes in determining your profit or loss. The diagram "Comparative Profit or Loss Statements" below explains the determination of profit or loss and the distribution of income for the different types of business organisations.

  Gross sales
  Gross sales are the income a business receives. For example, ABC Furniture Store sold R1 000 000 worth of furniture. Therefore, ABC Furniture Store had gross sales of R1 000 000.

  Cost of sales
  Cost of goods sold or cost of sales is the cost to the business to buy or make the product that is sold to the consumer. It would be simple to determine the cost of sales if you sold all your merchandise during the year. However, this seldom happens. Some of your sales during the year will probably be from stock that was bought in the previous year and some of the goods that were bought in the current year are not sold at the end of that year. To determine the cost of sales under these circumstances, you add the cost of goods bought during the current year to the cost of your stock on hand at the beginning of the year. From this total you subtract the cost of your stock on hand at the end of the year. For example, ABC Furniture Store had R120 000 worth of furniture in the store at the beginning of the year. During the current year R730 000 worth of furniture was bought from a manufacturer. At the end of the current year the store had R150 000 worth of furniture left. The cost of goods sold for the current year would therefore be:

Opening stock + Purchases – Closing stock = Cost of sales
R120 000 + R730 000 – R150 000 = R700 000

<u>Gross profit</u>

Gross profit equals gross sales less the cost of goods sold. ABC Furniture Store had gross sales of R1 000 000. The cost to the store for the furniture sold was R700 000. The gross profit is therefore R300 000 (R1 000 000 – R700 000).

<u>Business expenses</u>

Business expenses or operating expenses are the ordinary and necessary expenses incurred in the operation of the business. ABC Furniture Store incurred R200 000 expenses for wages, telephone, electricity, stationery, etc.

<u>Net profit</u>

Net profit is the amount by which the gross profit for a period exceeds the expenses for the same period. Net loss is the amount by which the expenses exceed the gross profit. ABC Furniture Store had a gross profit of R300 000, the business expenses were R200 000 leaving ABC Furniture Store with a net profit of R100 000.

<u>Businesses that provide a service</u>

In the case of a business that provides a service, i.e. no physical goods are kept or sold, the procedure to determine your business profit or loss is the same as mentioned above with the exception of cost of goods sold. A business that provides only a service will not have to calculate cost of goods sold. Business or operating expenses will be deducted from gross sales (e.g. professional fees, taxi fares and services rendered) to determine a net profit or net loss.

- Comparative profit or loss statements

SOLE PROPRIETORSHIP

gross sales

↓

less cost of sales

↓

equals gross profit

↓

less business expenses

↓

equals net profit or loss[2]

↓

The owner receives all the profit or loss from the business and is responsible for the payment of all taxes thereon in his personal capacity

PARTNERSHIP

gross sales

↓

less cost of sales

↓

equals gross profit

↓

less business expenses

↓

equals net profit or loss[2]

↓

net profit or loss is divided amongst the partners

↓

Each partner is responsible for the payment of taxes on his share of the profit

[2]See also "How to determine taxable income/assessed loss"

CLOSE CORPORATION

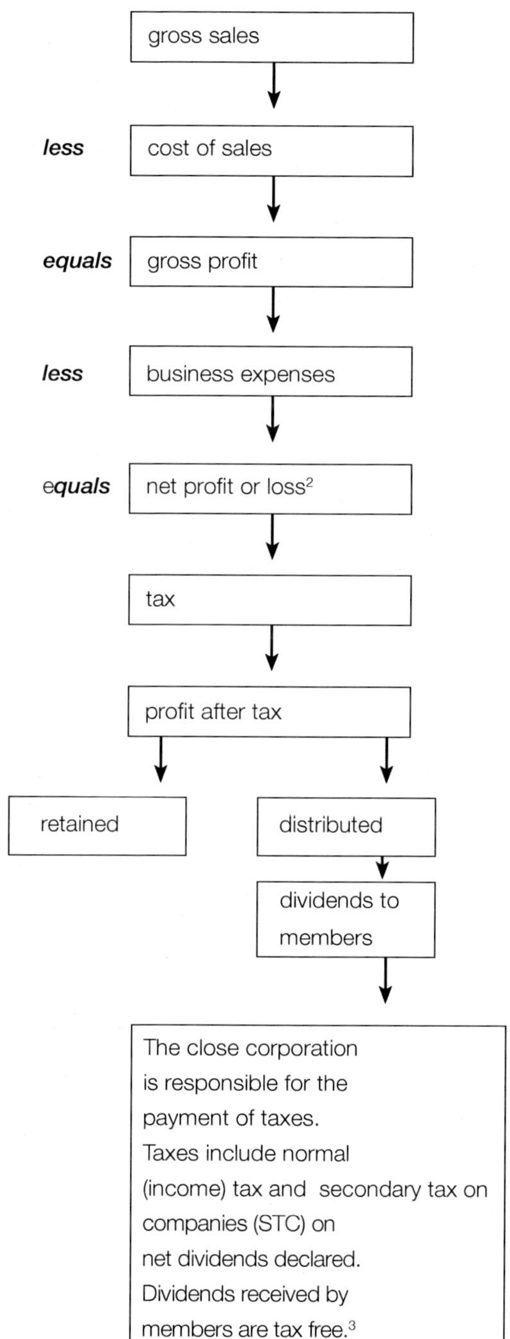

PRIVATE COMPANY

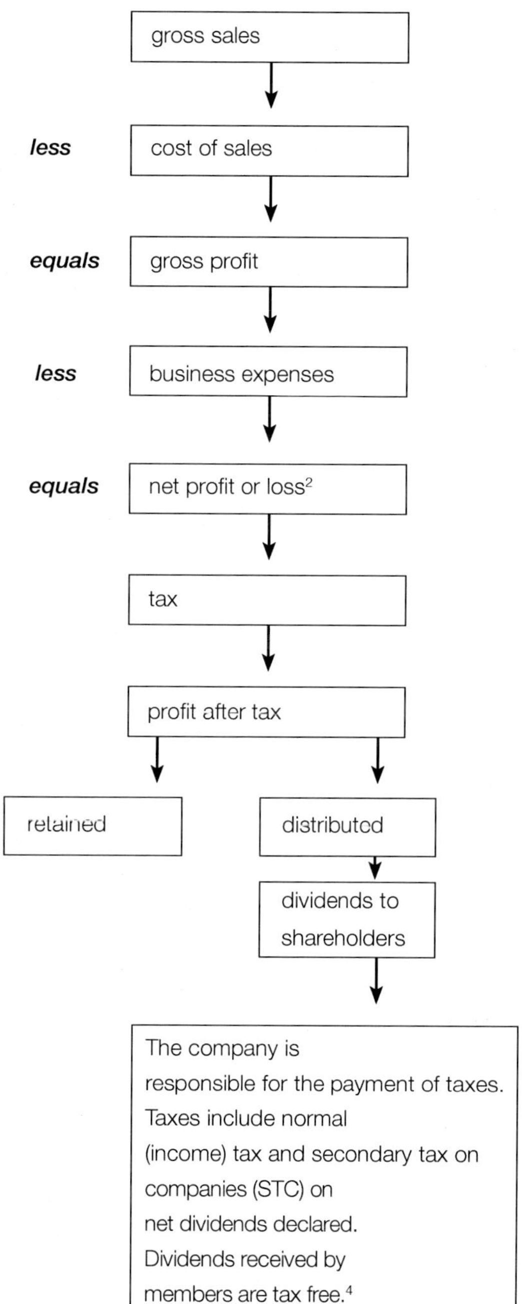

[3]Certain foreign dividends are, however, taxable
[4]Same as 3

- ### Link between "net profit" and "taxable income"

  Net profit is an accounting concept and is a term used to describe the calculation of the profit a business makes from an accounting point of view.

  Taxable income on the other hand is a tax term that is used to describe the amount calculated on which a business's tax is calculated.

  The amounts will often be different. The reason therefore is the basic differences in the income and deductions taken into account in determining the two amounts. For example, certain income of a capital nature may be fully included for accounting purposes, while only a portion thereof may be included for tax purposes. On the deduction side, there may be timing differences in respect of the depreciation of capital assets or special deductions/allowances for tax purposes which will cause differences in the deductions between accounting and taxation.

  Nevertheless, the determination of net profit from an accounting point of view is an important building block in the determination of the business's taxable income. Every business must first prepare a set of financial statements (income statement and a statement of assets and liabilities). From the income statement which determines the business's net profit/ loss, certain adjustments can be made to compute (normally referred to as the tax computation) the business's taxable income or assessed loss as explained below.

- ### How to determine taxable income/assessed loss

  The Act provides for a series of steps to be followed in arriving at the taxpayer's "taxable income". The starting point is to determine the taxpayer's "gross income". In the case of:

  - Any person who is a resident – the total amount of worldwide income, in cash or otherwise, received by or accrued to or in favour of such person during the tax year (subject to certain exclusions); or

  - Any person who is not a resident – the total amount of income, in cash or otherwise, received by or accrued to or in favour of such person from a source within or deemed to be within South Africa during the tax year.

  Receipts or accruals of a capital nature are generally excluded from gross income as the Eighth Schedule to the Act deals with capital gains and losses. However, "gross income" also includes certain other receipts and accruals specified within the definition of "gross income" regardless of their nature.

  The next step is to determine "income" which is the result of deducting all receipts and accruals that are exempt from tax in terms of the Act from "gross income".

Finally, "taxable income" is arrived at by deducting all the amounts allowed to be deducted or set off in terms of the Act from "income" and then adding any taxable capital gains. It can be illustrated as follows:

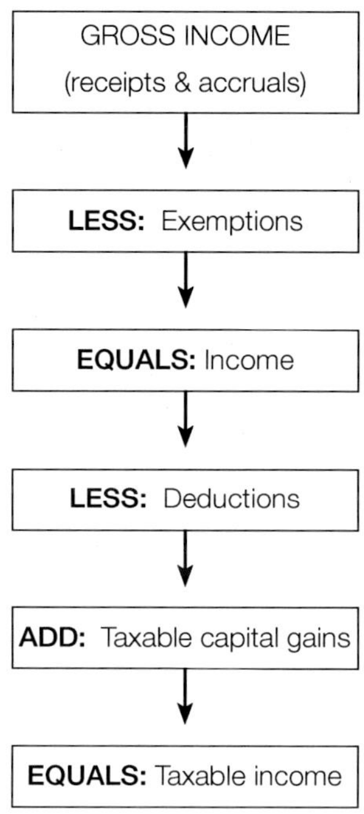

General deduction formula

The general deduction formula provides for the general rules with which an expense must comply in order to be deductible for normal income tax purposes. Other provisions of the Act allow for special deductions/ allowances. If no special deduction/allowance applies, however, the expense in question will have to comply with the general deduction formula.

The general deduction formula provides that for expenditure and losses to be deductible they must be –

- Actually incurred
- During the year of assessment
- In the production of income
- Not of a capital nature
- Laid out or expended for the purposes of trade

- Tax Rates

  A sole proprietor or each partner (individual) is subject to tax on his/her taxable income. The tax is levied at progressive rates ranging from 18% to 40%. For the 2007 tax year, the maximum marginal rate of 40% applies where the taxable income exceeds R400 000. Unlike individuals, a company or close corporation pays tax at a flat rate of 29% (except in the case of SBCs – see below) on its taxable income for the tax year and 12,5% secondary tax on companies (STC) on the net amount of dividends declared.

  Below is a summary of the different tax rates

Individuals

Tax rates for individuals: 2006/07

Taxable income (R)	**Rates of tax (R)**
1 - 100 000	18% of each R1
100 001 - 160000	18 000 + 25% of the amount above 100 000
160 001 - 220 000	33 000 + 30% of the amount above 160 000
220 001 - 300 000	51 000 + 35% of the amount above 220 000
300 001 - 400 000	79 000 + 38% of the amount above 300 000
400 001 and above	117 000 + 40% of the amount above 400 000

Rebates (Individuals only)	**2006/07**
Under 65 years	R7 200
65 years and older	R4 500

Tax thresholds	**2006/07**
Under 65 years	R40 000
65 years and older	R65 000

Standard Income Tax on Employees (SITE): Level: R60 000

Trusts

Tax rates – trusts (other than a special trust)

From Tax year	**Until Tax year**	**Normal Tax**	**From Taxable Income**
2001/02	2006/07	40%	On each rand of taxable income

Tax rates – Personal service trusts

From Tax Year	**Until Tax Year**	**Normal Tax**	**From Taxable Income**
2001/02	2006/07	40%	On each rand of taxable income

Corporates:

Companies (Standard)/Close Corporations

Tax years ending between	Normal Tax from R1 taxable income and above
01/04/06 to 31/03/07	29%

Secondary Tax on Companies (STC)

STC is payable on dividends declared by resident companies after being reduced by dividends receivable during a dividend cycle. South African branches of non-resident companies are exempt from STC. For more information see the *Comprehensive Guide to STC* on the SARS website.

From	Until	Rate
14/03/96	To date	12,50%

Small Business Corporations(SBCs)

Tax years ending between	Normal Tax	From Taxable Income	To Taxable Income
01/04/06 to 31/03/07	0%	R1	R40 000
	10%	R40 001	R300 000
	R26 000 plus 29% of the amount above R300 001		

Mining Companies

Companies Mining for Gold (taxed according to one of the following formulae "gold mining tax formula")

Tax years ending between	Not exempt from STC	Elected to be exempt from STC
01/04/2006 to 31/03/07	Y=35-175/X (Other income taxed at 29%)	Y=45-225/X (Other income taxed at 37%)

Where X = $\frac{\text{Taxable income from gold mining}}{\text{Total revenue (turnover) from gold mining}}$

Y = Rate of tax to be levied

Companies Mining for Oil and Gas

Taxed at the same normal tax rate applicable to standard companies plus an additional normal tax equal to 40%, remaining after the deduction of the normal tax. The normal tax and the additional normal tax may, however, be reduced in terms of section 5(2A)(b) of the Act.

Other Mining Companies

The rates applicable to ordinary companies also apply to all mining companies, other than companies mining for gold.

Insurance Companies

- Long-Term Insurance Companies – Four Fund Basis

Tax years ending between	01/04/06 to 31/03/07
Corporate Fund	29%
Individual Policyholder Fund	30%
Company Policyholder Fund	29%
Untaxed Policyholder Fund:	
• Retirement fund business	9%
• Other	Nil

- Short-Term Insurance Companies

  Companies carrying on a short-term insurance business are taxed at the same rate as is applicable to standard companies

Retirement Funds

Gross interest, net rental and foreign dividend income of retirement funds (i.e. pension, provident, retirement annuity funds) and untaxed policyholder funds of long-term assurance companies in respect of their retirement business are taxed as follows:

From	Rate
01/03/2006 to date	9%

Employment Companies

- Personal service company
- Labour broker that is a company without a labour broker exemption certificate

Tax years ending between	Normal Tax, from R1 taxable income and above
01/04/05 to 31/03/07	34%

Non-resident Companies

Non-resident companies which trade in RSA *via* a branch or agency

Tax years ending between	Normal Tax, from R1 taxable income and above
01/04/05 to 31/03/07	34%

- Special allowances

(a) Industrial buildings (buildings used in process of manufacture)

Wear and tear is normally not allowed on buildings or other structures of a permanent nature. However, an annual allowance equal to 5% (20 year straight line) of the cost of industrial buildings or of improvements to existing industrial buildings is granted.

This allowance was increased to 10% for industrial buildings erected between 1 July 1996 and 30 September 1999 and brought into use before 31 March 2000.

(b) Hotel keepers

- Buildings and improvements – 5% (20 year straight line)
- Machinery / improvements / utensils / articles – 20% (5 year straight line). The assets must be owned by the taxpayer or acquired as purchaser in terms of an instalment credit agreement as defined in the VAT Act.
- Refurbishment of buildings within existing exterior framework – 20% (5 year straight-line)

(c) Aircraft / ships

Where these are brought into use for the purpose of trade – 20% (5 year straight line). The assets must be owned by the taxpayer or acquired as purchaser in terms of an instalment credit agreement as defined in the VAT Act.

(d) Pipelines for transporting oil or gas and their derivative products

10% a year of the cost of the asset (10 year straight line)

(e) Electricity transmission lines

5% a year of the cost of the asset (20 year straight line)

(f) Telephone transmission lines

5% a year of the cost of the asset (20 year straight line)

(g) Railway tracks

5% a year of the cost of the asset (20 year straight line)

Note: Assets referred to in paragraphs (d), (e), (f) and (g) above must be owned by the taxpayer.

(h) Certain aircraft hangars, aprons, runways and taxiways

5% a year of the cost of the asset (20 year straight line)

(i) Machinery, plant implements, utensils and articles

An allowance, equal to the amount which the Commissioner may think just and reasonable which the value of the asset used by the taxpayer for the purposes of his trade has been diminished by reason of wear and tear or depreciation. The assets must be owned by the taxpayer or acquired as purchaser in terms of an instalment credit agreement as defined in the VAT Act. Small items costing less than R5 000 purchased on or after 1 March 2006 may be written off in full in the year of acquisition.

For more information, see Practice Note No. 19 available on the SARS website at www.sars.gov.za.

(j) Plant or machinery (manufacture)

An allowance for new or unused machinery or plant acquired on or after 1 March 2002 and brought into use and used directly by the taxpayer in a process of manufacture or similar process, is available. 40% of the cost of the asset will be deducted in the first year and 20% of the cost for the subsequent 3 years. The assets must be owned by the taxpayer or acquired as purchaser in terms of an instalment credit agreement as defined in the VAT Act.

(k) Small business corporations (SBCs)

- Plant or machinery

  100% of the cost of any plant or machinery brought into use in the tax year for the first time and used in a process of manufacture is deductible. The assets must be owned by the taxpayer or acquired as purchaser in terms of an instalment credit agreement as defined in the VAT Act.

- Machinery, plant, implement, utensil, article, aircraft or ship

  An accelerated allowance for the above assets (other than plant or machinery used in a manufacturing or similar process) acquired by the SBC on or after 1 April 2005 at 50% of the cost of that asset in the tax year during which that asset is or was brought into use for the first time, 30% in the second year and 20% in the third year.

For more information see under the heading Tax relief measures for / Small Business Corporations (SBCs), and Interpretation Note No. 9 on the SARS website.

(l) Patents, inventions, copyrights, designs, other property, etc

An allowance will be allowed as a deduction in respect of expenditure incurred during the year of assessment commencing on or after 1 January 2004 to acquire (otherwise than by way of devising, developing or creating) and which are, the following property—

(i) invention or patent as defined in the Patents Act, 1978 (Act No.57 of 1978);

(ii) design as defined in the Designs Act, 1993 (Act No. 195 of 1993);

(iii) copyright as defined in the Copyright Act, 1978 (Act No. 98 of 1978);

(iv) other property which is of a similar nature (other than Trade Marks as defined in the Trade Marks Act, 1993 (Act No. 194 of1993); or

(v) knowledge connected with the use of such patent, design, copyright or other property or the right to have such knowledge imparted.

The allowance is allowed in the year of assessment in which the abovementioned property is brought into use for the first time by the taxpayer for the purposes of the taxpayer's trade.

Where the expenditure exceeds R5 000, the allowance will not exceed in any year of assessment—

(a) 5% of the expenditure in respect of any invention, patent, copyright or the property of a similar nature or any knowledge connected with the use of such invention, patent, copyright or other property or the right to have such knowledge imparted; or

(b) 10% of the expenditure of any design or other property of a similar nature or any knowledge connected with the use of such design or other property or the right to have such knowledge imparted.

(m) Urban Development Zones

Taxpayers investing in one of the 15 demarcated urban development areas receive special depreciation allowances for construction or refurbishment of commercial and residential buildings located in these areas that are used solely for trade purposes. These areas are located within the boundaries of the municipalities of Buffalo City, Cape Town, Ekurhuleni, Emalahleni, Emfuleni, eThekwini, Johannesburg, Mangaung, Mbombela, Msunduzi, Nelson Mandela, Polokwane, Sol Plaatje, Tshwane and Matjhabeng.

The allowances are:

- in respect of the cost (or "deemed cost" in respect of a building purchased from a developer) of the erection of any new building or part thereof or the extension of or addition to any building or part thereof, an amount equal to -
    - 20% of the cost thereof to the taxpayer in the year of assessment that building or part thereof is erected, extended or added to is brought into use by the taxpayer solely for the purpose of that taxpayer's trade; and
    - 5% of the cost in each of the 16 succeeding years of assessment; and

- in respect of the cost (or "deemed cost" in respect of a building purchased from a developer) of improvements (including any extension or addition which is incidental to that improvements) to any existing building, an amount equal to -
    - 20% of the cost thereof to the taxpayer in the year of assessment in which the building or part thereof so improved, extended or added to is brought into use by the taxpayer solely for the purpose of that taxpayer's trade; and
    - 20% of that cost in each of the four succeeding years of assessment.

Where a building purchased from a developer, only a certain percentage of the purchase price will be deemed to be costs incurred by the purchaser in respect of the erection, extension, addition to or improvement of the building or part of the building, namely -

- 55% of the purchase price of the building or part thereof, in the case of a new building erected, extended or added to by the developer; and
- 30% of the purchase price of the building or part of the building, in the case of a building improved by the developer.

For more information see the *Guide to the UDZ Tax Incentive* on the SARS website.

(n) Agricultural co-operatives

Plant or machinery used for storing / packing farming products – 20% (5 year straight line). The assets must be owned by the taxpayer or acquired as purchaser in terms of an instalment credit agreement as defined in the VAT Act.

(o) Learnership Agreements

An allowance where-

a) the employer during the year of assessment entered into a registered learnership agreement with a learner in the course of any trade carried on by that employer; or

b) the learner completed during the year of assessment a registered learnership agreement entered into by the employer with that learner during the year or any previous year of assessment in the course of any trade carried on by that employer.

The allowance in respect of the entering into a learnership agreement is –

(i) in the case of a learner who was at the time of entering into that agreement employed by the employer, the lesser of-

(aa) in the case of a learnership with a duration of—

(A) less than 12 months, 70% of the total remuneration of that learner for the period of that learnership as stipulated in the employment agreement; or

(B) 12 months or more, 70% of the annual equivalent of the remuneration of that learner stipulated in the employment agreement; or (bb) R17 500 or R20 000 in respect of learnership agreements entered into on or after 1 March 2006; or

(ii) in the case of a learner who was at the time of entering into the agreement not employed by the employer, the lesser of-

(aa) in the case of a learnership with a duration of—

(A) less than 12 months, the total remuneration of that learner for the period of that learnership as stipulated in the agreement of employment; or

(B) 12 months or more, the annual equivalent of the remuneration of that learner stipulated in the agreement of employment; or

(bb) R25 000 or R30 000 in respect of learnership agreements entered into on or after 1 March 2006.

The allowance in respect of the completion of a learnership agreement is the lesser of -

(i) in the case of a learnership with a duration of—

(aa) less than 12 months, the total remuneration of that learner for the period of that learnership as stipulated in the agreement of employment; or

(bb) 12 months or more, the annual equivalent of the remuneration of that learner stipulated in the agreement of employment; or

(ii) R25 000 or R30 000 in respect of learnership agreements entered into on or after 1 March 2006.

Disabled persons

Given the additional expenses associated with employing disabled persons as learners, a more favourable allowance has been introduced in respect of contracts entered into on or after 1 July 2006. The allowances are set out below.

If the learner is a disabled person at the time of entering into the learnership agreement, the amount of the allowance in respect of—

(a) a registered learnership agreement entered into by the employer with the learner who at the time of entering into that agreement—

(i) was employed by the employer, is the lesser of—

(aa) in the case of a learnership agreement with a duration

of—

(A) less than 12 months, 150% of the total amount of the remuneration of the learner for the period of the learnership agreement as stipulated in the agreement of employment; or

(B) 12 months or more, 150% of the annual equivalent of the remuneration of that learner stipulated in the agreement of employment; or

(bb) R40 000; or

(ii) was not employed by the employer, is the lesser of—

(aa) in the case of a learnership agreement with a duration of—

(A) less than 12 months, 175% of the total amount of the remuneration of the learner for the period of the learnership agreement stipulated in the agreement of employment; or

(B) 12 months or more, 175% of the annual equivalent of the remuneration of the learner stipulated in the agreement of employment; or

(bb) R50 000; and

(b) the allowance at the completion of the registered learnership agreement, is the lesser of—

(i) in the case of a learnership agreement with a duration of—

(aa) less than 12 months, 175% of the total remuneration of the learner for the period of the learnership agreement stipulated in the agreement of employment; or

(bb) 12 months or more, 175% of the annual equivalent of the remuneration of the learner stipulated in the agreement of employment; or

(ii) R50 000.

A "disabled person" means a person who falls within the definition of "people with disabilities" as contained in section 1 of the Employment Equity Act, 1998 (Act No. 55 of 1998).

(p) Research and development

Assets of a capital nature exclusively used for research and development are depreciated at 40% of the cost of the asset in the year of assessment in which such asset is brought into use for the first time by the taxpayer, and 20% of such cost in each of the three succeeding years of assessment.

(q) Machinery, plant, implements, utensils and articles used in farming or production of renewable energy

– Farming

An allowance in respect of these assets, brought into use for the first time by the taxpayer in the carrying on of farming operations, is equal to-

- 50% of the cost of the asset to the taxpayer in the year of assessment in which the asset is so brought into use;
- 30% of such cost in the 2nd year of assessment; and
- 20% of such cost in the 3rd year of assessment.

– Production of bio-fuels

An allowance in respect of these assets, brought into use for the first time by the taxpayer for the purpose of the taxpayer's trade to be used for the production of bio-fuels (bio-diesel and/or bio-ethanol), is equal to-

- 50% of the cost of the asset to the taxpayer in the year of assessment in which the asset is so brought into use;
- 30% of such cost in the 2nd year of assessment; and
- 20% of such cost in the 3rd year of assessment.

– Generation of electricity

An allowance in respect of these assets, brought into use for the first time by the taxpayer for the purpose of the taxpayer's trade to be used in the generation of electricity from –

- wind;
- sunlight;
- gravitational water forces to produce electricity of not more than 30 megawatts; and
- biomass comprising organic wastes, landfill gas or plants,

is equal to -

- 50% of the cost of the asset to the taxpayer in the year of assessment in which the asset is so brought into use;
- 30% of such cost in the 2nd year of assessment; and
- 20% of such cost in the 3rd year of assessment.

Note: All the assets referred to in par (q) above must be owned by the taxpayer or acquired by the taxpayer as purchaser in terms of an agreement contemplated in paragraph (a) of an "instalment credit agreement" as defined in section 1 of the VAT Act.

(r) Film Owners

Special deductions are allowed in the determination of taxable income derived from their trade as film owners. These special deductions are contained in section 24F of the IT Act. Further information is available in a guide entitled *Taxation of Film Owners* which is available on the SARS website, www.sars.gov.za.

- Tax relief measures for:

– Tax Amnesty Small for Businesses

Introduction

Small businesses play an important role in stimulating economic activity, job creation, poverty alleviation and the general improvement of living standards. Many small businesses operate informally, were historically marginalised and were excluded from the economic mainstream, thus remaining outside of the tax system. During the 2006 Budget, the Minister of Finance announced that Government will introduce a tax amnesty for small business.

Purpose of tax amnesty

The purpose/objective of the tax amnesty is to-

- broaden the tax base;
- facilitate the normalisation of the tax affairs of small businesses;
- increase and improve the tax compliance culture; and
- facilitate participation in the taxi recapitalisation program.

Persons who may benefit

Small businesses which are unregistered for tax purposes at the end of the 2006 year of assessment or which are registered taxpayers but whose income from supplies (goods and/or services) made or employment taxes due in respect of small business activities have not been declared or has been understated during any year of assessment preceding the 2006 year of assessment, will benefit from the amnesty.

Persons who may apply for amnesty

Any individual (including the deceased or insolvent estate of the individual), unlisted company, close corporation, trust, co-operative, which meets certain requirements may apply for tax amnesty. These requirements are that –

- the individual or entity must have carried on a business;
- the gross income (turnover) of the business during the 2006 tax year was not more than R10 million;
- in the case of a company or close corporation all the shares or members interests were held directly by individuals throughout the 2006 year of assessment; and
- in the case of a trust all the beneficiaries of that trust throughout the 2006 year of assessment must have been natural persons.

Note: For purposes of the amnesty, the "2006 year of assessment" is defined as the year of assessment which ended during the period of 12 months from 1 April 2005 to 31 March 2006.

Method of application

An applicant must apply for amnesty at SARS on a form and at addresses prescribed by SARS. Application forms (available on the SARS website www.sars.gov.za or from any SARS office) should be submitted at any time during the period 1 August 2006 to 31 May 2007.

Information required in application

In the application for tax amnesty the applicant must:

- Disclose the taxable income from the carrying on of business during the 2006 year of assessment.
- Furnish an income tax return for the 2006 year of assessment and a statement of all assets (at cost) and liabilities as at the end of the 2006 year of assessment.

Where it is not possible to provide full particulars of any actual amounts in the application, reasonable estimates must be disclosed.

Payment of tax amnesty levy

In addition to the income tax payable for the 2006 year of assessment, the applicant must also pay an amnesty levy based on a sliding scale rate and is applied to the taxable income of the applicant for the 2006 year of assessment to the extent that the taxable income is attributable to any amount derived by the applicant from the carrying on of business (assessed losses brought forward must be excluded.)

The rates to be applied in the calculating of the tax amnesty levy are –

From	**To**	**Levy (R)**
Taxable income (R)	Taxable income (R)	
-	35 000	No levy payable
35 000	100 000	2% of the amount above 35 000
100 000	250 000	1 300 + 3% of the amount above 100 000
250 000	500 000	5 800 + 4% of the amount above 250 000
500 000	and above	15 800 + 5% of the amount above 500 000

Relief from payment of other taxes

Where an application for tax amnesty is successful, the applicant is not liable for the payment of –

- income tax in terms of the Act, in respect of any amounts received by or accrued to (or deemed to have been received by or accrued to) the applicant from the carrying on of a business in all years of assessment preceding the 2006 year of assessment;
- employees' tax in terms of the Fourth Schedule to the Act, in respect of remuneration as defined in that Schedule paid to employees for the tax periods or months ending on or before 28 February 2006;
- VAT in terms of the VAT Act, in respect of any supply or importation of goods or services for the tax periods or months ending on or before 28 February 2006;
- withholding tax on royalties in terms of the Act, in respect of any amount paid to a non-resident for the tax periods or months ending on or before 28 February 2006;
- STC in terms of the Act, in respect of any dividend declared or deemed to be declared in all years of assessment preceding the 2006 year of assessment;

- contributions payable in terms of the UIC Act, in respect of remuneration, as defined in that Act, for the tax periods or months ending on or before 28 February 2006; and
- levies payable in terms of the SDL Act, in respect of any leviable amounts as contemplated in that Act, for the tax periods or months ending on or before 28 February 2006.

The applicant will also not be liable for the payment of any additional taxes, interest and penalties which relate to the amounts for which relief has been granted.

Exclusion from the tax amnesty relief

The tax amnesty does not apply in respect of any tax, levy, contribution, interest, penalty or additional tax which—

- had already been paid by the applicant before the submission of the application;
- becomes payable as a result of any return, declaration or information submitted to SARS before the submission of the application;
- is payable by the applicant in terms of an assessment issued by SARS before the submission of the application; or
- relates to value-added tax not paid as a result of a false declaration of the acquisition, import or export of goods or services that did not actually occur.

Review of SARS's decision

An applicant whose application for tax amnesty is denied by SARS may object and appeal against that decision in terms of the normal dispute resolution procedures of the Act (see Dispute Resolution under General par 5 of this Guide).

Circumstances where approval of tax amnesty is void

The approval for tax amnesty granted is void if –

- the applicant fails to pay the full amount of the tax amnesty levy within 12 months from the date of approval or a longer period as SARS may allow;
- in the application for tax amnesty the applicant failed to make full disclosure of any information, including -
    - to disclose the taxable income from the carrying on of business during the 2006 year of assessment; and
    - to furnish an income tax return for the 2006 year of assessment and a statement of all assets (at cost) and liabilities as at the end of the 2006 year of assessment.
- Any estimates made by the applicant are materially incorrect.

Note: For more information, visit SARS website, www.sars.gov.za.

- Small Business Corporations (SBCs)

The small business corporation regime allows two major concessions to companies and close corporations which comply with all of the following requirements:

- The shareholders or members must be natural persons (individuals) and must hold the entire shareholding/member's interest of the company/close corporation.
- Shareholders or members may not hold any shares or interest in the equity of any other company [excluding shares in listed companies, a participatory interest in a collective investment scheme or an interest in a company as contemplated in section 10(1)(e)(i), (ii) or (iii) of the Act (body corporates)].
- The gross income of the corporation for the tax year may not exceed R14 million.
- Not more than 20% of the total of all receipts and accruals (other than those of a capital nature) and all capital gains of the company/close corporation may consist collectively of investment income and income from rendering a personal service. Investment income includes interest, dividends, royalties, rental and annuities. Personal services are services in the field of, for example, accounting, real estate and engineering which are performed personally by a person holding an interest in the company/close corporation. An SBC which is engaged in the provision of personal services will still qualify for the relief if it throughout the year of assessment employs at least four full-time employees who are on a full time basis engaged in the business of the SBC rendering that service.
- The company/close corporation may not be an employment company (i.e. a labour broker without an exemption certificate or a personal service company).

The first concession is to be taxed on the basis of a multiple rate system, viz SBCs pay tax at a rate of 0% on the first R40 000 of taxable income, 10% on taxable income in excess of R40 000 but not exceeding R300 000 and thereafter at a rate of 29% for every R1 in excess of R300 000.

The second concession is the immediate write-off of all plant or machinery used in a process of manufacture or similar process in the tax year it is brought into use for the first time. Furthermore, an accelerated write-off allowance for depreciable assets (other than manufacturing assets) acquired on or after 1 April 2005 is available at 50% of the cost of that asset in the tax year during which that asset is or was brought into use for the first time, 30% in the second year and 20% in the third year. [See also under Special Allowances, par (k)]

Note: For more information see Interpretation Note 9 on the SARS website www.sars.gov.za.

- Manufacturing

  Special allowances are granted to persons engaged in a process of manufacture or a process of a similar nature.

  SBCs as indicated above, may write off 100% of their manufacturing plant or machinery.

  An allowance for new or unused machinery or plant acquired on or after 1 March 2002 and brought into use and used directly by the taxpayer in a process of manufacture or similar process, is available. 40% of the cash cost of the asset will be deducted in the first year and 20% of the cost for the subsequent 3 years.

- Farming

  Farming operations include livestock farming, crop farming, milk production, plantation farming, sugar cane farming and game farming.

  Persons carrying on farming operations are required to account for the value of livestock and produce on hand at the beginning and end of a tax year in their tax returns. The values to be placed on livestock at the beginning and end of the tax year are the standard values as prescribed by regulation. (These values also appear in the tax brochures accompanying the annual tax returns). Produce, on the other hand, must be accounted for at cost of production or market value, whichever is the lower.

  Game is also regarded as livestock, but due to practical difficulties that can be encountered in establishing the actual numbers of game on hand at any given time, game is excluded from opening and closing stock.

  Game farmers must prove that the game is purchased, bred and sold on a regular basis with a genuine intention to carry on farming operations profitably in order to qualify as farmers. Income relating to accommodation and catering facilities for visitors does not qualify as income from farming operations and separate financial statements must be drawn up for such income.

  - Special concessions for farmers

    The deduction of capital expenditure, such as the development of and improvements to farming property, is permitted in the determination of taxable income. This deduction may not exceed the farmer's taxable income from farming operations in respect of that year. If the amount of such expenditure exceeds the income in that year, the balance will be carried forward and deducted in the succeeding year, subject to the same limitation. For further information, refer to the Information Brochure on Income Tax, which accompanies the yearly return of income forms, which is also obtainable from SARS offices.

    The cost of farming machinery, plant, implements, utensils or articles used by a farmer in farming operations or production of renewable energy is written off at the following rates:

    - First year of use : 50%
    - Second year : 30%
    - Third year : 20%

- Special measures in determining taxable income of farmers

  Since a farmer's income can fluctuate considerably from year to year, the Act contains provisions whereby the farmer may be taxed on the basis of his/her annual average taxable income from farming in the current and previous four tax years.

  Relief is also given to farmers whose income for any year includes income derived from:
  - The disposal of plantation and forest produce.
  - The abnormal disposal of sugar cane as a consequence of damage to cane fields by fire.
  - The disposal of livestock sold on account of drought.
  - Excess profits as a result of farming land acquired by the State or certain juristic persons.

– Mining

Mining enterprises are allowed to deduct capital expenditure incurred in full in the year the expense was incurred. Capital expenditure, for example, includes expenditure on shaft sinking and mining equipment. It also includes expenditure on development and general administration prior to the commencement of production or during a period of non-production.

The capital expenditure incurred on a particular mine is restricted to the taxable income derived from that mine only. Any excess (unredeemed) capital expenditure is carried forward and is deemed to be capital expenditure incurred in the next year in respect of the mine to which the capital expenditure relates. Furthermore, the capital expenditure of a mine cannot be set-off against non-mining income such as interest, rental, other trading activities, etc.

As stated above the capital expenditure of one mine may not be set-off against the taxable income of another mine. However, where a new mine commences mining operations after 14 March 1990 its excess (unredeemed) capital expenditure may also be deducted from the total taxable income derived from mining in respect of other mines operated by the taxpayer, as does not exceed 25% of such total taxable income derived from its other mines.

Taxpayers conducting mining operations are required to rehabilitate areas where mining has taken place. These taxpayers are, therefore, required to make provision for rehabilitation expenses, during the life of the mine. Amounts paid in cash to approved rehabilitation funds are allowed as a deduction for tax purposes.

The taxable income of a company derived from mining for gold is taxed in accordance with a special formula. A company which derives taxable income from other mining operations is taxed at the same rate (29%) that is applicable to other companies and also pays STC.

- Deduction of home office expenditure

  Expenses relating to your home office may be claimed as a deduction for tax purposes if-
  - a part of your home is occupied for purposes of your trade and that part is regularly and exclusively used for purposes of your trade; and
  - the part so used or occupied is specifically equipped for purposes of your trade.

If your trade is employment or the holding of an office no deduction is allowed unless-

- the income derived from that employment or office is mainly (i.e. more than 50% of your total income from employment or office) commission or other variable payments which are based on your work performance and your duties are not performed mainly in an office provided by your employer; or
- your duties are mainly performed in that part of your home.

If the above requirements are met you will be entitled to claim a portion of your total home expenses that relate to that part of your home used for business purposes, as a deduction against your income. Typical home expenses may include rent of the premises, interest on bond, rates and taxes, cost of repairs or maintenance to the property, etc. These expenses may be apportioned on the following basis:

A/B x Total Costs

Where: A = The area in m^2 of the area specifically equipped and used regularly and exclusively for trade

B = The total area in m^2 (including any outbuildings and the area used for trade) of your home

Total Costs = Total home expenses referred to above

Example

The total area (square metres) of your home office is 20 sq. metres in relation to the total area of your home which is 200 sq. metres. The percentage area of the home office in relation to the total area of your home is, therefore, 10% (20/200). You will, therefore, be entitled to claim 10% of your total home expenses as a deduction for tax purposes.

- Deductions in respect of expenditure and losses incurred prior to commencement of trade (start-up costs)

Taxpayers are entitled to a deduction for start-up costs incurred before the commencement of trade.

Start-up costs are not defined but they would include costs such as advertising and marketing promotion, insurance, accounting and legal fees, rent, telephone, licenses and permits, market research and feasibility studies, but excludes capital costs such as the purchase of buildings and motor vehicles.

Start-up costs incurred prior to the commencement of trade can only be set off against income from that trade.

- Ring fencing of assessed losses

  Section 11 of the Act provides for the general requirements for deducting expenditure and losses to the extent a person derives income from carrying on any trade. Not every activity is a trade, even if intended or labelled by a taxpayer as such. Whether or not an activity is a trade is a question of law depends on the "facts and circumstances" of each case. These "facts and circumstances" are deliberately left open to accommodate the wide range of trade activities existing in a modern world.
  However, more often than not, private consumption (i.e. a hobby) can be disguised as a trade so that individuals can set off these expenditures and losses against other income such as salary or business income.

  Due to the above, a new provision was added to the Act, namely section 20A, which aims to prevent expenditure and losses normally associated with suspect activities (i.e. disguised hobbies) to be deducted from income. This deduction limitation applies only to natural persons (i.e. an individual, including an individual as a partner). Section 20A is applicable in respect of years of assessment commencing on or after 1 March 2004. Further information is available in a guide entitled *Ring Fencing of Assessed Losses Arising from Certain Trades Conducted by Individuals*, which explains the ring fencing concept and is available on the SARS website, www.sars.gov.za.

- Tax on foreign entertainers and sports persons

  With effect from 1 August 2006 South African residents who are liable to pay amounts to foreign entertainers and sportspersons for their performances in SA must withhold tax at a rate of 15% from the gross payments and pay it over to SARS on behalf the foreign entertainers and sportspersons before the end of the month following the month in which the tax was withheld. Failure to withhold and / or to pay it over to SARS will render the resident payer personally liable for the tax.
  Where it is not possible for the withholding tax to take place (e.g., the payer is a non-resident), the non-resident entertainer or sportsperson will be held personally liable for the 15% tax and must pay it over to SARS within 30 days after the amount accrues or is received by the foreign entertainer or sportsperson.
  The 15% is a final tax, which means there will be no need to submit the usual return of income (income tax return).
  Where a non-resident entertainer or sportsperson is employed by a South African employer and he or she is physically present in South Africa for more than 183 days in aggregate in a 12-month period that commences or ends in a year of assessment, these persons will have to pay tax on the same basis as South African residents, that is at the usual tax rates, which may require the submission of an income tax return.
  Any person who is primarily responsible for founding, organising or facilitating a performance in SA and who will be rewarded therefor, must notify SARS of the performance within 14 days of concluding the agreement. (Visit the SARS website for more information.)

3.3 Residence Basis of Taxation (RBT)

All South African residents are subject to tax in South Africa on their worldwide income, i.e. income derived from sources within and outside South Africa. Relief is granted in respect of foreign taxes paid on income derived from foreign sources. Non-residents are taxable in South Africa on income they derive from South African sources.

Two tests apply to determine whether an individual is a resident or not. The **first test** is the ordinarily resident test (i.e. normally the place to which a person will naturally and as a matter of course return to from his/her wanderings). The **second test** is the physical presence test in South Africa (i.e. based on the number of days during which a natural person is physically present in the Republic).

A company or other entity which is incorporated, established, formed or has its place of effective management in South Africa is regarded as being resident in South Africa.
Income earned by certain foreign companies controlled by South African residents (controlled foreign companies – CFCs) can under certain circumstances be imputed and taxed in the hands of the controlling South African residents.

Further information is obtainable from SARS offices or on the SARS website under Tax Brochures and Interpretation Notes.

3.4 Capital Gains Tax (CGT)

CGT forms part of the income tax system. A taxpayer need not register separately for CGT if already registered for income tax.

Capital gains tax was introduced with effect from 1 October 2001. A capital gain arises when the proceeds from the disposal of an asset exceed the base cost of that asset. A capital loss occurs when an asset is disposed of and the base cost of that asset exceeds the proceeds from that disposal.

CGT only comes into effect when the taxpayer disposes of an asset. (The word "disposal" is described very widely – see paragraph 11 of the Eighth Schedule to the Act.) A capital gain forms part of a taxpayer's taxable income and must be declared in the income tax return for the tax year in which the asset is disposed of.

For individuals, only 25% of the net capital gain, after deducting the annual exclusion described below, is included when calculating the tax payable. For companies, close corporations and trusts, only 50% of the net capital gain on the disposal of assets is included in taxable income. Relief in the form of a deferral of the capital gain is available where the asset is either disposed of involuntarily and is replaced, or is disposed of in order to acquire another business asset that qualifies for a capital allowance.

The base cost of an asset is the amount the taxpayer paid for the asset plus whatever other cost was incurred directly related to buying it, selling it, or improving it. The base cost does not include any amount otherwise allowed as a deduction for income tax purposes. Some of the main costs that may form part of the base cost of an asset are:

- The price the taxpayer originally paid to buy the asset
- Transfer costs, stamp duty, VAT paid and not claimed or refunded on the asset
- Cost of improvements to the asset
- Advertising costs to find a buyer or seller
- The cost of having the asset valued in order to determine a capital gain or loss
- Costs directly relating to the buying or selling of the asset, e.g. fees paid to a surveyor, broker, agent or consultant for services rendered
- Cost of establishing, maintaining or defending a legal title or right in the asset
- Cost of moving the asset from one place to another upon acquisition or disposal
- Cost of installing the asset, including the cost of foundations and supporting structures

The taxpayer does not have to pay tax on the full profit when an asset owned before 1 October 2001 is disposed of. The base cost of the asset as at 1 October 2001 must be determined, and only the difference between the proceeds and that base cost is subject to CGT.

The base cost of an asset acquired before 1 October 2001 may be determined according to one of the following three methods:

(a) 20% X (proceeds less any expenditure incurred on or after the valuation date).

(b) The market value of the asset on 1 October 2001 (the valuation date) plus any expenditure incurred on or after the valuation date. The valuation must have been carried out before 30 September 2004.

(c) The time-apportionment method which is based on the following formulae:

$$P = R \times [B/(A + B)]$$

$$TAB = B + [(P - B) \times N/(N+T)]$$

Note:

1. The symbols used in the above formulae are as follows:

R = Amount received or accrued from disposal of asset

P = Amount determined using the proceeds formula, or where the formula does not apply, the proceeds.

A = Expenditure incurred on or after 1 October 2001

B = Expenditure incurred before 1 October 2001

N = Number of years before valuation date

T = Number of years after valuation date

2. The proceeds formula (P = R x [B/ (A + B)] must be applied where expenditure has been incurred before and after the valuation date.

3. Parts of a year are treated as a full year for the purpose of determining the periods before and after the valuation date ('N' and 'T' in the formula).

4. Where expenditure has been incurred in more than one year of assessment before the valuation date, N is limited to 20 years.

Example (where method (c) is used)

Zelda bought her holiday home on 1 June 1980 at a cost of R25 000. She sold it on 1 June 2004 for R850 000. The estate agent charged R50 000 in commission. The market value (MV) of the house on valuation date was R550 000.

<u>Solution</u>

Step 1 – Apply proceeds formula

The proceeds formula must be used because Zelda incurred R50 000 in respect of estate agent's commission after the valuation date.

P = R x [B/ (A + B)]

P = 850 000 x 25 000/(50 000 + 25000)

P = 283 333

Step 2 – Determine time-apportionment base cost (TAB)

TAB = B + [(P – B) x N/(N+T)]

TAB = 25 000 + [(283 333 – 25 000) x 22/25]

TAB = 25 000 + 227 333 = 252 333

Step 3 – Determine capital gain or loss

Capital gain = R850 000 – R252 333 – R50 000 = R547 667

<u>Comment</u>

Had Zelda done a valuation, her capital gain would be

Proceeds		R850 000
Less: Base cost		
MV on 1.10.01	R550 000	
Commission	<u>R50 000</u>	<u>(R600 000)</u>
Capital gain		<u>R250 000</u>

Compare: TAB R547 667 v MV R250 000

Note: Where there is a loss, the formula will reduce the original cost by the portion of the loss relating to the period before the valuation date.

Where no records have been kept, methods (a) or (b) must be used.

Individuals are entitled to an annual exclusion. This is the amount of an individual's net annual capital gain or loss that is disregarded for CGT purposes. The annual exclusion is R12 500 but is increased to R60 000 where an individual dies during a year of assessment.

Persons who operate **small businesses**[5] as sole proprietors, partners or owners of an interest (10% or more) in a company or close corporation are, subject to certain conditions, entitled to a concession which excludes capital gains of up to R750 000 on the disposal of active business assets when these persons attain the age of 55 years or the disposal is in consequence of ill-health, other infirmity, superannuation or death. For further information, see paragraph 57 of the Eighth Schedule to the Act.

CGT on disposal of foreign assets by residents

Residents are subject to CGT on the disposal of their worldwide assets. The method for determining the capital gain or loss depends on the nature of the asset. The relevant legislation is contained in the Eighth Schedule to the Act. Set out below are some examples of foreign assets and their CGT treatment.

- Immovable property held outside SA

  Where the property is acquired and disposed of in the same foreign currency, the capital gain or loss is determined in the foreign currency and translated to Rand at the spot rate applying at the time of disposal. With effect from 8 November 2005 individuals and non-trading trusts may alternatively elect to translate the gain or loss by using the average exchange rate applicable to the tax year in which the asset was disposed of. Special rules apply to immovable property bought in one foreign currency and disposed of in another, and where assets are attributable to a foreign permanent establishment.

- Foreign equity instruments (e.g. shares and interests in collective investment schemes) and deemed SA source assets (e.g. foreign endowment policies and other movable assets)

  The capital gain or loss is determined by translating the cost of the asset at the spot rate when incurred, and the proceeds at the spot rate when received or accrued. In the case of assets acquired before 1 October 2001 where the market value method for determining the base cost is adopted, the spot rate on that date is used to translate the market value into Rands.

  From 8 November 2005 individuals and non-trading trusts may elect to translate the cost of the asset and the proceeds upon disposal at the average exchange rate applicable in the year when the expenditure was incurred or when the proceeds were received or accrued as the case may be.

- Foreign currency assets and liabilities (foreign bank notes, traveller's cheques, bank accounts and foreign loans)

  Foreign currency notes and coins and traveller's cheques used for the regular payment of personal expenses (e.g. during a holiday) are exempt from CGT. A person is also allowed one foreign bank account (a call or current account) free of CGT, provided that it is used for the regular (e.g. monthly) payment of personal expenses.

  Foreign currency gains and losses on these assets became subject to CGT with effect from 1 March 2003. A foreign currency asset pool must be maintained for each foreign currency for the purpose of determining the base cost of a foreign currency asset. Additions to the pool are made at the average exchange rate in the year of acquisition. When an asset is disposed of its base cost will be the weighted average Rand cost of the pool. Proceeds are translated at the average exchange rate in the year of disposal.

[5] For purposes of CGT, a small business means a business of which the market value of all its assets, as at the date of the disposal of the asset or interest, does not exceed R5 million

CGT on disposal of property in RSA by non-residents

Non-residents must account for capital gains and losses made from the disposal of the following assets:

- Immovable property situated in SA or any interest or right in immovable property situated in SA. The term "interest in immovable property situated in SA" includes a direct or indirect holding of 20% or more of the shares in a company, where 80% or more of the current market value of the shares of that company are directly or indirectly attributable to immovable property situated in SA. Also included as immovable property is a vested interest in a trust where 80% or more of the value of that interest is attributable directly or indirectly to immovable property in SA.

- Assets attributable to a permanent establishment in SA (e.g. a branch or agency of a foreign company in SA).

Relief from double taxation is granted in the agreement for the avoidance of double taxation between RSA and the country of residence of the non-resident taxpayer, where applicable.

CGT Rates

Individuals (and special trusts)

Tax year	Annual exclusion	Inclusion rate
2006/07	R12 500	25% of net capital gain

Trusts

Tax year	Inclusion rate
2006/07	50% of net capital gain

Companies

Tax year ending between	Inclusion rate
01/04/2006 to 31/03/2007	50% of net capital gain

Further information on CGT is available on the SARS website or from any SARS office.

3.5 Donations Tax

Donations tax is payable on the value of property disposed of by means of a donation by a resident. The rate applicable is 20%. Apart from other exemptions such as donations to public benefit organisations, donations made by a natural person (individual) up to the value of R50 000 per year of assessment are exempt from tax. For other persons such as private companies, the exemption is limited to R10 000 in respect of casual gifts.

3.6 Value-Added Tax (VAT)

Value-added tax (VAT) is an indirect tax levied in terms of the VAT Act. VAT must be included in the selling price of every taxable supply of goods and/or services made by a vendor in the course or furtherance of that vendor's enterprise. VAT is also levied on the importation of goods into RSA. In certain instances, VAT is payable on the importation of services into RSA.

- Supplies

  There are two types of supplies, i.e. –

  - taxable supplies; and
  - exempt supplies.

  - o Taxable supplies

    A taxable supply is any supply of goods or services made by a vendor in the course or furtherance of an enterprise. A taxable supply is subject to VAT at either:

    - the standard rate, (currently 14%); or
    - the zero rate (0%)

    Standard-rated supplies

    Goods or services supplied by vendors in the RSA will generally be standard-rated unless a specific zero-rating or exemption applies. Imports of goods are also generally subject to VAT at the standard rate unless a specific exemption applies.

    Zero-rated supplies

    Section 11 of the VAT Act provides for certain supplies to be zero-rated. Examples of these supplies (goods and services) include:

    - Goods exported from RSA
    - Brown bread
    - Brown wheaten meal
    - Maize meal
    - Samp
    - Mealie rice
    - Dried mealies
    - Dried beans
    - Rice
    - Lentils
    - Fruit and vegetables
    - Pilchards and sardinella in tins or cans
    - Milk, cultured milk and milk powder
    - Vegetable cooking oil
    - Eggs
    - Edible legumes and pulse of leguminous plants
    - Dairy powder blends
    - Petrol, diesel and illuminating paraffin
    - Certain supplies made to VAT registered farmers of certain agricultural inputs

- Certain gold coins issued by the SA Reserve Bank, including Kruger Rands
- International transport and related services
- Services physically supplied outside RSA.

Any vendor applying the zero rate must obtain and retain certain documentary proof of the vendor's entitlement to apply the zero rate. VAT incurred on any goods or services acquired in order to make zero-rated supplies may be claimed as input tax.

o Exempt supplies

Exempt supplies are supplies of goods or services on which VAT is not levied. Exempt supplies are not taxable supplies and do not form part of your taxable turnover for VAT purposes. VAT incurred on any goods or services acquired in order to make exempt supplies may not be claimed as input tax. Examples of exempt supplies include:

- Certain educational services
- Public transport by road or rail
- The provision of medical aid
- Interest on loans
- Life insurance and retirement fund benefits

Section 12 of the VAT Act provides for those supplies that are exempt from VAT.

- Registration

o Compulsory registration

Any person who carries on an enterprise and whose total value of taxable supplies (taxable turnover) exceeds, or is likely to exceed, R300 000 in any 12 month period, must register for VAT.

o Voluntary registration

In certain instances, the VAT Act allows a person to register as a vendor, even though the turnover of potentially taxable supplies is below the R300 000 compulsory registration threshold. These are listed below:

- Any person who carries on an enterprise where the total value of taxable supplies (taxable turnover) exceeds R20 000 (but does not exceed R300 000) in the preceding 12 month period. (This rule does not apply in cases where other special rules are applicable. For example, welfare organisations and local authorities are not required to meet the minimum threshold of R20 000).

- Any person who intends to carry on an enterprise which is to be supplied to that person as a going concern and the total value of taxable supplies made by the supplier of the going concern has exceeded R20 000 in the previous 12 months;

- Any person who carries on an enterprise, where as a result of the nature of the activity, the person can only reasonably be expected to make taxable supplies exceeding R20 000 in a 12-month period after a period of time. For example plantation farmers.

It may be advantageous for a person to register voluntarily if supplies of goods or services are made mainly to other vendors so as to allow the purchasing vendor to claim the VAT incurred on the supply (i.e. input tax). However, where the person supplies mainly services to non-vendors, (i.e. people who are not registered for VAT), it will generally not be advantageous to voluntarily register for VAT.

Refusal of Registration

If you do not fall within the aforementioned categories, you will not qualify to register as a vendor. No registration will be allowed if the annual turnover is below R20 000.

In addition, where only exempt supplies are made, that person will not be conducting an enterprise for VAT purposes and will therefore not be able to register.

How to register?

Application for registration as a vendor must be made on form VAT101 (obtainable from your local SARS office or on the SARS website), within 21 days of becoming liable to register. The VAT402 guide will assist in completion of the VAT101 form.

- Accounting Basis
  - Invoice Basis

    Generally, a vendor must account for VAT on the invoice basis. In other words, output tax must be accounted for at the earlier of an invoice being issued or payment being received for a specific supply.

    Input tax may only be claimed when the vendor is in possession of a valid tax invoice, irrespective of whether payment has been made to the supplier or not. However, should payment not be made within 12 months after the expiry of the tax period within which the input tax was claimed, output tax must be accounted for on that portion of the payment that has not been made.

  - Payments Basis

    The Commissioner may, on written application by the vendor, direct that the vendor account for VAT on the payments basis. When using this method, output tax and input tax must be accounted for at the time that payments are received and made. It should be noted that it is still required for input tax purposes, for the vendor to be in possession of a valid tax invoice. Certain requirements must be met for the vendor to account for VAT on the payments basis. These include:

    - The vendor must be a public authority, local authority or an association not for gain; or
    - The vendor must be a natural person (other than the trustee of a trust fund) or an unincorporated body of persons of which all the members are natural persons. In this case, it is also required that the total value of the vendor's taxable supplies in the past 12 months has not exceeded R2.5 million, nor be likely to exceed that amount in the next 12 month period.

Refer to section 15 of the VAT Act for further information.

- Tax Periods

  It is the predetermined period in which a vendor is required to lodge a VAT return.

  Generally speaking, there are five different types of tax periods.

  - Monthly: known as Category C and applies to vendors whose turnover is more than R30 million a year.
  - Two monthly: known as Category A or B which is applicable to vendors whose turnover is less than R30 million a year. The applicable category is determined by the Commissioner.
  - Four monthly: known as Category F and applies to vendors whose turnover is less than R1 million a year (R1.2 million for tax periods commencing on or after 1 July 2006).
  - Six monthly: known as Category D and applies to small farmers with a turnover of less than R1 million a year (R1.2 million for tax periods commencing on or after 1 July 2006).
  - Twelve monthly: known as Category E and generally ends on the last day of the vendor's "year of assessment" as defined in section 1 of the Act. It only applies to vendors who are companies or trusts where the income consists solely of property rentals, management or administration fees charged to connected persons that are entitled to a full deduction of input tax on such fees.

  The above-mentioned categories have various requirements which must be satisfied before a vendor will be allowed to fall within a certain category. These requirements are contained in section 27 of the VAT Act.

- Calculation of VAT

  For ease of reference, the following terms are defined:

  Input tax – VAT paid by the vendor on the purchase of goods or services. VAT may, in certain circumstances, be claimed as input tax provided the goods or services are acquired for making taxable supplies and the vendor is in possession of a valid tax invoice. The following are examples of purchases where input tax cannot be claimed:

  - Purchase/lease/hire of a "motor car" as defined in the VAT Act.
  - Most expenses relating to entertainment.
  - Membership fees for sporting and recreational clubs (e.g. country clubs and golf clubs).

  Output tax – The VAT charged by a vendor in respect of the taxable supply of goods or services. This will also include certain payments which give rise to deemed supplies. (E.g. short term insurance payments received for loss or damage to assets).

  In determining the VAT liability, the vendor has to subtract the input tax claimed from the output tax charged. Where the output tax exceeds the input tax, the vendor has to pay the difference to SARS. Where the input tax exceeds the output tax charged, the vendor is entitled to a refund from SARS.

Where the vendor does not receive the refund within 21 business days after the date on which SARS received the VAT201 return and any defects on the VAT201 (if any) have been rectified and additional information requested by SARS has been supplied, interest will be paid by SARS at the prescribed rate, subject to various conditions being met.

- Small Retailers VAT Package

  - o What is the Small Retailers VAT Package?

    The Small Retailers VAT Package is a simpler VAT option for small retailers and forms part of SARS' drive to assist certain small businesses. If you qualify for this Package it means that you can satisfy the VAT Act without detailed recordkeeping or having to buy expensive cash registers to keep track of sales on the various types of products you sell.

    This Package also includes a free set of pre-printed books in which you keep track of the stock you buy and your daily sales. In short, you get to spend more time and money growing your business. This is not only important for the success of your business, but also supports the continued growth of our economy.

  - o Why was the Small Retailers VAT Package introduced?

    - *To make it simpler for small retailers who are registered for VAT*
      SARS recognises that small retailers find it difficult and time consuming to keep the detailed sales records required by the VAT Act. The Small Retailers VAT Package is designed to cut through these problems and make accounting for VAT simpler for small retailers.

    - *To make it simpler for small retailers who are not registered for VAT to satisfy the law*
      All retailers who have a turnover of R300 000 or more per year must register for VAT. There are many small retailers who should register for VAT but do not. However, SARS recognises that this is often due to a lack of knowledge or because small retailers feel that the process is too complicated and time consuming. While this is not a valid excuse for not registering, SARS has tried to resolve the problem by introducing the Small Retailers VAT Package. Unregistered retailers are thus encouraged to register for VAT and apply for the Small Retailers VAT Package.

    - *To reduce VAT fraud*
      SARS is aware that some retailers abuse VAT through dishonest reporting of sales information. There are also retailers who knowingly avoid registering for VAT when they are required to do so. These practices are regarded as serious criminal acts and SARS will increase its audit activity among retailers to identify such retailers.

  - o Who qualifies for the Small Retailers VAT Package?

    If you are not registered for VAT, you will first have to register for VAT before you can apply for the Small Retailers VAT Package. You can do so by visiting a SARS office or by calling the SARS Call Centre on 0860 121218. Alternatively, visit the SARS website at www.sars.gov.za for more information.
    If you are already registered for VAT, you qualify for the Small Retailers VAT Package only if you satisfy the requirements to become an approved vendor.

To be an approved vendor you must -

- sell standard-rated goods (i.e. goods taxed at 14% VAT) as well as zero-rated goods (i.e. goods taxed at 0%) from the same place of business;
- make taxable supplies (excluding VAT) of less than
- R1 million in any 12 month period; and
- not have adequate point of sale equipment i.e. an electronic scanning system; or a touch screen register; or a product-specific cash register which is able to separately record zero-rated and standard-rated sales.

If you meet all these requirements, you may apply by completing a form (VAT SRVP1) and delivering it to the nearest SARS office or mail box. If your application is approved, you will receive written notification on a form SRVP2, a set of pre-printed record books and a detailed guide that explains all aspects of the Package.

o Important points to take note of:

- If you have been accepted into the Small Retailers VAT Package and then decide, at some time in the future, to return to the normal VAT scheme you may apply to do so. Your reasons and circumstances will be taken into account when SARS assesses your application.
- Retailers who are not currently registered for VAT are encouraged to come forward and register voluntarily. SARS' Voluntary Disclosure Dispensation allows for the conditional waiving of penalties or additional tax provided that the taxpayer approaches SARS voluntarily before an investigation of his or her affairs has commenced.
- The industry mark-up percentage of 40% used in the Small Retailers VAT Package is an average rate used to simplify the calculation of VAT. It should NOT be interpreted as the mark-up you should actually charge your customers on zero-rated goods.
- The full technical detail of the Package is contained in a guide: SRVP 416.

o How does the Small Retailers VAT Package work?

The Small Retailers VAT Package allows you to determine your output tax liability by applying the following method:

Step 1 Calculate your daily gross takings inclusive of VAT over a period of 2 months.

Step 2 Calculate the value of your zero-rated sales by adding the value of the Industry Mark-up Percentage to total zero-rated purchases that you used to make zero-rated supplies.

Step 3 Calculate your standard-rated sales by deducting the zero-rated sales (from step 2) from your daily gross takings.

Step 4 Apply the 14% tax fraction to the total standard-rated sales determined in step 3.

Step 5 Account for the output tax in your VAT201 return.

Example

Corner Café was registered under the Small Retailers VAT Package with effect from 1 April 2005. Corner Café recorded the following transactions for the period 1 April 2005 to 31 May 2005:

Cash in till at end of day	R60 000
Cheques and cash banked	R25 000
Cash taken for purchases	R5 000
Daily float	R 250
Zero-rated stock purchases	R30 000
Standard-rated purchases	R34 200

The calculation of Corner Café's Daily Gross Takings (DGT) for the period 1 April 2005 to 31 May 2005:

Cash in the till at end of day	R60 000
Add: Cash/Cheques banked	R25 000
Add: Cash taken for purchases	R5 000
Less: Daily float	-R250
TOTAL Daily Gross Takings	R89 750

The calculation of Corner Café's zero-rated sales for the period 1 April 2005 to 31 May 2005:

Zero-rated purchases (from the purchases register)	R30 000
Less: Zero-rated purchases used to make standard-rated supplies	NIL
Equals: Total zero-rated purchases used exclusively to make zero-rated supplies	R30 000
Apply the 40% industry mark-up percentage to the zero-rated purchases to obtain the total rand mark-up on zero-rated sales	R12 000
Add: Total rand mark-up on zero-rated sales to zero-rated purchases to determine the TOTAL ZERO-RATED SALES	R42 000

The calculation of Corner Café's standard-rated sales for 1 April 2005 to 31 May 2005:

Daily Gross Takings	R89 750
Less: Zero-rated sales	R42 000
Total standard-rated sales	R47 750

The calculation of Corner Café's VAT liability for the period 1 April 2005 to 31 May 2005:

Standard-rated sales	R47 750	
Output tax (R47 750 x 14/114)		R5 864,04
Zero-rated sales	R42 000	
Less:		
Input tax (R34 200 x 14/114)		R4 200,00
Tax Payable (R5 864,04 – R4 200)		R1 664,04

- Requirements of a valid tax invoice

  A vendor must be in possession of a valid tax invoice in order to claim input tax. The following information must be reflected on a tax invoice:

  - The words "Tax Invoice" in a prominent place.
  - The name, address and VAT registration number of the supplier.
  - The name, address and VAT registration number of the recipient.
  - An individual serialised number and the date upon which the tax invoice is issued.
  - A full and proper description of the goods or services supplied (indicating, where applicable, that the goods are second-hand goods).
  - The quantity or volume of the goods or services supplied.
  - Either -
    - the value of the supply, the amount of tax charged and the consideration for the supply; or
    - where the amount of tax charged is calculated by applying the tax fraction to the consideration, the consideration for the supply and either the amount of the tax charged, or a statement that it includes a charge in respect of the tax and the rate at which the tax is charged.

  Where the consideration for the supply does not exceed R3 000, an abridged tax invoice may be issued. An abridged tax invoice contains the same information as a tax invoice, except that the quantity or volume of the goods or services supplied and recipient's particulars need not appear on the document.

- Submission of VAT returns

  o Manual submission

  Where a vendor manually submits a VAT201 return to SARS, it must be received by the 25th of the month following the end of the vendor's tax period. Where applicable, payment must accompany the VAT201 return.

  Where the 25th of the month falls over a weekend or on a public holiday, the VAT201 return and the payment must be submitted to the SARS office no later than the last business day before the 25th of the month.

  o Electronic submission

  Where a vendor has registered to submit the VAT201 return and payment electronically, the VAT201 return and the payment must be received by no later than the last business day of the month following the end of the vendor's tax period.

- Duties of a Vendor

  Once registered as a vendor, you have certain responsibilities including the following:

- Provide correct and accurate information to SARS
- Submit returns and payments on time
- Include VAT in your prices, advertisements and quotes
- Keep accurate accounting records
- Produce relevant documents when required by SARS
- Notify SARS about any changes in your business, namely its address, trading name, partners / members / shareholders, bank details and tax periods
- Issue tax invoices, debit and credit notes
- Notify SARS of any changes of the details of the representative person

Note: Failure to meet these responsibilities could result in penalties being payable and prosecution, additional fines and/or imprisonment.

- Exports

VAT is, usually, levied at the rate of 14%on the sale of goods supplied locally, but special concessions are made where goods are exported from South Africa. The basic rule is that if -

- **the seller controls the export**, (a direct export), the zero rate applies, (and the requirements as stipulated in Interpretation Note No. 30 must be met), and
- **the purchaser controls the export**, (an indirect export), the 14 percent standard rate applies. The purchaser may, however, claim a refund when the goods are exported in terms of Part One of the Export Incentive Scheme (the Scheme). Part Two of the Scheme offers the option to the South African vendor, at his own risk, to zero rate the supply of goods to be exported as an "indirect export" by sea or air).

The reason for this distinction is quite simple – if the purchaser controls the export, the seller cannot be sure that the goods will actually be exported from South Africa.

3.7 Estate Duty

Where the deceased was ordinarily resident in RSA his/her estate will, for estate duty purposes, consist of all property wherever situated, including deemed property (e.g. life insurance policies, payments from pension funds, etc). However, property situated outside RSA will be excluded from his/her estate if such property was acquired by him/her before he/she became ordinarily resident in RSA for the first time, or after he/she became ordinarily resident in RSA and acquired such property by way of donation/inheritance from a person which was not ordinarily resident in RSA at the date of such donation/inheritance. The exclusion also applies to property situated outside RSA, acquired out of profits/proceeds of any such property acquired in the above circumstances.

The estate of a non-resident is only subject to estate duty to the extent that it consists of certain "property" and "deemed property" of the deceased as defined in the Estate Duty Act. The Estate Duty Act unlike the Income Tax Act does not have a definition of the word "resident" and only refers to persons who are "ordinarily resident" or not "ordinarily resident". It therefore, follows that any natural person who is not ordinarily resident in South Africa, but who became a resident of South Africa, in terms of the physical presence test for income tax purposes, is still regarded as a non-resident for estate duty purposes, due to the fact that such person is not ordinarily resident in South Africa.

The duty is calculated on the dutiable amount of the estate. Certain admissible deductions are made from the total value of the estate. One such deduction is the value of property in the estate that accrues to the surviving spouse of the deceased. The net value of the estate is reduced by a R2.5 million general deduction to arrive at the dutiable amount of the estate.

Estate Duty Rates

From	Until	Deduction	Rate
01/03/2006	To date	R2 500 000	20%

Example of estate duty calculation

Net value	R 2 600 000
Less: Deduction	R 2 500 000
Dutiable amount	R 100 000
Duty payable on R100 000 at 20%	R 20 000

Interest at 6% per annum is charged on unpaid duty.

3.8 Stamp Duty

Stamp duty is levied on instruments such as leases of immovable property and unlisted marketable securities at different rates.

Leases of Immovable Property

For every R100 or part thereof of aggregate rent and any other consideration —	
Period not exceeding 5 years	25 cents
Period exceeding 5 years but not 10 years	40 cents
Period exceeding 10 years but not 20 years	55 cents
Period exceeding 20 years	70 cents

From 1 January 2005 the duty is calculated at 0,5% of the quantifiable amount of a lease. Where the rental is not quantifiable (e.g. turnover rental), duty will be payable when then amount becomes quantifiable.

Note: An exemption applies if the duty calculated over the period of lease does not exceed R200, but the exemption will not apply if the total consideration payable for the lease is not quantifiable, at the time of execution of the lease.

This exemption applies where the lease is executed in the year of assessment of the lessor who is a taxpayer commencing on or after 1 February 2006, or in the case of any other lessor, on or after 1 March 2006. With effect from 1 March 2006 the above amount of R200 was increased to R500.

The duty payable in this regard will not exceed 10 per cent of the value applicable for transfer duty purposes.

Marketable securities

Original issue of shares/stock

For every R20, or part thereof, the nominal value and any premium payable thereon (if transferable only by registration)	5 cents
If made out to bearer for every R20 or part thereof of the nominal value and any premiums payable thereon	20 cents

Note: Stamp Duty on the issue of shares was eliminated from 1 January 2006

The issue of a certificate or other like instrument representing an interest in shares/stock

If not transferable or only by registration for every R100 or part thereof of the price of issue	5 cents
If made out to bearer for every R100 or part thereof of the price of issue	20 cents

Note: Stamp Duty on the issue of shares was eliminated from 1 January 2006

Registration of transfer (other than through a stockbroker)

For every R10, or part thereof, of the amount or value of the consideration given, or less than the market value is given, the value of the marketable security transferred	2.5 cents

Note: With effect from 1 January 2006 no duty is payable if the duty is R100 or less during any six month period

Cancellation or redemption of company shares

For every R10, or part thereof, of the value of the consideration	2.5 cents

Acquisition by transferee from transferor

For every R10, or part thereof, of the amount or value of the consideration given , or where no consideration is given, the value of the marketable security transferred	2.5 cents

Notes: (1) With effect from 1 January 2006 no duty is payable if the duty is R100 or less during any six month period.

(2) Specific exemptions apply to each of the five items listed under Marketable securities.

3.9 Uncertificated Securities Tax (UST)

Uncertificated securities tax at the rate of 0.25% is payable in respect of every change in beneficial ownership in any securities which are listed on the JSE Securities Exchange. In the case of unlisted securities, stamp duty is levied at the same rate of 0.25%.

Note: UST on the issue of securities was eliminated from 1 January 2006

3.10 Transfer Duty

Transfer duty is levied on the consideration payable for the acquisition of fixed property. If, for some reason, no consideration is payable or consideration is not market related, the duty is levied on the fair market value of the property.

Amendments were introduced with effect from 13 December 2002 to counter the avoidance of transfer duty by placing residential property in companies, close corporations and discretionary trusts and selling the shares, members' interest and, arguably, contingent rights instead of the property. The definition of "property" was amended to include shares, members' interest and contingent rights in certain circumstances and to bring the transfer of these assets within the charging section.

All transactions relating to a taxable supply of goods and subject to VAT are exempt from transfer duty.

Transfer Duty Rates
From 01/03/2006 to date

Individuals

Consideration	Rate
On the first R500 000 of the consideration	0%
On the amount that exceeds R500 000 but not R1 million	5%
On the amount that exceeds R1 million	R25 000 plus 8% on the value above R1 million

A person other than a natural person (for example, a company, CC and trust), 8% of consideration.

3.11 Importation of Goods and payment of customs and excise duties and VAT

- Introduction

Goods arriving in South Africa may only enter through appointed places of entry. These goods must be declared to SARS within the prescribed time periods. The applicable customs duties, if any, must be paid when the goods are entered for home consumption, i.e. for use in the Southern African Customs Union comprising of the Republic, Botswana, Lesotho, Namibia and Swaziland. The rate of duty is dependant on the tariff classification (description) of the goods and duty is usually payable on the value (customs value) or the volume or quantity of the goods imported. The customs duty may however be –

- deferred if the importer is a participant in the SARS deferment scheme;
- or rebated if the goods meet certain conditions; or
- suspended if the goods are entered for storage in a licensed warehouse.

Imported goods may also qualify for a preferential rate of duty in terms of free or preferential trade agreements to which the Republic is a party. The goods may also be subject to import control, sanitary and photo-sanitary requirements.

In addition, VAT is also payable on goods imported and cleared for home consumption.

- **Registration as an Importer**

  Any person who intends importing goods into South Africa must register with SARS as an importer. Importers who import non- commercial goods of which the value for each consignment is less than R20 000, provided that this is limited to three importations per calendar year, are excluded from the registration requirement.

- **Goods imported through appointed places of entry**

  Imported goods can only enter South Africa through appointed places of entry, which include –

  - Customs appointed airports;
  - Customs appointed land border posts;
  - Customs appointed harbours; and
  - the postal service.

- **Import Declarations**

  The importer is required to complete the prescribed bill of entry declaration within the stipulated time period in respect of imported goods. Goods not declared within this time period will be detained and removed to a state warehouse. It is the responsibility of the importer to ensure that the declaration is fully and accurately completed and all supporting documents are produced. Declarations may either be submitted manually or electronically to SARS. Goods may be stopped or detained, on a risk basis in order to verify the correctness of the declaration. Where errors are detected by SARS or false declarations are made, whether duties were payable or not, the Customs and Excise Act, 1964 provides for penalties, in addition to the forfeiture of the goods. In instances of fraud, offenders may be prosecuted. Goods subject to import control will only be released on the production of the relevant permit at the time of clearance or seized if their importation is prohibited.

- **Tariff Classification**

  Tariff classification is the process whereby imported goods are categorized by virtue of what it is, or how it is made or what it is used for. According to this classification, the applicable rate of duty is levied.

- **Customs Value**

  Customs value is established in terms of Article VII of the General Agreement on Tariffs and Trade (GATT). Provision is made for six valuation methods. The majority of goods are valued using method 1, which is the actual price paid or payable by the buyer of the goods. The Free on Board (FOB) price forms the basis for the value, allowing for certain deductions (e.g. interest charged on extended payment terms) and additions (e.g. certain royalties) to be effected.

  In determining the customs value, SARS pays particular attention to the relationship between the buyer and seller, payments outside of the normal transactions, e.g. royalties and licence fees and restrictions that have been placed on the buyer. These aspects can result in the price paid for the goods being increased for the purpose of determining a customs value and thus directly affecting the customs duty payable.

- Duties and Levies

  Customs duty is protective in nature and the purpose of the duty is to protect local industries. Excise Duty, Fuel Levy and Environmental Levy are forms of indirect taxation used by government to primarily contribute to the fiscus, but also in certain instances to influence consumer behaviour. SARS also collects the Road Accident Fund levy.

  – Customs duty

    Customs duty is a consumption tax levied on imported goods and is usually calculated as a percentage on the value of the goods. However, goods such as certain meat and primary plastic products, certain textile products and certain firearms attract rates of duty that are calculated either as a percentage of the value of the goods, or as cents per unit, kilogram or metre, etc.

  – Excise duties

    Excise duty is a consumption tax levied on certain locally manufactured products. A counter-veiling Customs duty, equal to the rate of the Excise duty, is levied on imported goods of the same class and kind in addition to any customs duty payable. Excise duty or its counter-veiling Customs duty counterpart is fiscal in nature to raise revenue.

    – General Fuel Levy and Road Accident Fund Levy

    The general fuel levy and the Road Accident Fund levy are charged over and above the excise duty or counter-veiling Customs duty on certain fuel products.

  – Environmental levy (see also par 3.14)

    Environmental levy is currently levied on certain plastic carrier bags and flat bags.

  – Anti-dumping and countervailing duties on imported goods

    Anti-dumping, countervailing and safeguard duties are trade remedies to protect local industries against goods being dumped in South Africa or on subsidised imported goods or in the case of disruptive competition respectively. These goods are the subject of trade and industry investigations into pricing and export incentives in the country of origin and the rate imposed will depend on the result of the investigations.

    The above duties are either levied on an ad valorem basis (percentage of the value of the goods) or as a specific duty (percentage per unit, kilogram, litre, etc).

- VAT – Importation of goods

  VAT is, in terms of section 7(1)(b) of the VAT Act, 1991, levied at the rate of 14% on the importation of goods into South Africa from export countries, including Botswana, Lesotho, Namibia and Swaziland. However, the importation of certain goods into South Africa is, in terms of section 13(3) read with Schedule 1 to the VAT Act, exempt from VAT on importation.

The value to be placed on the importation of goods into South Africa is, in terms of section 13(2)(a) of the VAT Act,1991, deemed to be the value of goods for customs duty purposes, plus any duty levied in terms of the Customs and Excise Act, 1964 in respect of the importation of such goods, plus 10% of the said value. Section 13(2)(b) provides that the value is not increased by the factor of 10 percent where the goods have their origin in Botswana, Lesotho, Namibia or Swaziland.

- **Deferment, suspension and rebate of duties**

Participation in the SARS deferment scheme allows an importer to defer duty and VAT for a period up to 30 days after clearance of imported goods for home consumption. At the conclusion of the period of deferment the client is allowed a further seven days in order to settle the account. A requirement for participation in the deferment scheme is the furnishing of adequate security to cover the amount deferred.

The payment of duty and VAT is suspended for a period of up to two years when goods are entered into a licensed customs and excise storage warehouse for storage. Duty and VAT must be brought to account when the goods are cleared for home consumption.

Rebate provisions are provided for the suspension of customs duties on goods imported for inward processing (Industrial rebates) and outward processing (temporary admission for purposes of manufacture for export) subject to certain conditions. Value-added tax is suspended as well for goods temporary admitted for outward processing.

Relief (in the form of full or partial rebates) is also granted in respect of the use of excisable products in the manufacture of other non-excisable products and for the industrial use of these excisable products, e.g. spirits used in the manufacture of medicines, paints, adhesives, etc. and petroleum products used for farming, fishing and forestry purposes.

3.12 Exportation of goods and payment of export duty

- **Introduction**

Goods exported from South Africa may only be exported through places appointed for this purpose. Every exporter of any goods must within the prescribed period declare such goods for export. The goods may also be subject to export control being either totally prohibited from export or subject to the production of a permit from the issuing authority at the time of clearance. Although the Customs and Excise Act, 1964 makes provision for the imposition of export duty, no exports duties have been imposed.

- **Registration as an Exporter**

Any person who intends exporting goods from South Africa must register with SARS as an exporter. Exporters who export non- commercial goods of which the value for each consignment is less than R20 000, provided that this is limited to three exportations per calendar year, are excluded from registration.

- Export Declarations

  Every exporter of any goods must, before such goods are exported from South Africa deliver to the Controller a bill of entry in the prescribed form. Declarations may either be manually or electronically to SARS. Goods may be stopped or detained, on a risk basis in order to verify the correctness of the declaration. Where errors are detected by SARS or false declarations are made, the Act provides for penalties in addition to forfeiture of the goods. In instances of fraud, offenders may be prosecuted.

3.13 Free Trade Agreements and preferential arrangements with other countries

A number of agreements have been concluded or are in the process of being negotiated with other countries and trading blocs, which provides for preferential market access into South African (imports) as well as for South African products into other markets (exports). These are:

- Bi-lateral Agreements (Non-reciprocal)
  - Trade Agreement between the Governments of the Republic of South Africa and Southern Rhodesia (Zimbabwe); and
  - Trade Agreement between the Government of the Republic of South Africa and the Government of the Republic of Malawi,

  providing for preferential access of specific products into South Africa subject to specific origin requirements and quota permits.

- Preferential dispensation for goods entering South Africa (Non-reciprocal)
  Goods produced or manufactured in the Republic of Mozambique (Rebate Item 412.25), providing for free or reduced duties subject specific origin requirements

- Free or Preferential Trade Agreements (FTAs and PTAs) (Reciprocal)
  - SACU – The Southern African Customs Union consists of South Africa, Botswana, Lesotho, Namibia and Swaziland. Its aim is to maintain the free interchange of goods between member countries. It provides for a common external tariff and a common excise tariff to this common customs area.
  - TDCA - Agreement on Trade, Development and Cooperation between the European Community and its Member States, of the one part, and the Republic of South Africa, on the other part, which was implemented 1 January 2000.
  - SADC-Treaty of the Southern African Development Community, which was implemented on 1 September 2000.
  - A number of such agreements are in the process of being negotiated or being finalised which will come into operation during 2006. Notably will be the agreement with the European Free Trade Association (EFTA). Other agreements being negotiated are those with the United States of America, India, China and the Common Market of the Southern Cone (MERCOSUR).

- Generalised System of Preferences (GSPs) (Non- reciprocal)
  - AGOA

    Preferential tariff treatment of textile and apparel articles imported directly into the territory of the United States of America from the Republic as contemplated in the African Growth and Opportunity Act

  - EU

    Non-reciprocal preferential tariff treatment under the Generalised System of Preference granted to developing countries by the European Community

  - Norway

    Non-reciprocal preferential tariff treatment under the Generalised System of Preference granted to developing countries by the Kingdom of Norway

  - Switzerland

    Non-reciprocal preferential tariff treatment under the Generalised System of Preference granted to developing countries by the Swiss Confederation

  - Russia

    Non-reciprocal preferential tariff treatment under the Generalised System of Preference granted to developing countries by the Russian Federation

  - Turkey

    Non-reciprocal preferential tariff treatment under the Generalised System of Preference granted to developing countries by the Republic of Turkey

3.14 Environmental Levy

Since 1 June 2004 an environmental levy is charged on certain plastic carrier bags and flat bags (bags generally regarded as "grocery bags") at a rate of 3 cents per bag. Plastic bags used for immediate wrapping / packaging, refuse bags and refuse bin liners are excluded from paying this levy.

Apart from the payment of this specific Environmental Levy per quarterly excise account, VAT is also levied on these bags, calculated on a value which includes the amount of the levy.

Manufacturers of such bags must licence their premises as manufacturing warehouses with the local Controller of Customs and Excise and submit quarterly excise accounts to such Controller.

3.15 Skills Development Levy (SDL)

An employer must pay SDL if the employer pays annual salaries, wages and other remuneration in excess of R500 000. Employers with an annual payroll of R500 000 or less (whether registered for employees tax purposes with SARS or not) are therefore exempt from this levy.

This levy (currently 1%) is used for the funding of education and training of employees. It is calculated as a percentage of a leviable amount, which is more or less equal to the earnings of the employees. The application form to register for SDL is the same form that is used to register for employees' tax (EMP101). The monthly return for SDL is combined with the monthly return for employees' tax (EMP201) which means that the same terms and conditions apply for submission and payment. Further information in this regard is available in the SDL10 – "Guidelines to Employers" which is available at SARS offices and on the SARS website under SDL.

3.16 Unemployment Insurance Contributions

The Unemployment Insurance Fund insures employees against the loss of earnings due to termination of employment, illness and maternity leave. A monthly contribution has to be made by the employer (1%) and the employee (1%) based on the earnings of the employee. The contributions are calculated as a percentage of the remuneration paid to the employee for services rendered. An employer who is registered for employees' tax or the Skills Development Levy is automatically registered for U.I. contributions. (The forms used are the same forms that are used for SDL and PAYE purposes). An employer that is not liable for the payment of employees' tax or SDL must register for U.I. purposes with the Unemployment Insurance Commissioner at the Department of Labour.

UIF contributions are only paid or payable up to an amount of R11 662 remuneration per month. Any remuneration received by an employee which is in excess of R11 662 will not be taken into account for the calculation of UIF contributions. The threshold of R11 662 was effective from 1 July 2006.

Note must be taken of the following: Where an amount of an employee's contribution which has been deducted by an employer which is a company (other than a listed company) has not been paid over to the Commissioner or the Unemployment Insurance Commissioner, the representative employer and every director and shareholder of that company who controls or is regularly involved in the management of the company's overall financial affairs will personally be liable for the payment of that amount to the Commissioner or the Unemployment Insurance Commissioner and for any penalty which may be imposed in respect of that payment.

Further information in this regard is available in the Unemployment Insurance Contributions Guidelines to Employers which is available on the SARS website under "UIF". The Department of Labour's website, www.uif.gov.za also has useful information in this regard.

4. YOUR BUSINESS AND OTHER AUTHORITIES

4.1 Introduction

Before you commence with your business activities, it may be necessary for you to register with certain other authorities in order to comply with laws or regulations of a general nature or pertaining to your area of operation specifically. It will be in your own interest to make enquiries in this regard and to comply with all the requirements that might be set. Some of the requirements that might be applicable to you are mentioned below. The purpose of this section is merely to bring to your attention some of the authorities that might require your registration. The list below is not exhaustive.

- Municipalities

  – Regional Establishment Levy and Regional Services Levy

    These levies are levied (at fairly low rates) on turnover (viz, establishment levy) and payroll (viz, services levy). Any enterprise within the region of the municipality who has other persons in his/her employment or who carries on a business in the region must register with such municipality. Inquiries in this regard must be directed to the relevant municipality.

    It was proposed in the 2005 Budget that Regional Service Council levies would be abolished on 30 June 2006. Legislation has now been passed to repeal these levies with effect from 1 July 2006 (see section 59 of the Small Business Tax Amnesty and Amendment of Taxation Laws Act, No 9 of 2006).

  – Other

    Your local municipality will provide information with regard to the rules/regulations laid down in respect of businesses in their respective areas.

- Unemployment Insurance Commissioner

  Those employers who are not liable to register with SARS for PAYE and/or SDL purposes, but are liable for the payment of U.I. contributions must pay such contributions in respect of all its employees to the U.I. Commissioner at the Department of Labour. (See also under Unemployment Insurance Contributions.)

- South African Reserve Bank – Exchange Control Regulations

  Exchange control regulations restricting the in and out flow of capital in South Africa, still exist. For example, investments into South Africa must be reported and prior approval may be required if loan capital is invested in South Africa.

  Residents of South Africa wishing to remit/invest/lend amounts abroad are as a general rule subject to exchange control restrictions and will need to approach their local commercial banks in this regard.

  Individuals who are over 18 years and in good standing with their tax affairs may invest a total of R2 000 000 outside South Africa. However, individuals are also able to invest, without restriction, in foreign companies listed on South African bond and security exchanges.

  Companies may use unlimited South African funds for new approved foreign direct investments (strictly true investments in factories or businesses and not for portfolio investments). Companies will also be allowed to retain foreign dividends offshore, and dividends repatriated to South Africa after 26 October 2004 may be transferred offshore again at any time for any purpose.

  Application to the South African Reserve Bank's Exchange Control Department is still required for monitoring purposes and for approval in terms of existing foreign direct investment criteria, including demonstrated benefit to South Africa. The South African Reserve Bank, however, reserves the right to stagger capital outflows relating to very large foreign investments so as to manage any potential impact on the foreign exchange market.

Further information is available on the Reserve Bank website, namely: http://www.reservebank.co.za.

- **Department of Trade and Industry**

  Information on SMMEs, details of various assistance schemes, rebates, incentives and information such as how to start a business, type of business entities and requirements of registration of a business entity may be obtained from the Department of Trade and Industry or on their website www.dti.gov.za.

- **Broad-Based Black Economic Empowerment Act, No. 53 of 2003**

  The above Act provides a legislative framework for the promotion of black economic empowerment and for the issuing of the codes of good practice. For more information contact the Department of Trade and Industry or visit their website at www.dti.gov.za.

- **Environmental**

  Various Acts exist with regard to the control and management of pollution which are administered by different State Departments. Companies and individuals conducting businesses which may cause harm to the environment should approach the relevant Department to ensure that they comply with the relevant environmental standards. Acts in this regard may include the following:

  - National Environmental Management Act, 1998 (management of pollution in general)
  - Atmospheric Pollution Prevention Act, 1965 (management of air pollution)
  - National Water Act, 1998 (management of water resources)
  - Mineral and Petroleum Resources Development Act, 2002 (rehabilitation of mining areas)
  - Hazardous Substances Act, 1973

- **Safety and Security**

  Below is a list of some legislation relating to safety, security and health issues, which will enable businesses to ensure that their work places are safe and secure environments to work in.

  - Explosives Act, No 15 of 2003
  - National Nuclear Regulator Act, No 47 of 1999
  - Nuclear Energy Act, No 46 of 1999
  - Occupational Health and Safety Act, No 85 of 1993
  - Tobacco Products Control Act, No 83 of 1993

- **Labour**

  Various Acts, administered by the Department of Labour, govern the relationship between employers and employees. These Acts include the following:

  - Basic Conditions of Employment Act, 1997

- Labour Relations Act, 1995
- Employment Equity Act, 1998
- Skills Development Act, 1998
- Compensation for Occupational Injuries and Diseases Act,1993
    - Employers are required to make contributions calculated on a certain percentage of their employees' earnings to the Compensation Fund, from which compensation is paid for injuries/diseases sustained or contracted by employees in the course of their employment or for death resulting from such injuries/diseases (for more information visit the Department of Labour's website, www.labour.gov.za).

- **Promotion of Access to Information Act, No 2 of 2000**

  In terms of this Act, government departments, public and private companies, including registered close corporations and businesses are required to compile and publish manuals of their records. The initial deadline for publication of said manuals was 31 August 2003; however, the Minister of Justice has exempted small businesses and private bodies from submitting the manuals until 31 August 2005. The Department of Justice and Constitutional Development website www.doj.gov.za has more information in this regard. The SARS manual on the Promotion of Access to Information Act, 2000 is available on the SARS website under Brochures and Guides in three languages, namely English, Afrikaans and Xhosa.

- **Regulation of Interception of Communications and Provision of Communication-related Information Act, No 70 of 2002 (RICA)**

  The purpose of the RICA in broad terms is to regulate/control the interception of electronic and other communications. Senior persons in businesses using some form of electronic communications should take note of the provisions of RIC.

- **Electronic Communications and Transactions Act, No 25 of 2002 (ECTA)**

  The ECTA regulates the electronic communications, including digital signatures, electronic agreements and storage requirements. All persons making use of electronic communications are affected by this legislation.

- **Prevention of Organised Crime Act, No 121 of 1998 (POCA)**

  The purpose of the POCA is mainly to combat organised crime activities such as racketeering and money laundering. In terms of section 7 of POCA, businesses must report any unlawful activities and the failure to do so is an offence.

- **Financial Intelligence Centre Act, No 38 of 2001 (FICA)**

  The FICA sets up a regulatory anti-money laundering regime which is intended to break the cycle used by organised criminal groups to benefit from illegitimate profits. This Act aims to maintain the integrity of the financial system. Apart from the regulatory regime the Act also creates the Financial Intelligence Centre.

The regulatory regime of the FICA imposes 'know your client', record-keeping and reporting obligations on accountable institutions. It also requires accountable institutions to develop and implement internal rules to facilitate compliance with these obligations.

FICA imposes a duty on accountable institutions to establish and verify the identity of clients. Detailed records of clients and the transactions entered into by clients must be kept. Records obtained by an accountable institution must be kept for at least 5 years after a transaction was concluded and for a minimum of 5 years after the date which a business relationship was terminated and must be kept in electronic form.
Financial Intelligence Centre – contacts:

Pretoria
Private Bag X115
PRETORIA
0001
Tel: +27 12 309 9200
Fax: +27 12 315 0440

Cape Town
P O Box 6850
ROGGE BAY
8012
Tel: +27 21 443 4500

Further information on the FICA and what is meant by accountable institutions can be found on the National Treasury website, namely, www.finance.gov.za.

- Financial Advisory and Intermediary Services Act, No 37 of 2002 (FAIS Act)

  The FIAS Act has been enacted to regulate the provision of a wide range of financial and intermediary services to clients. This Act seeks to protect the public from unscrupulous and unprofessional investment advisors, intermediaries and representatives. It outlines areas such as codes of conduct, licensing requirements, the appointment of external auditors, reporting and retention obligations of financial advisors, and the declaration of 'undesirable practices".
  The Act became operational from 1 October 2004.

- Prevention and Combating of Corrupt Activities Act, No 12 of 2004 (PCCA Act)

  The PCCA Act aims to combat corruption and corrupt activities and lays out the offences relating to those activities. This Act requires that a person who holds a position of authority, who knows or ought to reasonably have known or suspected that any other person has committed a specified act of corruption or the offence of fraud, theft, extortion, forgery or uttering a forged document, involving an amount of R100 000 or more, must report such knowledge or suspicion to a police official.

- Companies Act, No 61 of 1973

  Section 173 of the Companies Act requires that private companies must submit annual returns with effect 1 May 2005 to CIPRO (Companies and Intellectual Property Registration Office). Annual returns refer to the information that companies must submit to CIPRO as confirmation that the company is still in business and that the information provided is still valid. For more information, visit www.cipro.gov.za.

- **Close Corporations Act, No 69 of 84 (CCA)**

  Close corporations (CCs) are governed by the CCA. CCs are simpler, less expensive corporate entities for single business persons or small groups of entrepreneurs. For income tax purposes a close corporation is classified as a company.

  A CC does not have to appoint an auditor, but only an "accounting officer" to draw up its financial statements. An accounting officer is a person who is a member of a recognised profession which as a condition for membership requires its members to have passed in accounting and related fields of study which would qualify such member to perform the duties of an accounting officer.

  The CCA also requires that a CC must keep accounting records to fairly represent the state of its affairs and business and must prepare annual financial statements. Furthermore, the CCA provides for penalties if certain requirements such as mentioned above are not carried out.

- **National Small Business Act, No. 102 of 1996**

  This Act provides for the establishment of an Advisory Body and the Ntsika Enterprise Promotion Agency; to provide guidelines for organs of state in order to promote small business in South Africa. The Ntsika Enterprise Promotion Agency is an agency of the Department of Trade and Industry and facilitates non-financial support and business development services to SMMEs through a broad range of intermediary organisations. For more information, refer to the Ntsika website, namely www.ntsika.org.za

- **Business Names Act, No 27 of 1960**

  This Act provides for the control of business names and related matters such as particulars to be disclosed regarding persons carrying on business, restrictions in respect of business names and prohibiting use of certain business names.

- **Lotteries Act, No 57 of 1997**

  Regulations under Lotteries Act provide the extent to which one may lawfully hold a lottery or other competition to promote the sale or use of any goods or services.

- **Mineral and Petroleum Resources Development Act, No 28 of 2002 (MPRD Act)**

  The MPRD Act affects the holders of "old order rights" (previous mining, prospecting or unused rights) held under the Minerals Act, 1991 (repealed by the MPRD Act) in the mining industry. In terms of the MPRDA the right to prospect, mine, explore, produce, etc for minerals vests in the State. Applications for the new forms of prospecting, mining, exploration, production rights, etc ("new order rights") must be made directly to the Department of Minerals and Energy. Holders of old order rights have until 30 April 2009 to convert their rights to the new order rights.
  The MPRD Act also facilitates the conversion of prospecting and mining rights currently held to the new forms of prospecting and mining rights contemplated by the MPRD Act.

- **Promotion of Administrative Justice Act, No 3 of 2000 (PAJA)**

  In terms of the Constitution of RSA, 1996 everyone has the right to administrative action that is lawful, reasonable and procedurally fair and that everyone whose rights have been adversely affected by administrative action has the right to be given written reasons. The PAJA gives effect to this right.

- Protected Disclosures Act, No 26 of 2000

  This Act provides for procedures in terms of which employees in both the private and public sectors may disclose information regarding unlawful or irregular conduct by their employers or other employees and for the protection of employees making that disclosure.

- National Credit Act, No 34 of 2005

  The purposes of the Act are, amongst others, to promote a fair, transparent, competitive, sustainable, responsible and accessible credit market and industry and to protect consumers. It also discourages reckless credit granting of credit, assists people who are heavily in debt and regulates credit information. For more information refer to the Department of Trade and Industry website, namely, www.dti.gov.za.

- Draft Consumer Protection Bill

  This draft Bill was published in Government Gazette No 28629 on 15 March 2006 for general information and comment. The aim of this Bill is to consolidate and integrate various existing consumer protection provisions that are currently contained in various other laws, for example, the Consumer Affairs Act and the Trade Practices Act, to name a few, and to protect consumers against unfair market practices and unsafe products.

5. GENERAL

- Record-keeping

  If you are involved in a business you must keep records that will enable you to prepare complete and accurate tax returns.

  You may choose a system of record keeping that is suited to the purpose and nature of your business. These records must clearly reflect your income and expenditure. This means that, in addition to your permanent books of account or records, you must maintain all other information that may be required to support the entries in your records and tax returns.

  Paid accounts, cancelled cheques and other source documents that support entries in your records should be filed in an orderly manner and stored in a safe place. For most small businesses, the business chequebook is the prime source for entries in the business records. It is advisable to open a separate bank account for your business so that you do not mix your private and business expenses.

  The records should include –

  - records showing the assets, liabilities, undrawn profits, revaluation of fixed assets and various loans;
  - a register of fixed assets;
  - detailed daily records of cash receipts and payments reflecting the nature of the transactions and the names of the parties to the transactions (except for cash sales);
  - detailed records of credit purchases (goods and services) and sales reflecting the nature of the transactions and the names of the parties to the transactions;

- o statements of annual stocktaking; and
- o supporting vouchers.

- Importance of accurate records

  Accurate records are essential for efficient management. The following demonstrates the need to keep accurate records:

  - Identify nature of receipt

    The records will show whether the receipts are of a revenue nature or capital nature.

  - Prevent omission of deductible expenses

    Expenses may be overlooked or forgotten when you prepare your tax return, unless you record them at the time they are incurred or paid.

  - Establish amounts paid out as salaries or wages

    Under normal circumstances amounts paid to employees for services rendered are taxable in the hands of the employees. In these cases employees' tax must be deducted from salaries or wages by the person paying such salaries or wages.

  - Explain items reported on your income tax return

    If your income tax return is examined by SARS, you may be asked to explain the items reported. Adequate and complete records are always supported by sales slips, invoices, receipts, bank deposit slips, cancelled cheques and other documents.

Availability and retention of records

You are required to keep the books and records of your business in order to make them available at any time for examination by SARS. The retention period commences from the date of the last entry in the particular document, record or book. In terms of Regulations issued under the Companies Act and the Close Corporation Act, records must be kept for 15 years. A list of the retention periods in terms of the Regulations is given below.

RETENTION PERIODS OF CLOSE CORPORATION RECORDS		
ITEM NO.	**RECORDS**	**RETENTION PERIOD**
1.	Founding statement (form CK1)	Indefinite
2.	Amended founding statement (forms CK2 and CK2A)	Indefinite
3.	Minute book as well as resolutions passed at meetings	Indefinite
4.	Annual financial statements including: • Annual accounts; and • The report of the accounting officer	15 years
5.	Accounting records, including supporting schedules to accounting records and ancillary accounting records	15 years
6.	The microfilm image of any original record reproduced directly by the camera - the "camera master"	Indefinite

RETENTION PERIODS OF COMPANY RECORDS		
ITEM NO.	**RECORDS**	**RETENTION PERIOD**
1.	Certificate of incorporation	Indefinite
2.	Certificate of change of name (if any)	Indefinite
3.	Memorandum and articles of association	Indefinite
4.	Certificate to commence business (if any)	Indefinite
5.	Minute book, CM25 and CM26, as well as resolutions passed at general/ class meetings	Indefinite
6.	Proxy forms	3 years
7.	Proxy forms used at Court convened meetings	3 years
8.	Register of allotments – after a person ceased to be a member (section 111)	15 years
9.	Registration of members	15 years
10.	Index of members	15 years
11.	Registers of mortgages and debentures and fixed assets	15 years
12.	Register of directors' shareholdings	15 years
13.	Register of directors and certain officers	15 years
14.	Directors attendance register	15 years
15.	Branch register	15 years
16.	Annual financial statements including: • Annual accounts • Directors' report • Auditors' report	15 years
17.	Books of account recording information required by the Act	15 years
18.	Supporting schedules to books of account and ancillary books of account	15 years

Record keeping as required in terms of sections 73A (Income Tax purposes) and 73B (Capital Gains Tax purposes) of the Income Tax Act and section 55 of the Value-Added Tax Act

In terms of the above mentioned sections, a taxpayer is required to keep records such as ledgers, cash books, journals, cheque books, paid cheques, bank statements, deposit slips, invoices, stock lists, registers, books of accounts, data in electronic form and records relating to the determination of capital gains or capital losses for a period of five years from the date on which the return for that year of assessment was received by SARS. However, in cases where objections and appeals have been lodged against assessments, it would be advisable to keep all records and data relating to the assessments under objection/appeal until such time that the objection/appeal has been finalised, even if the timeframe for finalisation exceeds five years.

- ### Appointment of Auditor/Accounting Officer

A company is required by law to appoint an auditor who will audit and sign an audit report in respect of its financial statements. Similarly a close corporation is required to appoint an accounting officer. Normally, the auditor or accounting officer will provide assistance in determining the taxable income and the amount of tax to be paid.

- Representative Taxpayer

Every Company/Close Corporation which conducts business or has an office in South Africa must, within one month from the commencement of business operations or acquisition of an office, for the purposes of section 101 of the Income Tax Act, appoint a representative as the Public Officer of the Company/Close Corporation. The name of the representative and his/her position in the Company/Close Corporation must be furnished to the SARS office for the district in which the Company/Close Corporation has its registered office, for approval. The representative must be a responsible officer of the Company/Close Corporation (for example, director, manager, senior member, secretary, etc.) and such position must constantly be kept filled by the Company/Close Corporation.

It is also advisable (although not a requirement of the Act) that a sole proprietor or partner of a business appoints a representative taxpayer such as an accountant to deal with his/her tax affairs.

- Tax Clearance Certificates

Exchange controls have been relaxed since 1 July 1997, allowing South African residents to invest funds abroad, or to hold funds in foreign currencies at local banks. The current permissible amount is R2 million over one's lifetime.

In terms of existing policy, South African individuals who are over 18 years and in good standing with their tax affairs may invest outside RSA. Such investors are required to apply for a Tax Clearance Certificate (TCC) from their local SARS office where they are registered for income tax purposes prior to any foreign investment being made.

A TCC may only be issued if all tax returns have been submitted (unless extension was granted) and no taxes (i.e. income tax, value-added tax and employees' tax) are outstanding and a statement of assets and liabilities has been provided. A person who is not registered for income tax purposes will also be required to apply for such a certificate.

Prospective tenderers will also be required to obtain a TCC from the SARS office where they are registered for tax purposes prior to submitting a tender for providing goods or services to Government.

The procedure to be followed when applying for TCC in respect of tenders and good standing can be accessed on the SARS Internet / Taxes / Operating Procedures.

The application forms used are:

- **FIA 001:** Application for tax clearance certificate (in respect of foreign investments)
- **FIA 002:** Application for tax clearance certificate (only for recurring foreign investments not exceeding R30 000 p.a.)
- **TCC 001:** Application for tax clearance certificate (in respect of tenders / good standing)

The above forms are obtainable from any SARS office and are also available on the SARS website.

- Non-Compliance with legislation

  Taxes are collected to enable the Government to provide essential services like education, health, security and welfare to the residents of South Africa. Therefore, if everyone pays their fair share, better services can be provided and tax rates can be reduced. Taxpayers who ignore their tax obligations such as not to register or failure to submit tax returns are actually defrauding their country and fellow residents/citizens.

- Interest, Penalties and Additional Tax

  The various tax/revenue laws also provide for the imposition of interest, penalties and additional tax up to 200% for non-payment or non-compliance of these laws. A person may also be liable for a fine or imprisonment on matters such as non-payment of taxes, failure to complete tax returns, failure to disclose income, false statements, helping any person to evade tax or claiming a refund to which he/she is not entitled to.

  Taxpayers who have not complied with tax legislation such as not to register or omission of income and who voluntarily approach SARS to meet their tax obligations will be received sympathetically.

- Dispute Resolution

  - Objections

    The procedure for taxpayers who are not satisfied with their assessments is to lodge an objection in writing stating fully and in detail the grounds on which the objection is lodged.

    The objection must be in the prescribed form, namely ADR 1 and must be submitted within 30 days after the date of assessment to the SARS office where the taxpayer is registered. This form must be completed as comprehensively as possible, and must include detailed grounds on which the objection is founded with supporting documentation where necessary.

    It must be signed by the taxpayer. Where the taxpayer is unable to personally sign the objection, the person signing on behalf of the taxpayer must state in an annexure to the objection:-

    - the reason why the taxpayer is unable to sign the objection;
    - that he or she has the necessary power of attorney to sign on behalf of the taxpayer; and
    - that the taxpayer is aware of the objection and agrees with the grounds thereof.

  - Appeals

    If the objection is disallowed wholly or in part, the taxpayer may appeal to a specially constituted Tax Board or to the Tax Court for hearing appeals. The notice of appeal must be in writing and must be made within 30 days of the notice of the disallowance of the objection.

  - Rules regarding objections and appeals

    Rules regarding objections and appeals have been formulated in terms of section 107A of the Act for assessments issued, objections lodged or appeals noted. These rules are available on the SARS website at www.sars.gov.za/dr and are also set out in the guide on Tax Dispute Resolution. Essentially, the rules set timeframes for both SARS and taxpayers' adherence in order that objections and appeals may be dealt with in an expeditious manner. It is important to note that objections need to be lodged at the address specified in the assessment in terms of these new rules. Additionally, these rules make provision for alternative dispute resolution.

- ADR

  Alternative Dispute resolution (ADR) is a form of dispute resolution other than litigation, or adjudication through the courts. It is less formal, less cumbersome and less adversarial and is a more cost effective and speedier process of resolving a dispute with SARS.

  If a dispute is resolved between SARS and the taxpayer, it must be recorded and be signed by the taxpayer and the SARS representative. SARS will issue, where necessary, a revised assessment to give effect to the agreement reached.

  Where the dispute is not resolved, the taxpayer may continue on appeal to the Tax Board or the Tax Court. In essence, a taxpayer has three options available when disputing an assessment:

  - Where the tax in question is less than R200 000, the Tax Board is to be utilised.
  - Where the tax in question is R200 000 or more, the Tax Court is to be utilised.
  - However, instead of going to the Tax Board or Tax Court, the ADR process can be used where the Commissioner decides it is appropriate.

  ADR applies to taxes such as –

  - Income Tax (including PAYE and CGT)
  - VAT
  - Transfer Duty
  - Stamp Duty
  - Skills Development Levies
  - Unemployment Insurance Contributions
  - Estate Duty
  - Donations Tax

- **SARS Service Monitoring Office (SSMO)**

The SSMO is a special office operating independently of SARS offices. The SSMO facilitates the resolution of problems of a procedural nature that have not been resolved by SARS offices through the normal channels. The SSMO reports directly to the Commissioner and provided regular reports to the Minister of Finance.

What is considered to be procedural problems?

- Delays in processing returns, decision making and the correction of administrative mistakes
- Failure to provide reasons for making an adjustment to a return
- Failure to respond to queries, objections and appeals
- The conduct and attitude of SARS staff

What is considered not to be procedural problems?

- Merits of disputes as to the amount of an assessment or schedules
- Complaints that have been referred to the Public Protector
- Matters that have been, or are, before the Courts
- Complaints about Government or SARS policy
- Changes to legislation

If you believe you have an issue that you want to bring to the attention of the SSMO, three steps must be followed:

STEP ONE

When you wish to raise an issue, it is usually best to do it in writing, by phone or fax, or by visiting your local SARS office. The relevant officer will try to resolve the issue as quickly as possible.

STEP TWO

If all avenues of communication have failed to solve your issue at Step One, contact your local Call Centre and request the Call Centre Agent to assist. If the problem can not be solved, the Call Centre Agent will register your complaint and provide you with a service request number. Your complaint will then be escalated to a Consultant/Manager to assist you.

STEP THREE

If you have received no resolution within a reasonable time at Step Two, you can ask the SSMO to look into the issue.

The SSMO can be reached on
Tel: 0860 12 12 16
Fax: 012 431 9695
Email: ssmo@sars.gov.za
For more information visit the website at **www.sars.gov.za/ssmo**

• Conclusion

Further information about the different taxes administered by SARS is available on the SARS website, www.sars.gov.za or from any SARS office.

Details on how to start a business, business opportunities, managing / financing your business, etc. is available on the SARS website under links (at bottom of the homepage) / Brain – Business Referral and Information Network". Information may also be obtained from the Department of Trade and Industry on their website www.dti.gov.za.

CITY	OFFICE	PHYSICAL ADDRESS	POSTAL ADDRESS	PHONE	FAX	
Alberton Revenue	Receiver of Revenue	49 New Quay Road, New Redruth, Alberton, 1451	P O Box 1003, Alberton, 1450	011 861 5500	011 861 5662	
Beaufort West Revenue	Receiver of Revenue	Church St, Beaufort West, 6970	Private Bag X548, Beaufort West, 6970	023 414 3235	023 414 4264	
Bellville Revenue	Receiver of Revenue	Teddington Street, Bellville, 7530	Bellville, SARS, Cape Mail, 8076	0860 12 12 18	021 943 8110	
Benoni Revenue	Receiver of Revenue	65 Howard Avenue, Benoni	P O Box 141, Benoni, 1500 (Docex 4)	011 421 1701	011 421 1726	
Bloemfontein Revenue	Receiver of Revenue	Central Government Building, Cnr Nelson Mandela Drive and Aliwal Street, Bloemfontein	P O Box 313, Bloemfontein, 9300	051 506 3000	051 448 4829	
Boksburg Revenue	Receiver of Revenue	146 Leeupoort & Short Streets, Boksburg	P O Box 206, Boksburg, 1460	011 841 1400	011 841 1445	
Brakpan Revenue	Receiver of Revenue	106 Kingsway Ave, Brakpan, 1540	P O Box 40, Brakpan, 1540	011 740-2900	011 740 1175	
Cape Town Revenue	Receiver of Revenue	17 Lower Long Street , Cape Town	SARS, Cape Mail, 8076	021 417 1413 0860 12 12 18	021 413 8900	
Cape Town	Enforcement Centre	22 Hans Strydom Drive Cape Town	SARS Cape Mail 8076	0860 12 12 18	(021) 413 8901	
Durban Revenue	Receiver of Revenue	201 West Street, Durban, 4000	P O Box 921, Durban, 4000	031 328 6000	031-333 7291-9 IT 031 332 8601 VAT 031 328 6012 PAYE 031 328 6013	
East London Revenue	Receiver of Revenue	C/o Station & Terminus St, East London	Private Bag X9012, East London, 5200	043 706 5400	043 706 5552/3	
George Revenue	Receiver of Revenue	93 York St, George, 6529	Private Bag X6585, George, 6530	044 874 7420	044 8840250	
Germiston Revenue	Receiver of Revenue	Outeniqua Builing, C/o Victoria & Plantation, Germiston	P O Box 116, Germiston, 1400	011 876 3000	011 873 3916	
Giyani Revenue	Receiver of Revenue	Parliament Building, Department of Justice, Main Road	Private Bag X9665, Giyani, 0826	015 811 6700	015 812 1988	
Johannesburg Carlton Centre	Receiver of Revenue	Level 200, Carlton Centre,C/o Commissioner & Von Weilligh Street, JHB	P O Box 1051, Johannesburg, 2000	0860 12 12 18 011 374 8000	IT: 011 374 8138 / 8080 PAYE: 011 374 8132 / 8532 VAT: 011 374 8200/8184 Other: 011 374 8254/8348	
Johannesburg	Large Business Centre	Megawatt Park Maxwell Drive Sunninghill	Private Bag X170 Rivonia 2128	(011) 602 2010	N/A	
Johannesburg	Gauteng West Enforcement	Megawatt Park Maxwell Drive Sunninghill	Private Bag X187 Rivonia 2128	(011) 602 2000	Criminal Investigation: (011) 602 3790 Collections: (011) 602 4705 or 602 4706 Audit: (011) 602 2934	
Johannesburg	SARS Academy	Megawatt Park Maxwell Drive Sunninghill	PO Box 5380 Rivonia 2128	(011) 602 2000	(011) 602 2833	
Kimberly Revenue	Receiver of Revenue	Old Main St, Hyescho Building, Kimberley, 8301	Private Bag X6068, Kimberley, 8300	053 831 2250	053 831 7616	
Klerksdorp	Receiver of Revenue	39 Leask Street, Revenues Building	Private Bag A4, Klerksdorp, 2570	018 464 1551	018 464 3917/ 3312	
Kroonstad Revenue	Receiver of Revenue	LMC Centre, C/o Hill & Steyn St, Kroonstad	Private Bag X01, Kroonstad, 9500	056 212 2151	056 212 1594/2974/2565	
Krugersdorp Revenue	Receiver of Revenue	40 Kobie Krige Street, Krugersdorp	P O Box 401, Krugersdorp, 1740	011 950 8000	011 953 2524	0
Lebowogomo Revenue	Receiver of Revenue	Old Lebowa Parliamentary Complex, Finance Wing, Lebowakgomo	Private Bax X34, Lebowakgomo, 0737	015 633 2000	015 633 6150	
Mmabatho Revenue	Receiver of Revenue	Revenue House, C/o Barokologabi & Bathlaping Road, Ground floor, Mmabatho	Private Bag X2131, Mmabatho, 2736	018 392 3071/2	018 384 1821/2546	
Mount Edgecomb Revenue	Receiver of Revenue	Lower Ground Floor, Blake House, 32 Flanders Drive, Mount Edgecombe, 4031	P O Box 921, Durban, 4021	031 538 3700	031 538 3729/30	
Nigel Revenue	Receiver of Revenue	C/o Hendrik Verwoerd Street & 4th, Ave, Nigel, 1491	P O Box 80, Nigel, 1490	011 814 6466	011 814 1662	0
Nelspruit Revenue	Receiver of Revenue	Nedbank Centre 6th Floor, 30 Brown Street, Nelspruit	Private Bag X11294, Nelspruit, 1200	013 759 4300	013 753 2197/6069	
Pietermaritzburg Revenue	Receiver of Revenue	209 Pietermaritz St, Westoe Building Lower, upper & 1st floor,Pietermaritzburg, 3201	P O Box 921, Durban, 4000	033 355 4500	033 355 4662 033 355 4698	
Polokwane Revenue	Receiver of Revenue	40 Landros Mare Street, Polokwane, 0699	P O Box 9384, Polokwane, 0700	015 299 7000	015 291 4019	
Polokwane	Criminal Investigations	The Mall, Ground Floor, C/o Biccard and Thabo Mbeki Street, Polokwane	Po Box 55600 Polokwane 0700	(015) 291 4670/1	(015) 291 4678	
Port Elizabeth Revenue	Receiver of Revenue	St Mary Terrace C/o White & Main Steet	P O Box 345, Port Elizabeth, 6000	041 505 7500	041 586 0618	
Pretoria Revenue	Receiver of Revenue	C/o Schoeman & van der Walt Street, Pretoria	P O Box 436, Pretoria, 0001	012 317 2000	012 317 2926/2328/ 2297/2666	
Pretoria East Revenue (Situated in Ashley Gardens)	Receiver of Revenue	46 Lebombo Street, Garsfonteitn, Ashlea Gardens	P O Box 436, Pretoria, 0001	012 425 2300	012 425 2390 Walk-in-service only	
Pretoria	Receiver of Revenue	299 Bronkhorst Street, Niew Muckleneuk	Private Bag X923 or P O Box 402, Pretoria 0001	012 422 4000	012 422 5181	
Randburg Revenue	Receiver of Revenue	C/o Kent & 25 Hill Street, Randburg	P O Box 1051, Johannesburg, 2000	Walk-in service only	Walk-in service only	
Randfontein Revenue	Receiver of Revenue	39 Stubb Street, Randfontein, 1759	P O Box 3, Randfontein, 1760 / Docex 10, Randfontein	011 411-7200	011 693-3700	
Robertson Revenue	Receiver of Revenue	48 Church Street	P.O Box 38, Robertson,6705	022 626 3040	023 626 4363	0
Roodepoort Revenue	Receiver of Revenue	Horizon View Shopping Centre, C/o Sonop & Ontdekkers Street, Roodepoort	P O Box 228, Roodepoort, 1725	011 271 9000	011 271 9123	
Rustenburg Revenue	Receiver of Revenue	135 Klopper Street, Rustenburg, 0299	Private Bag X82068, Rustenburg, 0300	014 592 2035	014 597 1001	
Sibasa Revenue	Receiver of Revenue	Old Post Office Building, Mphemphu Street, Sibasa	Private Bax X2338, Sibasa, 0970	015 963 3474	015 963 3377	
Springs Revenue	Receiver of Revenue	74 Third Street, Springs, 1559	P O Box 106, Springs, 1560	011 812 6000	011 812 6040	
Standerton Revenue	Receiver of Revenue	29 Church street / C/o Church & Princess Streets	Private Bag X2005, Standerton, 2430	017 712 2140	017 712 3760	
Uitenhage Revenue	Receiver of Revenue	1 Young St, Uitenhage, 6229	Private Bag 34, Uitenhage, 6230	041 991 0700	041 991 0327	
Umlazi	Receiver of Revenue	Umlazi Centre, Amawhele Building	P O Box 921, Durban, 4000	031 907 9062	031 907 1120	
Umtata Revenue	Receiver of Revenue	C/o Sutherland & Durham St, PRD 2 Building, Umtata	Private Bag X5027, Umtata, 5099	047 531 2162	047 531 1343	
Vereeniging Revenue	Receiver of Revenue	C/o Joubert & Merriman Ave, Vereeniging	Private Bag X07, Vereeniging, 1930	016 422 3621	016 422 4023/31	

The amnesty also covers all fines, interest and penalties and you will not have to pay any of these. Once you get amnesty SARS may not make a criminal case against you – as long as you have been honest about your income.

How to apply for the amnesty

Fill in the small business tax amnesty application form (SBA001). You can get it from any SARS office or download it from the SARS website: www.sars.gov.za.

You must also submit:
- The relevant income tax return for the 2006 tax year as required in the case of an individual or business.
- A statement of all assets and liabilities as at 28 February 2006.

What if you do not have accounting records or documentary proof of your taxable income?

If you do not have documents to prove what your taxable income is, you may give a reasonable estimate of these amounts.
When SARS has to decide whether your estimate is reasonable, we can look at your possessions, your lifestyle and any other information that can confirm your income.

What can you NOT get amnesty for?

You cannot get amnesty:
- For income you received in the form of a salary or wage.
- For taxes you have already paid.
- For taxes that become payable because you submitted a tax return before you applied for amnesty.
- If we have already informed you that we want to audit or investigate you.

Withdrawal of the amnesty

The amnesty will be withdrawn if you:
- Do not pay the full amount of the tax amnesty levy within 12 months
- Do not give full and honest information or amounts, including a statement of assets and liabilities as at 28 February 2006.
- Made an estimate which is not reasonable

What if you do not use the amnesty?

The amnesty is your one chance to become legal and to clear taxes you owe from the past. If you do not use the amnesty:
- You will always owe taxes from past years
- When you register or SARS catches you or you come forward voluntarily in the future, you will have to pay additional tax, penalties and interest
- SARS may take action against you and you could be charged with a crime.

For further information and assistance:
- Visit any SARS office
- Call the hotline on 0860 12 12 20
- Write to PO Box 292, Groenkloof, 0027
- Visit our website at www.sars.gov.za
- Email sbau@sars.gov.za

This document is a quick introduction to the draft small business tax amnesty. It does not go into technical and legal detail of the legislation. It should, therefore, not be used as a legal reference. For more information please refer to the legislation itself or consult SARS or your tax advisor.

This brochure is available in all official languages. To obtain a copy in your language of choice, visit our website at www.sars.gov.za or your nearest SARS branch.

Tax Amnesty for Small Business

1 August 2006 - 31 May 2007

SARS
At Your Service

Have you not paid taxes in the past?

Did you hide some of your income to avoid tax?

Do you want to legalise your business affairs?

Are you worried about getting into trouble or paying big fines if you register with SARS?

SARS can now offer you an amnesty – This means you can register your business and you do not have to pay all your old taxes.

Why?

Many small businesses and taxi operators did not pay tax in the past. All businesses are supposed to pay taxes like income tax, PAYE (employees tax) and VAT, but many small businesses never registered with SARS to pay tax.

It is illegal not to pay tax. But people who have never paid are scared to come forward because they are scared they will be fined or prosecuted.

In February 2006, the Minister of Finance announced in his Budget Speech that SARS will offer a tax amnesty to small businesses including taxi operators. This will give them a chance to sort out their tax affairs without being punished for not paying in the past.

Government uses tax money to provide social services for all South Africans. Our tax money pays for education, healthcare and policing. It pays for grants for poor people, and is used to build roads, power stations and dams. Without taxes government cannot build a better life for all.

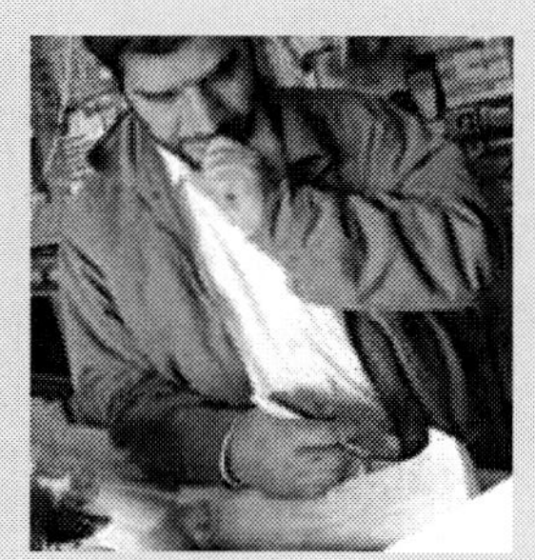

SARS is responsible for collecting taxes. We would like to make it easy for people to start paying tax – even if they evaded it in the past. The more people who pay, the more money government will be able to spend on providing services for the people of South Africa.

Who qualifies for the amnesty?

A small business can apply for amnesty as long as you had a turnover (gross income) of less than R10 million in 2006.

The business can be owned by an individual (including the insolvent or deceased estate of an individual), a close corporation, an unlisted company, a co-operative or a trust. If the business is owned by a close corporation, an unlisted company or a co-operative, the shares in it must be held by individuals. A similar rule applies to a trust.

Any small business that has not yet registered for the 2006 tax year, can apply for the amnesty. If you are registered but did not declare all your income or taxes, you can also apply for amnesty.

The 2006 tax year is defined as a tax year that ended during the period of 12 months from 1 April 2005 to 31 March 2006.

When can you apply for the amnesty?

You can apply from 1 August 2006 to 31 May 2007.

Where can you apply?

At any SARS office in the country except for an office that deals only with Customs or Excise matters. All applications will be treated confidentially.

What taxes can you get amnesty for?

When you apply for amnesty you still have to pay some taxes for the 2006 tax year:

- You will pay income tax on your profit (taxable income) for the 2006 year.
- You will pay a small levy to get the amnesty. This clears all your taxes from the past. The levy will be between 2% and 5% of your 2006 profit (taxable income) If your profits are less than R35 000 there will be no levy.

You can get amnesty for the following taxes up to the start of the 2006 tax year:

- Income tax on profits (taxable income).
- Secondary tax on dividends.

You can also get amnesty for the following taxes up to 28 February 2006:

- VAT (Value Added Tax).
- PAYE (Pay As You Earn).
- Contributions on payroll to skills development levies (SDL) and unemployment insurance fund (UIF).
- Witholding tax on royalties.

SARS At Your Service

WORLD TAX GUIDE LIBRARY-2006

Ultimate directories for conducting export-import operations in the country. Largest exporters and importers, strategic government and business contacts, selected export-import regulations and more...

Price: $99.95 each

TITLE
1. Albania Tax Guide
2. Argentina Tax Guide
3. Armenia Tax Guide
4. Australia Tax Guide
5. Austria Tax Guide
6. Azerbaijan Tax Guide
7. Belarus Tax Guide
8. Bermuda Tax Guide
9. Bolivia Tax Guide
10. Bosnia Tax Guide
11. Brazil Tax Guide
12. Bulgaria Tax Guide
13. Cambodia Tax Guide
14. Canada Tax Guide
15. China Tax Guide
16. Colombia Tax Guide
17. Croatia Tax Guide
18. Czech Republic Tax Guide
19. Ecuador Tax Guide
20. Estonia Tax Guide
21. Finland Tax Guide
22. France Tax Guide
23. Georgia Tax Guide
24. Germany Tax Guide
25. Global Offshore Tax Guide (Volume 1)
26. Global Offshore Tax Guide (Volume 2)
27. Global Tax Guide 2003
28. Global Tax Regulation Guidebook 2003
29. Greece Tax Guide

To order and for additional analytical and marketing information, please contacrt
International Business Publications, USA at:
P.O. Box 15343, Washington, DC 20003, USA. Phone: (202) 546-2103. Fax: (202) 546-3275.
E-mail: rusric@erols.com

TITLE
30. Guam Tax Guide
31. Hungary Tax Guide
32. India Tax Guide
33. Ireland Tax Guide
34. Italy Tax Guide
35. Japan Tax Guide
36. Kazakhstan Tax Guide
37. Korea South Tax Guide
38. Kyrgyzstan Tax Guide
39. Latvia Tax Guide
40. Lithuania Tax Guide
41. Luxembourg Tax Guide
42. Macedonia Tax Guide
43. Malaysia Tax Guide
44. Malta Tax Guide
45. Mexico Tax Guide
46. Moldova Tax Guide
47. Netherlands Tax Guide
48. New Zealand Tax Guide
49. Norway Tax Guide
50. Panama Tax Guide
51. Portugal Tax Guide
52. Romania Tax Guide
53. Russia Tax Guide
54. Singapore Tax Guide
55. Slovakia Tax Guide
56. Slovenia Tax Guide
57. South Africa Tax Guide
58. South Korea Tax Guide
59. Spain Tax Guide
60. Sri Lanka Tax Guide
61. Switzerland Tax Guide
62. Taiwan Tax Guide
63. Thailand Tax Guide
64. Trinidad and Tobago Tax Guide
65. Ukraine Tax Guide
66. United Kingdom Tax Guide
67. Uruguay Tax Guide
68. US Tax Guide
69. Uzbekistan Tax Guide
70. Yugoslavia Tax Guide

NEW! WORLD OFFSHORE TAX GUIDES– 2006

Price: $99.95 each

1.	Andorra Offshore Tax Guide
2.	Anguilla Offshore Tax Guide
3.	Bahamas Offshore Tax Guide
4.	Barbados Offshore Tax Guide
5.	Belize Offshore Tax Guide
6.	Bermuda Offshore Tax Guide
7.	British Virgin Islands Offshore Tax Guide
8.	Cayman Islands Offshore Tax Guide
9.	Cook Islands Offshore Tax Guide
10.	Costa Rica Offshore Tax Guide
11.	Cyprus Offshore Tax Guide
12.	Dubai Offshore Tax Guide
13.	Gibraltar Offshore Tax Guide
14.	Grenada Offshore Tax Guide
15.	Guernsey Offshore Tax Guide
16.	Hong Kong Offshore Tax Guide
17.	Ireland Offshore Tax Guide
18.	Isle of Man Offshore Tax Guide
19.	Jersey Offshore Tax Guide
20.	Labuan Offshore Tax Guide
21.	Liechtenstein Offshore Tax Guide
22.	Luxembourg Offshore Tax Guide
23.	Madeira Offshore Tax Guide
24.	Malta Offshore Tax Guide
25.	Mauritius Offshore Business and Investment Opportunities Handbook
26.	Mauritius Offshore Tax Guide
27.	Monaco Offshore Tax Guide
28.	Nauru Offshore Tax Guide
29.	Netherlands Antilles Offshore Tax Guide
30.	Panama Offshore Tax Guide
31.	Seychelles Offshore Tax Guide
32.	Switzerland Offshore Tax Guide
33.	Turks & Caicos Islands Offshore Tax Guide
34.	Vanuatu Offshore Tax Guide

To order and for additional analytical and marketing information, please contacrt
International Business Publications, USA at:
P.O. Box 15343, Washington, DC 20003, USA. Phone: (202) 546-2103. Fax: (202) 546-3275.
E-mail: rusric@erols.com